EDUCATION BY THE NUMBERS AND THE MAKING OF SOCIETY

International statistical comparisons of nations have become commonplace in the contemporary landscape of education policy and social science. This book discusses the emergence of these international comparisons as a particular style of reasoning about education, society and science. By examining how international educational assessments have come to dominate much of contemporary policymaking concerning school system performance, the authors provide concrete case studies highlighting the preeminent role of numbers in furthering neoliberal education reform. Demonstrating how numbers serve as 'rationales' to shape and fashion social issues, this text opens new avenues for thinking about institutional and epistemological factors that produce and shape educational policy, research and schooling in transnational contexts.

Sverker Lindblad is Professor of Education and Special Education at the University of Gothenburg, Sweden.

Daniel Pettersson is Associate Professor at the University of Gävle and Uppsala University, Sweden.

Thomas S. Popkewitz is Professor of Curriculum and Instruction at the University of Wisconsin-Madison, USA.

EDUCATION BY THE NUMBERS AND THE MAKING OF SOCIETY

The Expertise of International Assessments

Edited by
Sverker Lindblad, Daniel Pettersson,
and Thomas S. Popkewitz

NEW YORK AND LONDON

First published 2018
by Routledge
711 Third Avenue, New York, NY 10017

and by Routledge
2 Park Square, Milton Park, Abingdon, Oxon, OX14 4RN

Routledge is an imprint of the Taylor & Francis Group, an informa business

© 2018 Taylor & Francis

The right of Sverker Lindblad, Daniel Pettersson, and Thomas S. Popkewitz to be identified as the authors of the editorial material, and of the authors for their individual chapters, has been asserted in accordance with sections 77 and 78 of the Copyright, Designs and Patents Act 1988.

All rights reserved. No part of this book may be reprinted or reproduced or utilised in any form or by any electronic, mechanical, or other means, now known or hereafter invented, including photocopying and recording, or in any information storage or retrieval system, without permission in writing from the publishers.

Trademark notice: Product or corporate names may be trademarks or registered trademarks, and are used only for identification and explanation without intent to infringe.

Library of Congress Cataloging-in-Publication Data
A catalog record for this book has been requested

ISBN: 978-1-138-29582-7 (hbk)
ISBN: 978-1-138-29583-4 (pbk)
ISBN: 978-1-315-10043-2 (ebk)

Typeset in Bembo
by Apex CoVantage, LLC

CONTENTS

Preface   *viii*
Acknowledgments   *x*

1. Getting the Numbers Right: An Introduction   1
   Sverker Lindblad, Daniel Pettersson, and Thomas S. Popkewitz

SECTION I
Numbers: A History of a Style of Reasoning   **21**

2. Politics by the Numbers   23
   Theodore M. Porter

3. On the Contest of Lists and Their Governing Capacities: How 'Tax Havens' Became 'Secrecy Jurisdictions'   35
   Hans Krause Hansen and Anne Vestergaard

4. Time, Drawing, Testing: The Making Up of the Developmental Child and the Measuring of the Nation's Development   53
   Catarina S. Martins

5. And the World Has Finally Been Made to Measure   68
   Barbara Czarniawska

SECTION II
The Field of Making of Data: Problematics of Assessment 73

6. Producing the 'Right Kind of People': The OECD Education Indicators in the 1960s 75
   Regula Bürgi and Daniel Tröhler

7. Standards: Normative, Interpretative, and Performative 92
   Radhika Gorur

8. International Assessments and Its Expertise Fabricating Expert Knowledge for Policy 110
   Luis Miguel Carvalho

9. The Implications of Understanding That PISA Is Simply Another Standardized Achievement Test 127
   David C. Berliner

SECTION III
Large-Scale Assessment as the Production of Numbers 147

10. PISA as a Social Media Event: Powering the 'Logics of Competition' 149
    Miguel A. Pereyra, Antonio Luzón, Mónica Torres, and Daniel Torres-Salinas

11. Who Governs the Numbers?: The Framing of Educational Knowledge by TIMSS Research 166
    Christina Elde Mølstad and Daniel Pettersson

12. OECD as a Site of Coproduction: The European Education Governance and the New Politics of 'Policy Mobilization' 185
    Sotiria Grek

SECTION IV
The Dissolution of the Science/Society Distinction   **201**

13. Statistics Reasoning, Governing Education and Making
    Differences as Kinds of People   203
    Thomas S. Popkewitz and Sverker Lindblad

14. Anticipating the Future Society: The Cultural Inscription
    of Numbers and International Large-Scale Assessment   222
    Thomas S. Popkewitz

Index   *239*

PREFACE

Education by the numbers is signifying vital knowledge claims in current educational policy discourses as well as in research communication. Schools and educational systems are compared and evoking statements are made about both what went right or wrong and the attendant reasons why. What is regarded as valid knowledge on and in education is to a very high extent to know education by the numbers. And actionable knowledge is also formulated in terms of educational statistics. However, to our understanding, education by the numbers is an important and fascinating knowledge problematic given research on dynamic realism as studied by Ian Hacking and the history of statistics as analyzed by Ted Porter.[1] Thus, it is vital to analyze the preconditions and limits for educational knowledge by the numbers. In this anthology, the authors are doing so in different ways and with different foci. Taken together, it is our ambition that this book will contribute to improving educational discourses—academic as well as professional and political—and the making of educational knowledge.

This book is a result of a long intellectual journey for the editors: in 1999, Sverker Lindblad was a Fulbright scholar at the University of Madison-Wisconsin and worked with Tom Popkewitz on knowledge problematics in education governance. Educational statistics turned out to be vital here, and we wrote a research report and a few articles on this issue.[2] Daniel Pettersson started his PhD thesis work at about the same time and presented analyses of international large assessments in education—such as the OECD and PISA.[3] In 2014, the Swedish Research Council asked us to do a research review considering international large-scale assessments. This we presented in 2015 as a kind of systematic research review focusing on arguments and explanations.[4] Here, we used our previous work on statistics as a knowledge problematic. We noted an enormous amount of research publications in this field of study in combination with a fragmented knowledge organization. But what we also note was a high impact of such research, especially the OECD Programme for International Student Assessment (PISA), on and in education policy discourses. We also noted that International Large-Scale Assessments was developed in tandem with national and international discourses on education, for instance, the importance to measure performances by knowledge assessments rather than participation in education system. Given such processes, we considered it as highly important to analyze the construction and utilization of this way of doing education by the numbers.

Notes

1. Important texts were here Hacking, I. (1992). 'Style' for historians and philosophers. *Studies in History and Philosophy of Science Part A, 23*(1), 1–20.
   Porter, T.M. (1986). *The rise of statistical thinking, 1820–1900*. Princeton, NJ: Princeton University.
2. For instance, Lindblad, S., & Popkewitz, T.S. (2001). *Statistical information and systems of reason on education and social inclusion and exclusion in international and national contexts*. Uppsala Reports on Education 38. Uppsala: Department of Education, Uppsala University.
   Popkewitz, T., & Lindblad, S (2001): Estatísticas educacionais como um sistema de razão: relações entre governo da educação e inclusão e exclusão sociais. *Educação & Sociedade, 22*(75).
3. Pettersson, D. (2008). *Internationell kunskapsbedömning som inslag i nationell styrning av skolan*. Diss., Uppsala: Uppsala universitet. (Acta Universitatis Upsaliensis, Uppsala Studies in Education 120)
4. Lindblad, S., Pettersson, D., & Popkewitz, T. (2015). *International comparisons of school results: A systematic review of research on large scale assessments in education*. Stockholm: Vetenskapsrådets rapporter.

ACKNOWLEDGMENTS

The finalization of this book was supported by a research grant from the Swedish Research Council 'International Comparisons and the Reformation of Welfare State Education' (Project 2016–04520).

This book is not only a result of a long journey in research. It is as well a starting point for further analyses of educational knowledge—with a focus on international comparisons—at the agora between science and society.

We had support from a large number of actors: in June 2015, we had a symposium on Education by the Numbers at the University of Gothenburg with the support of the Swedish Research Council and Riksbankens Jubileumsfond. The symposium was organized with the efforts of the PoP-group (Pedagogik och Politik) and administered by Agneta Edvardsson at the Department of Education and Special Education. The Gothenburg symposium was followed up by a symposium at the AERA in Chicago, Illinois, in April 2016, where papers were presented and discussed by Bob Lingard and Gary Nutriello. In addition, several persons have reacted to the manuscripts in different versions, none mentioned and no one forgotten. Christine Kruger at the University of Wisconsin-Madison did the final organization and editing of the manuscripts. Last but first, our thoughts go to the authors of the chapters in this book!

Many thanks from us to all of you who made this intellectual journey and publication possible!

Fjärås, Hudiksvall, and Madison September 16, 2017
Sverker Lindblad, Daniel Pettersson, and Thomas S. Popkewitz

1
GETTING THE NUMBERS RIGHT

An Introduction

Sverker Lindblad, Daniel Pettersson, and Thomas S. Popkewitz

This is a book about knowledge on and in education. The focus is on numbers—on how numbers shape our understandings of education, its dynamics, practices, operations, goals and missions. Important are the comparative powers of numbers—how differences and similarities between kinds of people and performances are constructed by numbers, over time and over places. Numbers appear to be neutral and precise, but like all symbols (such as letters, flags, etc.), the relations between numbers and what they represent are to be socially produced and learned, and the techniques to translate the one to the other (the symbol to its representation), such as statistics, are built on specific systems of reasoning. Numbers say little as such, but as they have come to be powerful representations of the modern world, shown in tables, diagrams or percentages, they are today also highly embedded with what is, and is not, of value and importance. Numbers are not only tools for analyses, but also highly performative, as they are framing our thoughts and conceptions of things. If there were a modern purgatory, it would be a spectacle of numbers that translated into such things as diagrams and regression lines showing dramatically where we are and what to expect, fear or hope for. Numbers make us read the world in taken-for-granted terms of progress and crises, ups and downs, differences and similarities. From where, and how, do these powers of numbers come about—and what are their premises and preconditions as they have come to play a key role in large-scale assessments and other forms of science-based policies and governance?

Increasingly, social life and policy are presented in numbers over categories and over space and time, and by means of that in terms of graphs, lists and comparative tables showing progress or denials. Such presentations have become part of ambitions to increase transparency and accountability in science-based knowledge production. The categories embody representations and social relations that are never merely descriptive. As this book continually argues, numbers embody distinctions and differentiations about a desired future that the numbers 'act' as a technology to actualize. The seemingly descriptive categories of student achievement, for example, give expression to children as having 'a nature' that the assessments are 'to retrieve'. This changing of the child establishes relations of individuals connected to the norms and values ascribed to the visions existing within society. This forming of collective belonging, it is argued in this book, is given as universal through the use of numbers and its algorithms. The social and individuality inscribed in the knowledge by the numbers ARE also contested: for instance, technically, epistemologically and ontologically, as reduction of complexity and constraints and limits in making valid statements in statistical reasoning, or ideologically, in translating educational matters into instrumentalist and economistic measures. Numbers as 'act' is no less evident than in the field of education, educational research and the international assessments that circulate to define what is and should be the successful school system. Given current global developments, an urgent task for educational research is to analyze the making and meaning of international large-scale assessments, their development and use in interaction with professional and policy discourses.

We are dealing with these and similar tasks in this book as contributions to current discourses on education, educational knowledge and the intersection of science and society. Here, we have the ambition to identify a set of knowledge problematics in educational contexts and to clarify implications of knowledge by the number in education.

How do we then understand numbers as a knowledge problematic? Numbers, Hacking (1983) argues, are parts of a system for communication with technologies creating a distance from phenomena by appearing to summarize complex events and transactions (cf. Porter, 1995). The production and use of numbers are vital in governing as well as governmentality (Rose, 1999). A specific aspect of this problematic is categorizing practices in statistics (Popkewitz & Lindblad, 2010) and looping processes (Hacking, 1992) in the making of human kinds by means of categorization and reflexivity. Rigor and uniform numbers also have their advantages in enabling transport across time and space not requiring intimate knowledge and personal trust as appearing to exclude judgments in the joint struggle of science and policies against subjectivity.

As such, numbers were interwoven into the project of modernity and democracy as guarantees for '*fairness*', '*accuracy*' and '*impartiality*'. A central position in the project of modernity and democracy is occupied by education and all the societal expectations inscribed into education. These expectations can be summarized in education as a central requirement for individual and social as well as economic development. In times of a dominating comparativistic paradigm based on ranking and efficiency measures, rather than understandings of educational cultures and ways of dealing with educational problems, international benchmarks are regarded as an important tool for accomplishing betterments. One contemporary example of this is noted in the statement of OECD: 'It is only through [. . .] benchmarking that countries can understand relative strengths and weaknesses of their education systems and identify best practices and ways forward' (OECD, 2006, p. 18). This exemplifies the significance ascribed to comparisons as a tool for the standardization and legitimacy of national educational systems (cf. Kamens, 2009; Steiner-Khamsi & Waldow, 2012).

While the comparativist paradigm is evident in the formation of the social sciences in the 19th century (Popkewitz, 2008), in this era of an expanding comparativistic paradigm, international organizations come to function as '*containers*' for knowledge as well as producing new knowledge based on statistical analyses. From this context, Carvalho (2012) has stated that international organizations come to function as mediators for exchange and create and reshape ideas and programs, thereby fabricating a specific knowledge-policy instrument. In particular, international large-scale assessments, the organizations producing them and research based on these kinds of data have become a powerful instrument for the change, standardization and legitimization of national education systems.

Numbers for Educational Understanding

The International Association for the Evaluation of Educational Achievement (IEA) was one of the first organizations to focus on large-scale assessments of individual students' achievements. The organization was created on a reasoning to conduct comparative educational studies in the late 1950s—staging their first assessment in the early 1960s (Pettersson, 2014). The first study performed by the IEA differed from other comparative education studies undertaken at that time in that it tried to introduce an empirical, number-based approach into a field dominated by cultural analysis (Foshay et al., 1962). Before the first IEA study was undertaken, comparing education had been undertaken more from out of humanistic ideals, but with the formation of the IEA by scientists with an interest in psychometrics and with an outspoken interest in educational outputs, social sciences and behavioral science came to be the ideal on which comparative achievement tests rested (cf. Kazamias & Massialas, 1982). In 1935, an unknown book written by the Frenchman Marc-Antoine Jullien in 1817 was donated to the International Bureau of Education in Geneva. The book was read by Pedro Roselló, who then was working at the Bureau. In 1943, Roselló published a text that presented Jullien as the father of comparative education (Roselló, 1943). What Jullien tried to do in his book from the early 19th century was to introduce positivism as the foundation for all comparative studies. In this, numbers came to be the objective facts that had to be gathered for enabling educational claims. In relation to the first IEA study, it was, therefore, possible, even though the study was something new, to claim a rather long history of performing comparative studies based on numbers. With that, the IEA could argue for a historical legitimacy of the study, which came to be of importance during the 1950s and 1960s, especially in an American research context where positivism gained in importance (cf. Anderson, 1961). The statement that Jullien was the founding father of comparative education is something most contested in the field of comparative education (e.g. García Garrido, 1996; Noah & Eckstein, 1969), and even today there is a vivid discussion within the field of comparative education about its roots and historical trajectories (Epstein, 2008). However, Jullien's thinking was used for legitimating a study like the one undertaken by the IEA as a science-driven endeavor and served well for giving the study a history and a legitimacy. Another way to look at this problematic is to state that the IEA created something new in the history of comparing education. It focused on educational output that could be represented in numbers: they created hierarchies of students and educational systems as well as nations based on these numbers, and as a result, IEA created a specific positivistic reasoning on education. The IEA has continued to conduct various assessments such as the TIMSS, CIVED and the ICCS. Eventually, another important actor came to be engaged within the field—the OECD. Starting in the early 21st century, the OECD has, with the assistance of their Programme for International Student Assessment (PISA) study, come to be one of the most important actors in performing large-scale assessments, and more organizations came to walk the same line.

This development, exemplified by PISA, was a result of an international conflict starting in the 1980s, according to Cussó and D'Amico (2005). They show that in international educational statistics, UNESCO, who at that time was the main producer of statistics, was criticized by the World Bank and the OECD, who demanded more of hierarchical classifications and information on student performances. Cussó and D'Amico (a.a., p. 200) state:

> It became necessary not only to know how many graduates an education system produced in comparison to those of other countries but also at what cost, with what objectives, and what knowledge and exact skills were gained by the students.

What we find here is a shift in emphasis in international comparisons. What matters are comparisons of education systems presenting hierarches and rankings in performances and efficiency. This in contrast to international comparisons focusing on a cultural understanding of education and how educational tasks and problems are dealt with in different contexts. We are here doing a distinction between *comparatistic* analyses emphasizing educational qualities and understanding of educational matters, and *comparativistic* analyses, where the focus is on ranking and hierarchizing measures. Though international comparative studies often have comparatistic as well as comparativistic characteristics, the point made here is that currently, comparativistic analyses matter most, and that we since the 1990s have turned into a *comparativistic paradigm*. In this paradigm, education by the numbers is dominating. But the main point is the hierarchization of education—which is better and which is worse—according to the standards or criteria used.

But what is actually happening when education is transformed into something possible to demonstrate in numbers, and what kinds of people and what kinds of hierarchies and typologies are created? As an example of this, we can start by looking into one of the offspring of the PISA study on students' well-being presented in April 2017. The study is presented in the following words:

> Are students happy at school? Do they have good relations with their peers, teachers and parents? Is there any link between the quality of students' relationships in and outside of school and their academic performance? These questions are central to 'Students' Well-Being: PISA Results 2015 (volume 3)', the first OECD PISA report that analyses students' performance in school, their relationships with peers and teachers, their home life, and how they spend their time outside of school
> *(www.oecd.org/newsroom/first-oecd-pisa-report-on-students-well-being-launches-wednesday-19-april-2017.htm).*

Within another PISA report, the arguments for studying students' performances and highlight schools as important settings continues with the following lines:

> Schools are not just places where students acquire academic skills; they also help students become more resilient in the face of adversity, feel more connected with the people around them, and aim higher in their aspirations for their future. Not least, schools are the first place where children experience society in all its facets, and those experiences can have a profound influence on students' attitudes and behaviour in life.
> *(PISA 2015 Results [Vol. III] Students' Well-Being, 2017a, p. 3)*

The previous quotes from recent OECD assessments would seem on the surface as not only reasonable but, in fact, necessary. Modern schooling '*makes*' students' success in schools as linked to their psychological happiness and security in a world that continually seems to pose new challenges to its youth. Students' personal lives, feelings of satisfaction and relations with parents, peers and society are regarded as indicators of performance and pathways for individual success in society as well as the health of society in preparing for the future. OECD's venture in the new study of students' well-being seems as a likely extension of how schooling is understood as promoting the multiple goals of enabling individual feeling of satisfaction, providing for students' achievement and promoting of national prosperity.

In the literature on large-scale assessments, this kind of reasoning orders what is said and done through its measurement. This epistemological commonalty is addressed in the subtitle of this book, in which the plural of 'international assessments' is placed with the singular of 'its expertise'. The inscriptions, management and orchestrations of graphs, statistics and charts map a rationality or a system of reason for telling the truth about organizations, institutions and people. The data statements of population taxonomies of gender, socioeconomic distinctions, connected with the classifications of school designs and education systems, together with assessments of school performances or other kinds of measurements. Such data statements about schooling and society embody deficits and hopes as directives for professional or political action that is never merely descriptive but anticipatory.

The expression of student well-being is a normative statement about who the child is but also should be. This reconfiguration of knowledge expressed in Table 1.1 embodies a particular kind of calculative rationality and '*communicative objectivity*' (Halpern, 2014) that reformulate the epistemological principles of the social and policy sciences and the field or agora of policy in education, although that reformulation has implications for circulation of the expertise. The participating countries in Table 1.1 are compared and graded by measurements of student life satisfaction over gender and socioeconomic differences as well as school performances. Within a comparativistic paradigm, we note that in Mexico there is the largest share of students who are satisfied with their lives, whereas Korean students are measured as being least satisfied.

The normative qualities expressed in the international student assessment of schooling are not what is conventionally thought of philosophical relation of the '*is*' and '*should be*'. Nor are the assumptions about health, normalcy and the future empirically derived facts. This production of statements on education and schooling is constructed in styles of reasoning about '*the nature of the child*' and in networks of actors in different positions, for instance, considering what to measure and classify as well as what conclusions that are possible to make and how to act. The research embodies inscription devices about kinds of people that appear as universal qualities that contribute to children's school performance in different contexts, which simultaneously articulate normative boundaries about what matters—and should matter—and facts for people to act on. This coproduction of research and society in the education sector (see, e.g. Nowotny, Scott, & Gibbons, 2003; Kullenberg, 2012), paradoxically, seeks to actualize what is expressed as describing—the fabrication of individuality and society that is to usher in the future that is to be.

TABLE 1.1 Snapshot of Students' Life Satisfaction

- Life satisfaction in countries/economies with values above the OECD average
- Life satisfaction in countries/economies with values not significantly different from the OECD average
- Life satisfaction in countries/economies with values **below** the OECD average

	Students' life satisfaction[1]			Gender difference in life satisfaction (B-G)	Socioeconomic disparity in life satisfaction (top–bottom quarter of ESCS[2])	Difference in life satisfaction between high-achieving and low-achieving students in science (top–bottom quarter of science performance)
	Average	Students who are very satisfied with life (9–10)	Students who are not satisfied with life (0–4)			
	Mean	%	%	Dif.	Dif.	Dif.
OECD average	7.31	34.1	11.8	0.58	0.44	0.12
Australia	m	m	m	m	m	m
Austria	7.52	39.7	11.1	0.86	0.49	0.16
Belgium (excl. Flemish)	7.49	32.8	8.3	0.57	0.46	0.23
Canada	m	m	m	m	m	m
Chile	7.37	38.1	12.1	0.47	0.49	0.04
Czech Republic	7.05	30.7	13.8	0.65	0.63	0.19
Denmark	m	m	m	m	m	m
Estonia	7.50	37.0	9.3	0.46	0.70	0.15
Finland	7.89	44.4	6.7	0.74	0.47	0.18
France	7.63	36.6	7.4	0.45	0.49	0.35
Germany	7.35	34.0	11.1	0.80	0.50	0.26
Greece	6.91	26.2	14.7	0.64	0.48	0.20
Hungary	7.17	31.7	13.1	0.74	0.68	0.33

(*Continued*)

TABLE 1.1 (Continued)

	Students' life satisfaction[1]					Gender difference in life satisfaction (B-G)	Socioeconomic disparity in life satisfaction (top–bottom quarter of ESCS[2])	Difference in life satisfaction between high-achieving and low-achieving students in science (top–bottom quarter of science performance)
	Average	Students who are very satisfied with life (9–10)		Students who are not satisfied with life (0–4)				
	Mean	%		%		Dif.	Dif.	Dif.
OECD average	7.31	34.1		11.8		0.58	0.44	0.12
Iceland	7.80	46.7		9.5		0.93	0.73	0.55
Ireland	7.30	32.4		11.9		0.56	0.19	0.04
Israel	m	m		m		m	m	m
Italy	6.89	24.2		14.7		0.79	0.39	0.09
Japan	6.80	23.8		16.1		-0.12	0.38	0.31
Korea	6.36	18.6		21.6		0.47	0.48	0.13
Latvia	7.37	31.5		8.9		0.16	0.64	0.20
Luxembourg	7.38	36.1		11.1		0.78	0.49	0.24
Mexico	8.27	58.5		6.4		0.12	0.12	0.06
Netherlands	7.83	32.5		3.7		0.55	-0.03	-0.38
New Zealand	m	m		m		m	m	m
Norway	m	m		m		m	m	m
Poland	7.18	32.4		12.6		0.69	0.47	-0.02
Portugal	7.36	31.0		8.9		0.51	0.22	-0.17
Slovak Republic	7.47	39.4		11.3		0.59	0.43	0.06
Slovenia	7.17	32.5		13.5		0.91	0.07	-0.05
Spain	7.42	33.0		9.5		0.37	0.49	0.23
Sweden	m	m		m		m	m	m
Switzerland	7.72	39.6		7.4		0.65	0.22	0.23

The Emergence of a Reasoning

The idea of the social sciences as embodying desired futures to be actualized through number was visible in the European Enlightenment from the late 18th century. If we look at David Hume and British theorists of wealth, society and political economy in the early 18th century, the naturalist philosophy considers a desired world of equity and equivalence as less of questions of knowledge than as about justice in the law governing market exchange. Numbers did not play a part in deciding justice and equity. Adam Smith's *The Wealth of Nations* (1776), in contrast to Hume, recast the calculations about markets into questions of science as standardized 'markets' in a manner that could be projected into resemblances of the future. The market, theoretically the heart of Smith's moral economy, was an agent to increase national wealth through '*the invisible hand*' of human motives and competition. Smith invented ways to gain numerical representation through setting up ways of "measuring and calculating as if they did exist in order to say something about wealth and governing" (Poovey, 1998, pp. 240–241). The numbers were not descriptive but 'embodied [Smith's] *a priori* assumptions about what the market system *should be*' (Poovey, 1998, p. 216, italics in original).

Smith's sciences of society and wealth can be understood as embodying the movement from systemic philosophical claims about universals (human nature), to descriptions of abstractions (the market system), and then to the quantifications. The quantifications were of the effects or products of the abstractions (labor, national prosperity). The later became the 'social facts' that enable comparisons (Poovey, 1998, p. 237). The philosophical operations of abstracting and generalizing markets inscribed the philosopher's hope that its knowledge would lead to action and 'if the action was diligently pursued, it could actualize the future of which the philosopher was the first to dream' (Poovey, 1998, p. 247).

The quantifications as descriptions of the theory became a historical agent of '*human nature*', a philosophical universal that could be named and could quantify the effects of the abstraction. Constructing aggregates was to 'register the significance of these phenomena which could only be known in retrospect and discounting what diverged from type so as to describe "nature"'' (Poovey, 1998, p. 226). The historical schema gave importance to domesticity, manners, women and commercial society as

> the most sophisticated incarnation of human sociality through which the human mind would be collectively revealed [...] The second order abstractions such as labor and happiness that was no longer a universal claim but a non-rhetorical (nonsuasive) place for a kind of representation that described what *could be* as if this potential was simply waiting to materialize.
> *(Poovey, 1998, p. 248, italics in original)*

We focus on Smith's science of wealth, as it provides a way to think historically of '*society*' not as a domain but as something that is assembled as a way to speak and act about people and collective belonging. Prior to the 18th century in Europe, for example, 'society' was a word to describe an association or guild of people. Society in the late 18th century came to refer to anonymous forces and structures that gave organization to human life. The appearance of individuality with an independent existence paradoxically was in reference to principles about society. Adam Smith's notion of the invisible hand of markets gave focus to the abstract forces through which the individual pursued self-interest in the promotion of the good of society. John Locke's political theory embodied principles about the consciousness of the self to the knowledge gained through the experiences of society. Jean-Jacques Rousseau's notion of the social contract related government and individuality as central in determining '*the general will*'. While different in the relation of the social and the individual, the two do not stand in opposition but are embodied in the same phenomenon.

The inscription of '*the social*' gave reference to the abstract relations through which individuality was linked with Enlightenment notions of the cosmopolitan and later brought into the political theories of the citizen and collective belonging in the new republics. The German sociologist Tönnies' (1887/2007) Lutheran-inspired notions of *Gemeinschaft* (based on personal interaction) and *Gesellschaft* (based on indirect interaction), for example, were to consider how urban societies could reestablish its prior pastoral communities of belonging. The distinctions of *Gemeinschaft* (pastoral) and *Gesellschaft* (urban society) traveled and were translated into American Calvinist salvation narratives about rural pastoral communities to deal with the perceived moral disorder of early 20th century urban populations. The concepts about primary groups and symbolic interactionism generated principles about how social belonging and '*home*' can be established in the abstract and anonymous conditions and qualities of industrial and urban '*society*'.[1]

Our interest, most visible in the fourth section of this book, is how this making of society and collective norms and values of belonging is inscribed in international assessments through its expertise of quantification. The making of these inscription devices about schools are not only about children's performances but also historically embody principles about '*the nature of people*' as a society. For instance, Porter (2012) points out that the making of thin descriptions is based on thick networks and processes that cannot be assumed when looking at the tables, charts and graphs about nations and school performances. Kullenberg (2012) analyzes the production of surveys, for example, and examines how making a quantification of society is possible. He suggests that the use of quantitative facts regarding a society shapes and fashions what becomes the problems within that same construction of the social. Methodologically, there is no need for interpretation. The common production of '*the social*' does not require a detour via the '*signifier*' or '*discourse*'. It is possible, as long as empirical material can be assembled properly, to follow references to texts, instruments, scales, practices, people and so forth in a very concrete sense.

The inscriptions of numbers are a method of thought, a grid of cultural and sociological analysis, an imagination and a method of governing that moves into non-economic phenomena focusing on attributes and correlations that reference behavior rather than process (Foucault, 2004/2008, p. 218). Current international assessments, the concern of this book, embody theories about individuality and society in the categories inscribed into the comparative statistics of assessment. Those categories and the construction of equivalences through the application of statistics are not, in fact, about assessing what is, but about what is to become. The numbers are cultural practices that embody changing social conditions that also change people.

The uniformity given by numbers brings unlike orders in social life into a system of magnitudes that regularize relations among social and psychological components (Rose, 1999). If I use the contemporary policy and research about poverty in for example, the United Kingdom and the United States, numbers establish categories of equivalence and correlate them to identify factors about the family '*unit*' such as physical, social and psychological characteristics of the home and parental relations. By correlating the statistical magnitudes of these characteristics of populations to achievement levels of children, it is thought that a more equal and democratic society can be achieved. Numbers perform as technologies to map boundaries and the internal characteristics of the spaces to be managed as a strategy to make judgments outside of the subjective. Yet while the things of numbers 'act' as real, they embody implicit choices about 'what to measure, how to measure it, how often to measure it and how to present and interpret the results' (Rose, 1999, p. 199).

Numbers as Inscription Devices

The thinking of numbers as '*inscription devices*' is important when viewing international assessments and its visual culture in which the graphs, tables and charts are taken as a mode of telling the truth. The collection and aggregation of numbers participate in a 'clearing' or space where thought and action can occur (Rose, 1999, p. 212). That cultural space in schooling entails the fabrication of human kinds. Fabrication focuses on the distinctions and classifications about people as having double and simultaneous qualities. The categories about children and the school subjects in the assessments are fictions. What constitutes mathematics, physics and literature education in the assessments draw on the modes of representation and processes of thinking about children's learning found in particular historical European and North American models of the curriculum. This performs as the '*back stage*', or assembly of different sets of principles that connect and make reasonable the models of curriculum through which the assessments are formed.

If we use the analogy of alchemy, the assessments are based on a range of different activities that occur before the assessments are ever constructed through measurement practices (Popkewitz, 1984, 2008). The curriculum models are translations and transmogrifications of the historical relations that form the disciplinary fields of school subjects. Translation into curriculum models are necessary, as schools have different sets of cultural relations and patterns of communication, among others, then the disciplinary fields of physics or mathematics. These school models of curriculum design are shaped and fashioned through psychological and sociological theories that were invented to understand science, history or mathematics as fields of knowledge production. The psychologies of learning were formed in governing the moral order in which children develop that anticipates a desired adulthood (see Lesko, 2001). This fiction about who the child is and should be was expressed in the psychological notion of adolescence of the early 20th century American child studies. The psychologies were invented to change the ways in which the inner qualities and moral values of new populations were coming into mass schooling—particularly urban, immigrant and racialized children and families (Popkewitz, 2008).[2]

The abstractions are chimeras of the first order: what are given as the school subjects to be assessed are alchemies and chimeras. If one examines the contemporary McKinsey report on '*youth*' (Mourshed et al., 2013) and the recent OECD report on the '*well-being*' of the child, the classifications and distinctions of the child studies are formed without any recognition of '*the back stage*' in the curriculum models and psychologies that structure what is assessed. The cultural practices embodied in the numbers are elided. Youth is given as a particular representation and identity to order and organize the study of schooling, crime, family and community, among others. Its inscription as an independent space shapes and fashions technologies that produce kinds of people, act on particular populations and function as cultural theses for people to act for themselves. In this sense, international large-scale assessments (ILSA) are actors, producing relations of individuality and the social that are not only descriptive but anticipatory of what should be.

Objective of the Book

We have entitled the book *Education by the Numbers and the Making of Society: The Expertise of International Assessments*. With this as a title, we engage into the international emergence of a particular international style of reasoning about society, science and governing through numbers. The book moves in two directions at the same time: (1) case studies of international comparisons of education performances and (2) science and technologies studies to consider the historical and social/political changes of the science and society relations. By speaking of the book in this way, we bring what are often two disparate fields of research into a conversation that is vital in order to understand and analyze current discourses in educational knowledge production and governing.

International large-scale assessments (ILSA have become of increasing importance in educational research as well as for policymaking and professional work.

It is also observed as an expanding field. Since the 1990s, a number of research programs, for example, initiated by the IEA, the OECD and the European Union (EU), are carried out and published, which are then disseminated, discussed and criticized within policy, research and media. Consequently, ILSA is producing a vast amount of educational research products considered to be highly relevant in key areas like policymaking and educational reforms all over the world.

However, ILSA is also highly contested as a reference in policymaking as well as criticized by researchers because of its methodological assumptions and operations. The ILSA research programs—such as the OECD *Programme for International Student Assessment* (PISA) or the IEA *Trends in International Mathematics and Science Study* (TIMSS)—have led to a large set of research studies performed by independent academic scholars. In a research review initiated by the Swedish Research Council, more than 11,000 such publications were located (Lindblad, Pettersson, & Popkewitz, 2015). This phenomenon of using data from international large-scale assessments is not merely about education and international agencies. Its style of reasoning (cf. Hacking, 1992) circulates, for example, also in the World Bank as it talks about economic indicators, the role of the state and comparative ranking about health of societies and the political progressiveness of nation. By acknowledging that the reasoning within ILSA also influences other activities taking place within an international discourse on education, we are in a position to also study some of the historical and social/political changes that occur effecting the science/society relation, and by that we are able to start a discussion about how education is thought of and interpreted today within a specific reasoning on how numbers are used.

The book's contribution moves as such through two different layers of contemporary scholarship. First, the scholarship opens up new avenues for thinking about nexus of actors—institutional and epistemological—that produce educational policy, educational research and school programs in a transnational context. Second, the project of the book is related to the social science studies, which consider how numbers and technologies in producing these numbers are historically inscribed in social and cultural practices as ways of '*producing valid and accurate statements*' about who '*we*' are and should be.

As a result of this framing of the book, the individual chapters draw attention to new institutional actors outside what is ordinarily viewed as the nation and the state. These international actors that are highlighted as important influences how educational phenomena are interpreted and organized as systems of intervention. International organizations assessments of student performance, however, are viewed as not only descriptive and comparative measures of school system performance. They have also an effect on what is thought and done. These effects steer models of change and how the context is ordered in national policy and research.

At a different and related layer of analysis—related to the sociology of knowledge—the book explores how particular categories and distinctions inscribed in numbers and their magnitudes function as '*actors*' in narratives of educational practice and reforms. Numbers and statistics are, as shown in these discussions, central features of how contemporary societies present valid data about social life and narratives of progress and development. The construction of the categories and correlations of measurements are in these discussions considered as cultural practice that embody principles about '*the nature of society*', its '*kinds of people*' and '*what matters*' as the social context of change brought into national imaginaries and the futures in their development. Our intent is to explore the social and cultural principles embodied in the international comparative assessments as '*rationales*' to shape and fashion what is (im)possible for intervention to rectify social issues.

When the institutional and sociology of knowledge analyses are explored, it becomes apparent that the distinction between society and science is not oppositional categories, but one that is in a constant relation. Further, these relations entail new nodal points both in nations and also outside through the increasing visibility and involvement of international assessments that are important in an education discourse.

We believe that it is important for academia to comprehend and discuss implications of large-scale international studies to the meaning and making of educational knowledge in contemporary society. We also take seriously the questions raised about how to intervene, taking the position to challenge the common sense and to question the seeming causality of today's orthodoxy as important to processes of thinking about the possibilities of alternatives.

Overview of the Chapters

The book engages in the issues of science and numbers as an '*actor*', providing an intellectual and historical view to the particular contributions. The contributions are divided into four sections:

I. Numbers: A History and Style of Reasoning
II. The Field of Making of Data: Problematics of Assessment
III. Large-Scale Assessment as the Production of Numbers
IV. The Dissolution of the Science/Society Distinction

The different sections provide concrete case studies on how numbers become an '*actor*' in governing social and educational phenomena. In doing so, it explores how a particular style of reason enters and is transformed into material processes in shaping and fashioning research, policy and reform programs, with transnational education sectors as its central focus. The second section through the fourth section examines the distinctions, differentiations and categories that are inscribed in the discourses and measurement procedures for making principles visible about how judgments are made, conclusions drawn, solutions given plausibility and the daily life made manageable and intelligible. In doing so, we are not arguing that the nation as a specific sphere for educational discourse has disappeared in the process of globalization, but we do argue that there are new sets of actors—institutional and epistemological—that are working through international performance assessments such as organizations like OECD, IEA, EU and McKinsey that changes the role of the nation in terms of educational knowledge production and governing.

The first section of the book provides also a historical discussion that intersects philosophy and history of science and '*the state*' with the specific problems set up within the book. In this, we introduce scholarship that is often seen in other places then explicitly educational. By including these scholars into discussions on educational policy, we are able to visualize a discussion where '*the state*' is analyzed in terms of changes in knowledge production and governing. By doing so, we are able to highlight ILSA as something '*new*' in the contemporary in producing educational knowledge as well as how '*the state*' has to govern education. Consequently, on the basis of these notions, we believe that it is important for academia to comprehend and discuss implications of international large-scale assessments to the meaning and making of educational knowledge in contemporary society. We also take seriously the questions raised about how to intervene, taking the position to challenge the common sense and to question today's orthodoxy as important for analyzing the premises for the '*doxa*' and to engage in a critical discussion about alternatives to this '*doxa*'.

In the first section of the book, the production of numbers in and on education is analyzed. Theodore M. Porter starts with a piece on the history of sciences. In his chapter, *Politics by the Numbers*, he presents a history of statistics as developed in the social sciences for governing and preserving national populations by means of information collection and decontextualization. Porter also show how statistics has been a matter of control as well as sources for visibility of societal categories and their struggle for social recognition and challenge of oppression. Hans Krause Hansen and Anne Vestergaard analyze a particular use of numbers in for example, ranking lists, in their chapter, *On the Contest of Lists and Their Governing Capacities: How 'Tax Havens' Became 'Secrecy Jurisdictions'*. Such lists are reducing complexities by classifications and operations in order to get lists that seem to be highly transparent, but are based on sets of complex activities in need to be clarified. A historical study by Catarina S. Martins analyzes universal stages in child development by means of technologies of comparison. Her chapter, *Time, Drawing, Testing: The Making Up of the Developmental Child and the Measuring of the Nation's Development* presents the framing of contemporary assessments and the identification of abnormalities. Barbara Czarniawska analyzes how the world of science is meeting the world of commerce in her chapter, *And the World Has Finally Been Made to Measure*. She notes how meta-organizations such as OECD are regulating other organizations. Given current developments, Czarniawska argues for the vital importance to analyze such meta-organizations and think tanks and their role in shaping education.

Within the second and third sections of the book, the development of large-scale assessments is problematized from different angles for investigating what kind of knowledge is gained and what is the reasoning behind these assessments. In the chapter by Regula Bürgi and Daniel Tröhler—*Producing the 'Right Kind of People': The OECD Education Indicators in the 1960s*—we are given the opportunity to understand how the OECD already in the 1960s was inspired by how education was compared within the reasoning in the IEA and how this was interpreted within the OECD sphere constituting an effort to create indicators for not only understanding, but also managing education. Creating indicators on education have a lot in common with the struggle to standardize, which is the focus in Radhika Gorur's chapter—*Standards: Normative, Interpretative and Performative*—where the author tries to find some of the reasoning behind standardization within education. Organizations like the IEA and the OECD developed into important agencies attracting scientists and other kinds of experts. Within this milieu of knowledge-intensive activities based on specific reasoning, a specific kind of expertise is created, with a special focus on policy change. Luis Miguel Carvalho's chapter—*International Assessments and Its Expertise Fabricating Expert Knowledge for Policy*—makes an argument on how this functions and what the results are of this activity. In David Berliner's chapter—*The Implications of Understanding That PISA Is Simply Another Standardized Achievement Test*—we are given the opportunity to better understand in what ways PISA, as an example of an international large-scale assessment, is simply another standardized achievement test, which, if true, cannot as much be used for comparing nations as for testing kids. All four chapters in Section II help us to better understand what international achievement tests are about, what reasoning lies behind them, what are the problematics framing them and how can this be understood in the making of society and its citizens.

It is not just that international large-scale assessments are parts in constituting the society and its citizens by chance. For this to happen, the results from the tests have to gain or, at least, claim legitimacy. This is a central discussion in the third section of the book. One way of doing this is to blot out the borders between the results presented in reports emanating from the organizations performing the tests, science, policymaking and media. PISA's use of the social media platform Twitter for communicating their findings is investigated by Miguel A. Pereyra, Antonio Luzón, Mónica Torres and Daniel Torres-Salinas in their chapter, *PISA as a Social Media Event: Powering the 'Logics of Competition'*. They capture principles on PISA at work on Twitter such as the decoupling of policy, research and practice. Another example of how the results emanating from international large-scale assessments are traveling is done in the chapter by Christina Elde Mølstad and Daniel Pettersson—*Who Governs the Numbers? The Framing of Educational Knowledge by TIMSS Research*. In this study, the dissemination of '*facts*' from TIMSS into the field of science is investigated. By doing bibliometric research on where and by whom the data from TIMSS are used, they are in a position to present the scientific field of what they call TIMSS research. The third chapter in this section—*OECD as a Site of Coproduction: The European Education Governance and the New Politics of 'Policy Mobilization'*—is written by Sotiria Grek. The study illustrates how lines are blotted out and how a specific reasoning is gaining legitimacy. The chapter is a fine example on how the OECD invites other actors and how in that process legitimacy can be further gained. Conclusively, Sections II and III of the book try to bring together different aspects on how a *'comparativistic paradigm'* influences the activity of comparing education and how this gains legitimacy by creating it as a specific branch within the comparative education with a constructed historical, societal, organizational and scientific legitimacy. In this, international large-scale assessments are portrayed as important actors.

In the fourth section of the book, Thomas Popkewitz and Sverker Lindblad in their chapter, *Statistical Reasoning, Governing Education and the Making of Differences as Kinds of People* explores statistics as a particular style of reasoning and technology in the making of people into populations. The use of populations invents inventories or profiles of people that are not descriptive but anticipatory. Anticipatory as they embody cultural and social principles about desired futures about who children, but also families and communities, should be. The chapter explores the inscription produced by the distinctions and classifications of the successful and failing schools that bring into being epistemological principles that are no longer fictions but principles of reflection and action. The numbers of ILSA are inscription devices about desired kinds of people and societies that are to be actualized through the categories, distinctions and classification through numbers are given intelligibility. The chapter by Thomas Popkewitz, *Anticipating the Future Society: The Cultural Inscription of Numbers and International Large-Scale Assessments* examines how OECD's PISA and the McKinsey reports of education bring into action technologies that govern what is seen, talked about and done. Its expertise is a particular kind of science that creates the abstraction of the school as '*a system*' whose parts function to order and classify how judgments are made, conclusions are drawn, rectification to social and educational programs are proposed and the fields of existence are made manageable and predictable in school reform. The chapter also explores how the very categories and distinctions embodied in the numbers and magnitude of ILSA fabricate not only narratives and images of society, but in practice, also kinds of people. If we focus on OECD's PISA 2015 *Students' Well-Being* report (OECD, 2017b), the qualities and characteristics of students' relationships to family and community are not empirically derived but abstractions that, if we return to the previous, move from a philosophical universal into measurements of representations to be materialized about what is hoped for. The abstraction of the school as a system is codified and standardized through numbers as social facts. These facts enable comparisons to trace differences and identify its '*pathways*' to its realization, to use the phrases in the OECD and McKinsey reports discussed.

The End of a Beginning

By inviting these scholars to present their arguments and texts, and by putting it together in a book, we hope to start a discussion on the phenomenon of ILSA in a more elaborated manner. We have no intention that this book will function as an encyclopedia for researchers and an interested public on ILSA, the contemporary role of ILSA or the activities influenced by it, but hopefully it can be the start for a further discussion on these matters, matters that are of importance for understanding education discourses of today.

Of special interest is the notion of a comparativistic paradigm in comparative education and how this is influencing understandings of education and educational knowledge. What are the implications of such a comparativistic turn in educational policy and in the making of education and schooling?

Notes

1. The concept of 'primary group' of Charles Horton Cooley (1909), one of the founding members of the American Sociological Society, and the symbolic interactionism of George Herbert Mead (1934) gave expression to human agency within the grid of practices associated discussions about the social conditions of American urban life.
2. 'Adolescence' was a word that existed prior to Hall but brought into a realm of the new sciences of psychology to rationalize, classify and administer children.

References

Anderson, C. A. (1961). Methodology of comparative education. *International Review of Education*, 7(1), 1–23.
Carvalho, L. M. (2012). The fabrications and travels of a knowledge-policy instrument. *European Educational Research Journal*, 11(2), 172–188.
Cooley, C. H. (1909/2009). *Social organization: A study of the larger mind*. Ithaca, NY: Cornell University Press.
Cussó, R., & D'Amico, S. (2005) From development comparatism to globalization comparativism: Towards more normative international education statistics. *Comparative Education*, 41(2), 199–216.
Epstein, E. H. (2008). Setting the normative boundaries: Crucial epistemological benchmarks in comparative education. *Comparative Education*, 44(4), 372–386.
Foshay, A. W., Thorndike, R. L., Hotyat, F., Pidgeon, D. A., & Walker, D. A. (1962). *Educational achievements of 13 year olds in twelve countries*. Hamburg: UNESCO Institute of Education.
Foucault, M. (2004/2008). *The birth of biopolitics: Lectures at the Collège de France, 1978–1979*. New York: PalgraveMacmillan.

García Garrido, J. L. (1996). *Fundamentos de Educación Comparada* (Editorial). Madrid: Dykinson S. L.
Hacking, I. (1983). *Representing and intervening: Introductory topics in the philosophy of natural science*. Cambridge: Cambridge University Press.
Hacking, I. (1992). "Style" for historians and philosophers. *Studies in History and Philosophy of Science Part A, 23*(1), 1–20.
Halpern, O. (2014). *Beautiful data: A history of vision and reason since 1945 (experimental futures)*. Durham, NC: Duke University Press.
Kamens, D. H. (2009). Globalization and the growth of international educational testing and national assessment. *Comparative Education Review, 54*(1), 5–25.
Kazamias, A., & Massialas, B. G. (1982). Comparative education. In H. E. Mitzel (Ed.), *Encyclopedia of educational research* (Vol 1). New York: Free Press.
Kullenberg, C. (2012). *The quantification of society: A study of a Swedish research institute and survey-based social science*. Gothenburg: Gothenburg University.
Lesko, N. (2001). *Act your age: A cultural construction of adolescence*. New York & London: Routledge Falmer.
Lindblad, S., Pettersson, D., & Popkewitz, T. S. (2015). *International comparisons of school results: A systematic review of research on large scale assessments in education*. Stockholm: Swedish Research Council.
Mead, A. G. H. (1934). *Mind, self, and society from the standpoint of a social behaviorist*. Chicago: Chicago University Press.
Mourshed, M., Farrell, D., & Barton, D. (2013). *Education to employment: Designing a system that works*. Chicago: McKinsey & Company.
Noah, H. J., & Eckstein, M. A. (1969). *Toward a science of comparative education*. New York: Macmillan.
Nowotny, H., Scott, P., & Gibbons, M. (2003). Introduction: Mode 2 revisited: The new production of knowledge. *Minerva, 41*(3), 179–194.
OECD (2006). *Education at a glance: OECD indicators 2006*. Paris: OECD Publishing.
OECD. (2017a). *PISA 2015 results (Vol. III): Students' well-being PISA*. Paris: OECD Publishing.
OECD. (2017b). *PISA 2015 results (Vol. III): Students' well-being*. Paris: OECD Publishing. http://dx.doi.org/10.1787/9789264273856-en
Pettersson, D. (2014). The development of the IEA: The rise of large-scale testing. In A. Nordin & D. Sundberg (Eds.), *Transnational policy-flows in European education: Conceptualizing and governing knowledge* (pp. 105–122). East Greenwich: Oxford Studies in Comparative Education. Symposium Books.
Poovey, M. (1998). *A history of the modern fact: Problems of knowledge in the sciences of wealth and society*. Chicago: University of Chicago Press.
Popkewitz, T. S. (1984). *Paradigm and ideology in educational research: The social function of the intellectual*. London & New York: Routledge.
Popkewitz, T. S. (2008). *Cosmopolitanism and the age of school reform: Science, education, and making society by making the child*. New York: Routledge.
Popkewitz, T. S., & Lindblad, S. (2010). Educational governance and social inclusion and exclusion: Some conceptual difficulties and problematics in policy and research. *Discourse: Studies in the Cultural Politics of Education, 21*(1), 5–44.
Porter, T. M. (1995). *Trust in numbers: The pursuit of objectivity in science and public life*. Princeton, NJ: Princeton University Press.
Porter, T. M. (2012). Funny numbers. *Culture Unbound, 4*, 585–598.

Rose, N. (1999). *Powers of freedom: Reframing political thought.* Cambridge: Cambridge University Press.
Roselló, P. (1943). *Marc-Antoine Jullien de Paris: Père de l'Education Comparée et Précurseur du Bureau International de l'Education.* Geneva: International Bureau of Education.
Smith, A. (1776). *An inquiry into the nature and causes of the wealth of nations.* London: Methuen & Co. Ltd.
Steiner-Khamsi, G., & Waldow, F. (2012). *World yearbook of education 2012: Policy borrowing and lending in education.* Milton Park: Routledge.
Tönnies, F. (2007). *Community and society (Gemeinschaft und Gesellschaft).* New Brunswick, NJ & London: Transaction Publishers.

SECTION I
Numbers
A History of a Style of Reasoning

This section brings together historical discussions that intersect philosophy and history of science and '*the state*' to think about how numbers become a way of thinking about reality and change. This scholarship often seen in other places then explicitly educational. By including this scholarship, our intent is to think about educational phenomena as part of larger social, cultural and political formations and changes in knowledge production and governing. By doing so, we are able to highlight ILSA as something '*new*' in the contemporary in producing educational knowledge in the governing of education. We believe that this historicizing is important for comprehending and discussing the implications of international large-scale assessments to the meaning and making of educational knowledge in contemporary society.

In this section, Theodore M. Porter starts with a text on the history of sciences. In his chapter *Politics by the Numbers*, a history of statistics as developed in the social sciences for governing and preserving national populations by means of information collection and decontextualization is presented. Porter also shows how statistics has been a matter of control as well as sources for visibility of societal categories and their struggle for social recognition and challenge of oppression. Hans Krause Hansen and Anne Vestergaard analyzes particular use of numbers in for example, ranking lists, in their chapter: *On the Contest of Lists and Their Governing Capacities: How 'Tax Havens' Became 'Secrecy Jurisdictions'*. Such lists are reducing complexities by classifications and operations in order to get lists that seem to be highly transparent, but are based on sets of complex activities in need to be clarified. A historical study by Catarina S. Martins analyzes universal stages in child development by means of technologies of comparison. Her chapter, *Time, Drawing, Testing: The Making Up of the Developmental Child and the Measuring of the Nation's Development* presents the framing of contemporary assessments and the identification of abnormalities. Finally, Barbara Czarniawska analyzes how the world of science is meeting the world of commerce in her chapter, *And the World Has Finally Been Made to Measure*. She notes how meta-organizations such as OECD are regulating other organizations. Given current developments, Czarniawska argues for the vital importance to analyze such meta-organizations and think tanks and their role in shaping education.

2
POLITICS BY THE NUMBERS

Theodore M. Porter

'*In the beginning was the word*'. The poet Goethe revised the famous words of John the evangelist into '*Im Anfang war die Tat* [*In the beginning was the Act*]'. History of science in former times was very reluctant to confuse scientific knowledge with human deeds. My graduate advisor, Charles Gillispie, insisted on the conceptual purity of objective science even as he devoted most of his scholarly career to research on its tight historical relations with the French state during the last years of the Old Regime and the Revolution. He also was highly skeptical of the poet's pretended contributions to science, depicting him instead as the very model of anti-science. Goethe's bitter denunciation of Newton's *Opticks* was a sign of the problem, whose core lay in his effort to humanize science, to make it speak to human needs and embody human values. In 1960, Gillispie was highly skeptical of claims for science as a vital source of practical technologies. The leaders of the rising discipline of history of science generally agreed on this. Gradually, over the next decade, he changed his mind. The tools and concepts of science, he now acknowledged, were becoming important for technology by the 18th century. He did not—and neither can we—accept that technological breakthroughs always or even usually begin as basic science. The claim for science as the unique basis for bold new technologies was also a claim for public funding, and engineers appreciate the dignity that comes from an association with disinterested knowledge. Yet there is no sharp divide between science and technology, knowledge and practical action, but at most a highly porous one, surviving, perhaps, only for the sake of more advantageous trespassing. Much of the most important scholarship now in history of science is about their intersections.

And what of social science? It has never been fully distinguishable from natural science, and it, too, runs together with a wide range of social technologies. We confront a still wider range of interactions if we speak instead of '*human sciences*'. The term, familiar in French, is not quite a synonym for social sciences. Michel Foucault, with whom it is often identified in English, did not invent the term, but he put new emphasis on its active side, as a developing set of technologies designed to alter human behavior and even human consciousness. This aspect of human science is, I think, then its association with any particular subject matter. It takes in medicine, architecture, management and parts of natural science as well as psychology, anthropology and sociology. Now that medical enterprise has pulled ahead of military ambition as the dominant factor in the economy of science, human science has become fundamental.

In this respect, Goethe proves to be right, at least for historians of science and STS[1] scholars. Our subject matter demands a focus on actions rather than just words, and often the recognition of words—and numbers—as actions. I do not accept the necessity of choosing between things and ideas, or of privileging objects over people. Nor is there any need. With only a little irony, we can defend an interest in the human side of science with this slogan: *People are things too*. The key point is not to require a clear boundary between science and other knowledge forms. That doesn't mean we accept every truth claim as equally valid, and, of course, we still need to make distinctions. But whatever functions as knowledge in the world must be regarded as knowledge, even when we doubt its correctness.

Here, the topic is numbers. They are brought to bear on every subject matter and for a multitude of purposes. The forms of quantification that are most respected by institutionalized science are not necessarily the most important, and may not be the most truthful for every purpose. The urge to set up rigorous criteria of validity is irrepressible, yet they remain out of reach. The power of the statistical significance test in science as in administrative matters arose as a beacon of objectivity, a promise of incorruptibility, resting on the supposition that measurement and calculation stand above self-interested manipulation. Are these, therefore, free of politics? It scarcely rises even to the point of irony to point out that the determined pursuit of apolitical neutrality represents a political ideal. That does not make it an easy goal to attain, and the determination to let numbers decide leads to striking unintended consequences. There are good reasons for investing trust in science, but to pretend that it can rise wholly above ordinary human foibles and provide easy, formulaic answers to complex questions is to turn it into politics by other means.

While numbers are not synonymous with science, much or most science can be summed up in numbers, and this is not less true for science that has been decked out for power. We may think of economic measures of unemployment or GDP,[2] medical measures of therapeutic effectiveness or risk factors or educational measures of student achievement or teacher effectiveness. Tools of precise measurement are always somewhat technical, even when the concepts seem simple. Indeed, all of science is in some way technical, and is often, though misleadingly, defined in terms of technicality. The ascent in human sciences of statistical reasoning has incorporated this veneration for the technical, even when its conclusions provoke opposition. Technical knowledge is the business of experts and specialists, and seems, therefore, (again, misleadingly) to be remote from human interests. Statistics has become a mathematically demanding and specialized field, but statistics also has its ways of reducing technical complexity to apparent simplicity. Complex questions are often summed up as a comparison of just two numbers, perhaps with significance levels or error bars lurking in the margins. The suppression of complexity is often irresistible, even if, on any serious issue that people care about, such radical simplification will provoke dissent. Few disciplines have generated such persistent dissent as statistics, just as few are so often bound up with corrupt practices as accounting. Yet both are commonly pushed aside, either as boring and routine or as so encumbered with minute rules as to be incomprehensible. The beguiling goal of quantitative transparency, rising out of incontrovertible rigor, remains in our sights, often just out of reach.

In fields like education and therapeutic medicine, the processing or '*reduction*' of observations is now a well-developed set of methodologies associated with principles of mathematical probability. The most basic tools arose in sciences of the observatory, especially in astronomy, where they achieved a reasonably standardized form in the early 19th century. Similar tools came into use to estimate errors and variation around mean values, whereas more complex tools to define relationships between variables in biology, psychology and social science took off near the end of the 19th century. These techniques have, of course, continued to develop, and the discipline of statistics is now understood as an applied mathematical field.

Whether to regard the deployment of these tools as a triumph of mathematics is another question. The physicist Eugene Wigner (1995) spoke famously of the unreasonable effectiveness of mathematics. While his title limits this unreasonable effectiveness to the natural sciences, he interpreted the thought in a very sweeping way. How stunning, he declared, that such a product of human thought as mathematics should apply at all to physical things in the external world. His essay returns several times to Galileo's law of falling bodies, which he treated as almost miraculous even in its application to stones falling from towers on Earth, and still more so when it could be shown to correspond to the circulation of planets in the heavens. Perhaps it was too good to be true. The relationship of mathematics to the world, he proposed, may not be unique:

> We are in a position similar to that of a man who was provided with a bunch of keys and who, having to open several doors in succession, always hit on the right key on the first or second trial. He became skeptical concerning the uniqueness of the coordination between keys and doors.
> *(Wigner, 1995, p. 535)*

A statistician might enter a few other reservations, for it is no simple task to reduce such data to a form that can be compared with theoretical calculation. If, to a Platonist like Galileo, mathematical regularities in the world appear as wonderful and even mysterious, a craftsman or calculator might point to the modeling tools and techniques of approximation that often are required in practice to produce a satisfactory agreement between Galileo's or Newton's laws and the observed revolutions of the planets.

While it has become in many ways a mathematical field, '*statistics*' came into the world as a social science, or more precisely as a state science, since that word '*state*', is part of its name. It was definitely also a human science, crafted to work its effects in politics, administration, law, medicine, agriculture and industry. In its 18th-century form, it was a descriptive science, with no pretentions to the mystical possession of pure or abstract truth. Informed descriptions of what was happening out beyond those places the duke, king or emperor could inspect with his own eyes should contribute to effective government. It is still in part the object of statistics, and especially of official agencies such as census bureaus, to contribute to good government. The tools of state and social statistics have evolved considerably since 1800, and we may note that, despite his insistence on natural science, Wigner began his essay with an example from human science. He imagined a conversation between a statistical demographer and an arts graduate. The humanist wants an explanation of a formula this statistician is using. Well that symbol is just ϖ, he says, the ratio of the circumference to the radius of a circle. The humanist now scoffs. His friend must be playing a joke on him. 'Surely a population has nothing to do with the circumference of the circle' (Wigner, 1995, p. 534). Indeed, the population as such does not. Measures of error and precision, however, do.

Indeed, if you had to pick just one formula to exemplify mathematical mysticism, the Gaussian normal distribution—the bell curve—would be a very an excellent candidate. The appearance together of those great irrational constants, e and ϖ, in a formula so basic remains striking, and it appears in many guises that have little to do with error. This formula has become fundamental to public health, evaluation of medical treatments, school testing, engineering, demography and almost every kind of measurement. The physicist Joseph Fourier was already impressed by its amazing range in 1819, from errors of observations to heat diffusion to insurance. Adolphe Quetelet, who labored to make statistics the basis for social science '*social physics*', viewed this 'law of error' with great reverence, and the physicist James Clerk Maxwell was duly impressed by its application to distributions of molecular velocities in gas physics. Francis Galton, a Victorian polymath with a particular devotion to statistics as a basis for the study of human heredity and eugenics, called it '*the supreme law of Unreason*'.

These scientists wrote mathematically, but with a keen sense of the things in the world to which it applied. Nineteenth-century statistical mathematics stressed the order that appeared in mass phenomena, including stable mean values and distributions of traits within populations. At its core, statistical thinking referred to something more basic still, the natural and social order that appears spontaneously in the presence of large numbers, even when, at the individual level, these events elude our understanding. A favorite example from the social sciences was suicide, whose regularity in the mass became famous in the 1830s, and could not easily be understood as the reflection of a providential order. The numbers for suicide, according to Quetelet, had to be understood in terms of the order of society, although no really satisfactory explanation could be given for the decision of particular individuals to take their own lives. In Maxwell's time, the very existence of molecules was still in doubt, and there certainly was no prospect of following the motions of individual molecules. Yet laws of gases, involving relations of pressure, volume and temperature, were as exact as any other physical principle. For the kinetic gas theory, this was a statistical relationship.

Gillispie noticed already in the early 1960s that statistical reasoning came out of the social sciences, from which it was appropriated by physics, geology, biogeography, evolutionary biology and population genetics. Quetelet regarded social science as allied to astronomy and meteorology, a science of the observatory, and Stephen Stigler has pointed out that his social science was more nearly social meteorology than social physics. It remains necessary to emphasize that the compilation and sorting of social numbers was no mere spinoff of physical science, with its traditions of mathematical reasoning going back beyond Galileo to the ancients. Quetelet, a trained mathematician and astronomer, was astonished in the late 1820s to discover that disorderly, decentralized human acts such as marriages or murders were highly stable in the mass. He regarded it as a wonderful and yet disturbing demonstration of mathematical order in social relations. It created problems for the moral doctrine of human free will while showing that society could be subject to science. Society, he announced, is a real entity, no mere sum of autonomous individuals. We see that there is some sense to the word statistics for this science of state and policy, even in relation to a mathematical field whose business is to specify sampling procedures and to establish the bounds of random error. Natural science was not accustomed to explaining exact law, such as those of thermodynamics, in terms of averages of disorderly individuals. Now, the new statistical mechanics of the second half of the 19th century appears as the entirely reasonable effectiveness of mathematics.

The statistical model of social order was in many respects liberal in its implications. A new book on historical sociology of censuses criticizes the familiar view associated with Michel Foucault that statistics has served primarily as a way of projecting the power of the state over populations. Many counts have been initiated by non-state actors as a challenge to official declarations or a strategy for organizing activity apart from political authority. It is true that during the period of industrialization, workers and farm laborers who lacked effective political standing were key objects of statistical study. Local officials, landholders and factory owners used data to keep them under observation, and in this way to regulate their behavior. But workers, too, took a great interest in numbers, and even learned to deploy them to define and defend their interests. Political reformers defended numbers as a strategy to evaluate and to challenge the state. Jean-Jacques Rousseau made it very simple in his Social Contract: 'The government under which [...] the citizens do most increase and multiply is infallibly the best' (Rousseau, 1762/1960, p. 280). He had in mind that population growth, good in itself, must follow as a consequence of prosperity, and that governments unable to achieve this were to be condemned. After Malthus, people were more nervous about exploding populations and more conscious of the potential for long-term industrial expansion arising from technology and enterprise. Political economists of the 19th century looked specifically to increased prosperity as a mark of a well-functioning political order. Such figures as crime rates, death rates and levels of literacy also sometimes came into the picture. In 1892, Alfred de Foville in France offered statistics as the infallible judge of good government. Rest assured, he declared, 'that whenever the struggle resurfaces between the champions of the general interest and that of private interests, you will find us at our post, armed and ready to march'. In modern times, this role is assigned above all to GDP.

In relation to political forms, statistics has a rather complex legacy. The census grew up in most states as a form of public information or collective self-knowledge and a democratic ritual. The census mirrors, in a way, the ballot box in an election, providing assurance that the state will take the views and needs of its citizens into account. The old fear that a census or survey will be followed by new taxes or the conscription of our children to fight vainglorious wars is mostly forgotten. State access to such information about its citizens is ensured now by registration processes, and no longer depends on the census. With the growth of neoliberal opposition to state-directed economic activity, there has been a resurgence of opposition to certain economic general of trade, income and environmental health. But in the 19th century, and for much of the 20th, census figures advertised demographic and industrial growth in successful countries, and especially in settler societies like the United States, while provoking alarm in nations whose birth rates sagged, most famously France. The preoccupation with gross numbers reflected an era of imagined homogeneity of the citizens. The census has more recently become a site of contestation over ethnic composition. With the 19th-century rise of the nation-states, ethnicity—they called it '*race*'—became a concern almost everywhere. The United States was perhaps the first country in which minority groups began campaigning effectively to redefine the terms in which they would be represented. Paul Schor, a French historian of the US census, documents these struggles over how race and ethnicity should be classified. The racialized divisions that grew up around slavery seemed a most undesirable model of human difference to immigrants from Asia and Latin America. They certainly did not want to be classified as '*colored*'. A new politics of race and ethnicity, growing up in the 20th century and mainly after World War II, regarded disparities as undesirable and looked for policies that might lessen them. In the context of this new ethno-racial management, minorities of all kinds began making new demands about how they should be represented on the census. Statistics has become a fundamental instrument for creating and shaping public visibility.

The use of statistics to assess policies and to judge elected officials has become almost routine, even if these judgments rarely achieve consensus. It is not easy, however, to know how people balance the official numbers against their own experience. Immigration is one of the great issues of the present moment. European news presents abundant images of migrants crossing from Lesbos or Lampedusa, or lining up to board trains in Vienna to reach a suitable country in which to apply for refugee status. In the United States, undocumented immigrants are less visible as they quietly travel, rarely confronting state officials unless they are found and deported or reach the point of applying for work permits. We may encounter on the streets or in gardens, construction sites and restaurants, people we suppose may be illegal. They are not at all eager to confirm such suspicions. In political discussion, we hear numbers on the order of 11 million. Would the politics be different if this number were 5 million or 20 million?

Similar uncertainties apply to measures of the economy. A weak economy is experienced at the personal level with lost jobs or reduced hours, lower wages and canceled benefits, or on the employer's side, abundant, cheap labor but lowered demand. In any case, the industrial nations put out a barrage of data pertaining to growth and prosperity. On these questions, there is now much meta-discussion. It has become normal in the respectable press as well as in more openly politicized outlets to question the reliability of new economic numbers. There are even challenges to the validity and appropriateness of the most familiar measures: not just objections in detail, but critiques of fundamental concepts. An important recent object of this critique has been GDP. A report commissioned by Nicolas Sarkozy, the former French president, and involving a considerable roster of economists and other social scientists, has, as its principal authors, Joseph Stiglitz, Amartya Sen and Jean-Paul Fitoussi.

I have on my shelves three new books on the history of GDP. One of them purports to be an '*affectionate*' history, yet agrees with the least affectionate author that GDP was shaped by the urgency of fighting the Great Depression and then mobilizing for a world war, and that it was never suited to be a measure or even a reliable indicator of economic value. GDP incorporates a host of contradictions, most famously, if a man marries his housekeeper, the salary he once paid her disappears from GDP, whose atomic unit is the nuclear family. The most critical of these books emphasizes the high values assigned by GDP to things like armies, prisons and security systems, whereas home-cooked food or clean air and water, along with most other public goods, are ignored or assigned an inadequate value. This rule applies also to public health measures, whereas cosmetic surgery is valued at whatever sum can be extracted from the customer. In its traditional form, GDP discounts the future very steeply. It we set off on a track that would suddenly end life on Earth in two centuries, the initial effect on the GDP measure would barely amount to a rounding error. How far will people follow the logic of such numbers? And do we apply them to the things that are closest to us? Americans, at least, are famous for despising the Congress but approving their Congressman, and bemoaning the crisis of education while defending their own local school.

Until perhaps a century ago, it was common even for statistical experts to make light of pretended measures of vital but subtle things like health and education. They said that such numbers functioned merely to satisfy expectations of a credulous and ill-trained public. Here is a comment in a book on the difficulties, procedures and results of statistics by a French author, written in 1904, which reached its fifth edition in 1927:

> To make a comparison so complex as this demands sustained attention, and a mind accustomed to the relativity of things. For purposes of influencing the general public, an argument loses force in proportion as it takes more terms and comprehends a wider field. Statistical problems are not questions of elementary arithmetic for the common crowd.
>
> *(quoted from Porter, 1995, p. 81)*

We find such sentiments repeatedly in the 19th and early 20th centuries. This author envisioned statistical measures as a loose guide for experts, to be applied with discretion, and as useful propaganda for the public. I don't think it was ever so easy, and it certainly is not now. Experts in statistics and social science cannot dominate discourses of number any more than they can control words and sentences. The public may not have the opportunity to vote down new definitions of unemployment, medical effectiveness or educational achievement, but they can file lawsuits, challenge budgets, change political parties or vote down a European agreement. Measurement for policy is powerful, and it can be dangerous.

Two decades ago, when I published my book *Trust in Numbers* (Porter, 1995), it seemed clear to me that the United States relied on what we can call technologies of quantitative objectivity to a degree that was unknown in Europe. I don't think this is true anymore. The European project, as Roser Cussó argues, has been in various ways a technocratic one, and some key policy initiatives at the level of Europe have relied heavily on the power of accounts and statistics. Much of this involves the imposition of uniform standards. EU ambitions for free movement of labor, including professional labor, depend on enforceable definitions of educational qualifications to allow evenhanded comparisons. Academic exchange within and beyond Europe have helped to create a class of impressively cosmopolitan scholars and scientists with an unprecedented level of cosmopolitanism. One crucial and, for some, highly burdensome aspect of the new standards is the insistence on communication and publication in English. An international system of monoglot publication opened up new opportunities for international comparison of scholars and scientists, of research institutions and of universities. Even the divorce of the UK from the EU seems unlikely to undermine the European condition as a linguistically heterogeneous continent, divided by a common language. '*The world is flat*', according to the triumphant title of a technology-infatuated American journalist. Difference of location and geography no longer matter. This may be doubted. In any case, flatness is a project, anchored in no small measure in numbers, and does not happen by itself. How should we evaluate it?

The crucial point here is that regimes of quantification cannot be regarded as neutral knowledge, a mere language of precision, but as programs of interventions. Perhaps the most fundamental limit rule by numbers is precisely the inseparability or quantification and action. Politics by the numbers dreams of bypassing the need for skill and judgment, and even of critique. However, once we take on the task of making numbers uniform and cosmopolitan, and especially if we think of using them as an algorithm of evaluation, their descriptive adequacy begins to erode. Numerical projects cannot escape the burden of responsibility for changing the world, even when they propose first to know, and only afterwards to act, now on the basis of tested schemes of measurement. They find, however, that their policy machine starts up and shoots off before they can even begin to draw a map to guide it. They may think of their measurements as indicators, but once they are taken as the basis for choices, the indicators are magically transformed into the very thing in question. If schools or hospitals know they will be judged by their performance in regard to some particular measurement, there is every incentive to labor to maximize this measurement. The agencies that preside over this testing may be fully aware of the limits of the measures, including what I call their '*Spaces of Exploitable* Ambiguity'. This means, for example, achieving a desired measure in a simple or cheap way without being bound to achieve what the measure was designed to require. In institutions such as schools and hospitals, it is extremely difficult to define measures that are neutral with respect to what is outside their control: family backgrounds, prior conditions of health, wealth or poverty and so on. The sagacious statistician may imagine quietly accommodating such discrepancies. But that requires trust in the expertise and good will of the sage. The ideal of assessment based on impartial measurement cannot accommodate expert decisions to override the verdict of the numbers with ad hoc adjustments.

We are very far then from the French statistician's comment that an implicit faith in numbers is really only for simple people. Here, the preference for quantitative rules over (claimed) depth of understanding is backed up by state power, or perhaps by the authority of international organizations. Such issues loom large in the Programme for International Student Assessment, whose acronym PISA instantly recalls the tower in a historic Italian city, famous above all for leaning. Like the American educational reforms under the *No Child Left Behind Act*, these efforts rely heavily on statistical comparisons. I do not have the knowledge or standing to sit in judgment, except to say that these initiatives display the extreme difficulty of producing true comparability between systems with different goals, different histories and different forms of institutional embeddedness.

Should different schools, perhaps with legitimately different goals, be held to the same standard? Can uniform testing really capture cultural or economic analysis, historical comprehension, clear or literary expression? Is it even the right measure for mathematical or scientific competence?

The ideal of rule by numbers raises fascinating issues on the moral as well as epistemic character of rules. Labor organizations are noted for their insistence— some for their insistence on inflexible and inappropriate rules. The justification, or excuse, is that workers with little negotiating power are otherwise subject to the whims of their employers. Even a generous patron uses charity, which transcends rules, in part to reaffirm this authority. Bosses, too, may find it convenient to rely on strict rules, but rules of work and pay are not all the same. Trade unions insist on job requirements that are within the power of the workers to fulfill without undue strain. (They may, of course, protect idleness.) Are such rules specifically adapted to repetitive, and hence (often) unskilled, labor? We reasonably suppose that what can be measured reliably is not unique or intuitive, and does not embody any distinctive craft. Expert professionals are protected less by union rules than by the possession of skills for which there are no ready substitutes. Each new task, if it is unique, requires adaptability and judgment. It may be supposed that professional labor resists measurement. Physicians, in particular, have long insisted on this point. The recent push to standardize measures of professional work suggests a process of deskilling and a sacrifice of professional dignity, associated with the power of hospital managers, insurance institutions and state regulators.

Academic life in recent decades has become a key site of assessment and regulation by measurement, still more so in much of Europe than in the United States. The modern way is to judge researchers by some combined measure of productivity and impact. It has become common to let measured journal quality stand in as a proxy for that of the particular paper. This facilitates evaluation without understanding, perhaps without reading, or even from outside the discipline. Such practices have grown up partly in the context of the Bologna process, which aspires to make university programs in different nations interchangeable. International rankings of universities are, of course, also key to the process. Universities as well as primary and secondary schools may live or die according to their performance in relation to such standards. To be sure, professional self-regulation persists to some degree, since peer evaluation retains its ritual role in publication decisions and awards of research grants. Perhaps we should be less disturbed by the loss of professional self-regulation than by the enhanced opportunities for gaming, the exploitation of ambiguity, that accompany any system of routinized measurement. It is no accident that the new power of science indicators has coincided with proliferating scandals involving doctored or invented data, plagiarism and other forms of research fraud. I find it curious and damning that researchers in many fields, especially the social sciences, have not resisted simplistic measures of research success, but even embraced them. Should we sacrifice genuinely creative research for the sake of a convenient system of evaluation?

As my examples here suggest, the function of numbers in schooling has much in common with their role in medicine. The application of quantitative technologies to medical care and public health is one of the great themes of contemporary medicine, and is widely recognized as such. I would pick out three principal dimensions of this story. First is the effort to regulate the practice of medicine in the face of traditions that grant extraordinary discretion to doctors. Here, the key quantitative technology is the controlled clinical trial as the basis for a statistical assessment of pharmaceuticals, and in general for medical evidence. Second is the need or desire to impose on medicine a more uniform and perhaps centralized system of planning and regulation of expenditures. This is interwoven with attempts to control costs. Third is increasing attention to the behavioral dimension of public health, including attempts to alter lifestyles and to control health by prescribing long-term prophylactic drugs and pushing for lifestyle changes. We think immediately of smoking and of drugs to control blood pressure and cholesterol. Some of these measures emerge out of insurance investigations—in the first instance, life insurance—though by now it extends much more widely. Insurers have long treasured their access to numbers.

The numerical aspect of topics like health and education is expressed in highly technical tools of analysis, and in iconic numbers that often enlighten but may also conceal or mislead. While there is no alternative to technical competence, it is never sufficient. Good numbers depend on scrupulous social and historical analysis. We need critiques of analytical tools and even of data, critiques that take account of the power behind numbers. Numbers, properly designed and presented, can help to reveal the play of power and even to provide a basis for challenging it. There is no easy reconciliation between technical inaccessibility and false transparency. Clear, scrupulous interpretation, including effective visual tools, has to be part of the mix. Numbers, certainly, have an important and constructive role in politics and public administration as well as in the private economy. Yet it is not enough for them to be placed at the service of power. It is equally important to generate numbers that can be used to challenge power. The 19th-century ambition to cultivate statistics as a basis of public information and criticism remains vital. A French initiative presents good statistics as a moral and political cause, under the banner of *Statactivism*. I laughed when first encountered this fusion of 'statistics' and 'activism', but it is serious as well as funny. Numbers matter. They can be brought to bear on inequality in its many dimensions, on public services, on land, transportation, schooling, nutrition, policing, health and environment. A critical perspective on the claims of numbers has a vital role, but the purpose is not to expunge numbers from public life, which would certainly be harmful if it were possible. We might, however, want to reconsider the notion that numbers should replace, rather than inform, moral and political debate. It is true that letting political leaders and privileged experts modify or adjust the message of numbers can do more harm than good, perhaps by opening up new spaces for corruption. But insisting on inflexibility will never suffice to close them, and we are unlikely to improve our lives by denying out shared humanity.

Notes

1. Acronym for Science and Technology Studies
2. Gross Domestic Product

References

Porter, T. (1995). *Trust in numbers: The pursuit of objectivity in science and public life*. Princeton, NJ: Princeton University Press.

Rousseau, J. J. (1762/1960). The social contract. In E. Barker (Ed.), *Social contract*. Oxford: Oxford University Press.

Wigner, E. P. (1995). *Philosophical reflections and syntheses*. Berlin & Heidelberg: Springer-Verlag.

3
ON THE CONTEST OF LISTS AND THEIR GOVERNING CAPACITIES

How 'Tax Havens' Became 'Secrecy Jurisdictions'

Hans Krause Hansen and Anne Vestergaard

> *The list is the origin of culture.*
> (Umberto Eco, 2009)

Introduction

At first glance, the production of lists, written on paper or computer screens, does seem an extraordinarily boring topic to explore, with no significance whatsoever beyond the most ordinary. Lists are, nonetheless, crucial for the coordination of human activity across time and space. Listing, and enlisting, transforms the complex, continuous flow of everyday practices and things into discrete and discontinuous items, which help to order and sort out things in practice. Lists open up social spaces for individual and collective control by mediating between two epistemic orders (Stäheli, 2016): on the one hand, the flow, which the list is tasked to break up, reorganize and give visual form, and on the other hand, the reading and interpretation of the list, that is, of its visual and condensed representation, especially once it has 'gone public'. This way, the list helps us to see and act upon certain, prechosen aspects of the flow, but certainly not everything.

As a puzzling side effect, the list also helps create an illusion of '*complete*' transparency and understanding (Hansen, 2015). This includes the sense of objectivity, a strange view from nowhere, even though, or perhaps because, the list rarely reveals the judgments and decisions on coding and classifications taken in the process of its making. The invisibility of this process also suggests why the effects of the list, which we tend to associate with its public appearance and circulation, actually begin to take shape well in advance, back stage. On closer inspection, and perhaps unsurprisingly, lists and listing practices turn out to be one of the foundations of modern science and bureaucracy: 'The material culture of bureaucracy and empire is not found in pomp and circumstance, nor even on the first instance at the point of a gun, but rather at the point of a list' (Bowker & Star, 2000, p. 137).

Recent research shows that lists like rankings, ratings, benchmarking and blacklists have come to play a central role in contemporary transnational governance. Shaped by the classifications of their designers, such lists operate as technologies of knowledge condensation, comparison, organization and coordination. They help to reduce complexity, providing important foundations for policy- and decision making and governing at a distance. Lists are frequently linked to quite conventional mechanisms of state or inter-state power for achieving their effects. Consider how national governments withhold development aid to other states on the basis of governance indicators that rank countries as good and bad performers (e.g. Löwenheim, 2008). Other recent examples include national governments steering public resources toward educational institutions, on the basis of their performance in international rankings (Scott, 2013), and international organizations publicly blacklisting companies from future engagement in mega-projects because of their involvement in fraudulent behavior (Hansen, 2012). Lists are linked to the activities of the private sector and corporations in transnational governance. Examples include private credit rating agencies establishing the creditworthiness of sovereign governments and public institutions on the basis of rating schemes and scores, with drastic implications for those having the '*wrong*' scores, as evidenced during the financial crisis.[1]

The pervasiveness of lists in contemporary transnational governance makes it important to scrutinize how they are formed and come to govern across time and space. In short, we are interested in analyzing the politics of lists (de Goede, Leander, & Sullivan, 2016;. Contrary to the predominant analytical focus, we shed light on how several lists operating within a transnational field can feed and interact with one another in struggles for truth and power. We provide a snapshot of how such struggles take place in the transnational arena of taxation. The issue of tax is notorious for its extreme complexity and the propensity among observers for developing shorthand reductions and simplifications of knowledge, frequently authorized by experts. It also provides an interesting laboratory for exploring what we term the contest of lists. By devising alternative lists, non-state actors can exert pressure on state actors whose '*official*' lists are responded to, contested and denounced, in prolonged struggles over truth and power. The recent revelation of the financial arrangements set up by political and financial elites to avoid and evade taxation, also referred to as the Panama Papers, provides a well-suited backdrop for investigating the contest of lists across time and space and from different points of view. The metaphor of '*Tax Haven*' has dominated the way of representing the problems of tax avoidance and tax evasion since World War II, conveying the well-known image in public blacklisting of small tropical island jurisdictions being the main actors to blame. In recent years, however, an alternative way of approaching the problem has arrived: the Financial Secrecy Index, developed by expert-activists to rank jurisdictions according to their secrecy and global financial impact. This new framing turns the problem on its head and instead locates it at the heart of major Western countries. The index has made its way to the public and policymaking circles internationally, contesting basic elements of the traditional tax haven metaphor and associated techniques of blacklisting. The contest of lists shares some affinity with the phenomenon of '*statactivism*', a contraction of both 'statistics' and 'activism' (Bruno, Didier, & Vitale, 2014). Statactivism demonstrates how lists often play a dual role. They are developed to represent reality, making visible or disclosing certain features of it, but can also be deployed to criticize it, if designed differently. When used for social mobilization, lists can play an important role in constructing a shared understanding of reality to denounce the dominant version of it. Lists can bring new processes and social categories into being at the intersections of disclosure and affirmation: The invention of new social categories—and their criticism—is as such an important terrain of statactivism (Bruno, Didier, & Vitale, 2014, Desrosières, 2014).

One typical way to approach the question as to what lists do is to analyze the actors behind a specific list, that is, those producing and issuing it, including their degree of legitimacy and trustworthiness. This approach is commonplace in studies concerned with the strengths and weaknesses of lists, including whether they actually reflect '*reality*' and especially to what degree the actor issuing the list can have a particular interest in conveying the listed items in exactly one way and not another. It is also common among practitioners. The discussions around the lists relating to the taxation debates briefly illuminated here display that logic, in which the list is still seen as an instrument or tool for political processes exterior to the list. While recognizing this important point, our approach to list and listing practices is inspired by the notion that lists can be '*reactive*' or '*performative*' (Espeland & Sauder, 2007; Hansen & Porter, 2012) if not simply '*constitutive*' of knowledge production and coordination within and across organizations and in social life more generally (Bowker & Star, 2000). In short, lists help to constitute the objects they target. In this regard, scholars have also analyzed lists under the heading of '*soft power*' or '*informational governance*', emphasizing the capacity of lists to help generate informal social pressure as opposed to more traditional, hard and legally based forms of state power (Kelley & Simmons, 2014). While that view tends to obscure that lists can be intimately related to and entangled with traditional hard power and algorithmic forms of governance (Johns, 2016), it nonetheless highlights the centrality of lists in the exercise of power.

While this focus on the centrality of lists is timely, it is important not to overstate their '*autonomy*'. While lists and especially rankings seem to be everywhere these years, their effects of power and truth must be analyzed in relationship to a more thorough examination of the knowledge circuits in which such lists are flowing, including the schemes of coding, classification, artefacts, technologies and networks that make their dissemination and consumption possible, as well as their accompanying narratives and stories. Just as lists mediate between different epistemic orders, so too is their formation and circulation associated with two orders of surveillance, which indicate the entangled character of listing practices (Hansen, 2012). First, lists are fabricated on the basis of the primary surveillance of particular processes, their coding, (numerical) classification and ordering into visualized hierarchies, back stage. Second, these hierarchies are published and reach one or more audiences, whether intentionally targeted, who then turn them into tools for surveillance, and translate observations into something meaningful, front stage. There is also a sense in which lists, from the lens of second-order surveillance, can appear as '*non-narrative*' statements detached from messy contextual narratives (Stäheli, 2016). But it would be misleading to locate them analytically '*outside*' wider discursive and institutional processes. The classificatory work that goes into the construction of lists as well as the wider discursive field, which shapes the lists, that is, their narrative points of anchoring, forms the space where the potentially ordering and governing effects of lists can be identified. In this way, lists can undoubtedly entangle and enroll audiences into a project of some sort—political, commercial and the like.

The Contest of Lists: An Extended View

Before we turn to a more detailed investigation of these dynamics with respect to the issue of taxation, we briefly look into another field in which lists and their politicization are equally prolific: education and research. The use of rankings to measure and compare education and research performance has become ubiquitous on a global scale over the past couple of decades. New rankings are continuously developed by a thriving industry of rankers, spearheaded by commercial media and international organizations (e.g. Lindblad, 2008; Wedlin, 2010; Scott, 2013). It is remarkable that the increasing concern with tax havens has expanded in roughly the same period, together with the rise of a vibrant private industry providing financial services such as wealth management. The connection between the rise of tax haven lists and rankings and the rankings in the field of education and research is subtle and indirect, suggesting huge differences but also some possible intersections. Not least, as some experts and NGOs have argued, when it comes to the draining of governments from resources that could otherwise have been invested into publicly funded education and research, among other public goods. As Oxfam has put it:

> This global system of tax avoidance is sucking the life out of welfare states in the rich world. It also denies poor countries the resources they need to tackle poverty, put children in school and prevent their citizens dying from easily curable diseases.
>
> *(Hardoon et al., 2016, p. 5)*

While the influence of rankings in education and research has been shown to vary a lot relative to national contexts and at specific moments of time (Martens &

Niemann, 2013), their impact has been described as considerable. At the level of public schools and universities, rankings influence work practices, organizational identities and strategic decisions such as the allocation of resources and other substantial priorities (e.g. Espeland & Sauder, 2007). In national policymaking, the ranking of national education and research is linked to indicators for success in the global political economy, such as national competitiveness, and anchored in methodologies of international comparison developed by organizations like the OECD. More generally, international rankings in education and research tend to initiate public and political debates, creating an 'air of competition around state performance or policies by attributing relative positions' (Martens & Niemann, 2013, p. 314). As to academia, the focus on positioning and competition at the levels of institutions and faculty is, of course, not a novelty. What is new is the extended use of increasingly sophisticated technologies for positioning universities in the shape of performance indicators and rankings that compare institutions, faculties and researchers through global media, with implications for research funding and research substance and, by implication, publication patterns (Mingers & Willmott, 2013).

A mix of factors associated with globalization, neoliberalism, individualization and mediatization of social life is usually emphasized to explain the advent and proliferation of rankings in education and research: the promotion of the market and competition in the public sector; the use of management practices known from business, such as performance-based management, which comes at the expense of traditional trust in the authority and expertise of teachers and researchers; the development of mass education and the associated public appetite for knowledge and participation in education and research, which was previously considered rather autonomous and elitist; and, not least, mediatization and commercialization, including the rise of commercial publishers of rankings keen on stimulating and satisfying knowledge and competition thirsty education and research managers, policy makers and decision makers, and wider publics. Part and parcel of all this is the emphasis on accountability and transparency in public policy. Here, rankings are claimed to provide the public and policy makers with '*information*' in the name of accountability and transparency (Scott, 2013).

Scholars point to a number of additional basic problems with rankings in education and research (e.g. Espeland & Sauder, 2007; Lindblad, 2008; Wedlin, 2010). Rankings always involve classifications and aggregations, which by their very nature can never be unbiased. The continuous advent of new and more advanced methodologies for making rankings will never remove such bias. Moreover, rankings are always general abstractions of complex local realities and qualities. Deeper nuances can rarely be captured by quantification since the latter, by definition, always entails a reduction of complexity. Finally, and related, rankings tend to have harmonizing and mainstreaming effects. Their operations are not as '*soft*' as often claimed by those who promote and use them actively, especially professionals and decision makers. Rankings have performative effects in the sense that the actors listed will usually try to adapt to the ranking by adopting as explicit target the goal of improving the position on the list.

Faced with such daunting perspectives, and reflecting on what to do, Lindblad (2008) revives Albert Hirschman's classical conceptualization of exit, voice and loyalty. In essence, Hirschman asked how an actor would respond to a change in the environment (Hirschman, 1970). The change can be accidental or random, but also rather deliberate, for example the result of a change in public policies or commercial activity. Consider here as an example the production and dissemination of rankings to measure education and research quality. Whereas exit means to refuse to participate in the ranking, denying its hierarchy and the authority behind any loyalty (which may imply to leave the university entirely and find something else to do), voice means to go against the ranking. In other words, choosing to use voice means non-acceptance but also implies contestation and an effort to pressuring the authority issuing the ranking through protesting and campaigning. Protesting may include the proposal of alternative or better rankings. Finally, loyalty means to adapt and accept things as they are, playing the ranking game with all its advantages and disadvantages. From a Gramscian viewpoint it can be argued here that sometimes people may choose to exit or remain loyal without even thinking of voice as an option. This can indicate that people have not realized that they could successfully change the behavior of others. This is the operation of hegemony: the order of things it is taken for granted, things are depoliticized. In turn, and, of course, depending on circumstances, voice can be interpreted as manifestation of social critique.

It is noteworthy that social critique has historically often relied on statistical arguments, that is, on the construction and use of statistics to articulate and make visible discrimination, injustice and inequality. Desrosières observes that while the 'dominant classes' produce statistics 'to suit their own interests', their hegemony 'is often founded on implicit, unchallenged evidence, lived as "natural"'. This means that dominated classes can articulate different arguments, also based on statistics, with a specific view to breaking down 'the old order' and making 'injustice visible'. Such recourse is often taken by the 'dominated fraction of the dominant class, the more educated middle class, endowed with the resources to construct such arguments' (Desrosières, 2014, pp. 349–350). Thus, while statistics can be mobilized as a tool of power for both the dominating and dominated, to be successful, it is not sufficient that statistics are technically innovative—their creators must have allies that enable the translation of the statistics in question within and outside the domain of their production. In other words, the language of statistics 'cannot rely simply on the justness of the arguments, but depends largely on the political and social network in which it is inscribed' (Desrosières, 2014, p. 355).

Such dependency is very much the case with university rankings, irrespective of what opinion one may have of the justness of the arguments associated with endorsing such rankings: 'This spread of management based on benchmarking, which is to say, a permanent competition based on quantified indicators, profoundly transformed university practices, by unifying these around a single objective: climbing upwards' (Desrosières, 2014, p. 357). An analysis of this transformation would focus on two areas:

One, micro-sociological, would follow the trajectory of the innovation, beginning in China, its actors, its vectors, its retranslations from one continent to another. The other, more macro-sociological, would analyze how this innovation was coherent with the neoliberal turn symbolized by the 'Washington consensus', founded on free exchange and competition generalized to global scale.

(Desrosières, 2014, p. 357)

If nowadays statistics and not least university rankings are often contested, it is also the case that forms of emerging collective action use numbers and indictors as means of criticism, struggle and emancipation, suggesting 'shared understanding' (Bruno, Didier, & Vitale, 2014, pp. 199–200). Mobilizations are led by experts, NGOs or laypersons, private actors or even local administrative bodies reacting to evaluative criteria and indicators, set up by national governments or international organizations, which are perceived as wrong and discriminating. In other cases, statactivism is not against a particular set of indicators as such, but rather consists in quantifying and qualifying original data to make an issue visible and relevant. For example,

> Workers whose jobs are precarious point out their real numbers to defend their rights, pro-migrant activists estimate the cost of deportation policy to show that it is too expensive, the Blacks use statistics to shed light on the discrimination they are subjected to.
>
> *(Bruno, Didier, & Vitale, 2014, p. 200)*

In all cases, statactivism covers a variety of practices ranging from individual ones to those explicitly collective, and its effect is double. First, it demonstrates the possibility of an aggregate reality other than the one put forward by typically official public institutions. At the same time, it suggests, and in effect denounces, the capacity of the official institution to mold if not occasionally produce a misleading account of reality. In the following section, we turn to the transnational arena of taxation to explore in more detail such dynamics, especially the dynamics of lists, and their contestation.

'Geographies' of Tax Havens and Secrecy Jurisdictions: A Contest of Lists

In an article from 2015 headlined 'Tax Blacklists. EU Hypocrites! The Naming and Shaming of Tax Havens Is Fraught With Folly', *The Economist* made the following illustrative comment in connection with a recent EU initiative aimed at listing tax havens:

> [Blacklists] affect public perceptions and give NGOs a rod with which to beat perceived offenders. Moreover, inclusion on a list damages more than just reputation. The information is fed into commercial risk software, making banks that use it less willing to deal with blacklisted countries. Few will want to open local outposts in places regularly denounced as financial rogues.
>
> *("EU Hypocrites", August 20, 2015)*

Since the late 1990s especially, blacklists have been an important albeit highly controversial ingredient of internationally coordinated actions against so-called tax havens, spearheaded by the OECD, the EU and later civil society organizations such as the Tax Justice Network. The term 'tax haven' has been widely used since the 1950s, but the listing of such '*havens*' much more recent. While tax havens now span the globe and provide services and facilities for all the major financial and commercial centers, the complex of activities and instruments the term as such commonly denotes stretches far back in history. Palan (2009) has identified three pillars of the modern '*offshore world*' (which is another and competing term for the matter at hand): (1) US state laws of the 19th century permitting states to attract non-resident companies by liberalizing incorporation laws and offering them preferential regulatory treatment, (2) British law courts allowing companies to incorporate in Britain without paying tax, and (3) Switzerland instituting secrecy in its Banking Act of 1934, under protection of criminal law, which makes enquiry or research into the trade secrets of banks and other organizations a criminal offence:

> Not surprisingly, very few academics and journalists have been prepared to risk jail for their research. The law ensured that once past the borders, capital entered an inviolable legal sanctuary guaranteed by the criminal code and backed by the might of the Swiss state.
>
> *(Palan, 2009, p. 3)*

Since the 1990s, tax havens have increasingly attracted public attention because of the sheer proliferation, culminating during and in the aftermath of the financial crisis of the late 2000s.

While there is little agreement on what 'tax havens' more precisely means, in part because of the highly politicized character of taxation, tax avoidance and tax evasion, it is usually taken to refer to the processes whereby a jurisdiction provides services and facilities that make it possible for people or entities to avoid or violate the rules and regulations of other jurisdictions. The provision of anonymity and secrecy offered by jurisdiction plays an important role in maintaining the system (Cobham, Janský, & Meinzer, 2015; Palan, 2009). The prime example of a financial construction that lends itself to a tax haven is the shell company. A shell company is an empty or hollow structure, which, unlike a regular company, has no employees, assets or operations. A shell company is created for the purpose of performing financial maneuvers rather than trading in services and goods, and the identity of the person or organization to which the company belongs, the beneficial owner, is generally anonymous and secret, hidden behind a registered holder with no de facto influence and, in most cases, with no formal duty or desire to report public about the de facto ownership structure.

The types of lists pervading the field of taxation and related issues are not limited to blacklists, but include rankings produced and published by a wide range of organizations. In recent years, two lists have captured the attention in public media and research: the OECD list on uncooperative tax havens and the Tax Justice Network's Financial Secrecy Index. These lists are interesting to analyze because they reflect variation in listing practices while illuminating commonalities. More than anything, they demonstrate how the construction and dissemination of lists convey different geographies of taxation, tax avoidance and tax evasion (Cobham, Janský, & Meinzer, 2015). The images connected to these geographies matter as they can become aligned to wider political projects, programs and technologies aimed at shaping and anticipating the future of tax governance (Anderson, 2010).

It was back in the early 1990s that efforts to combat so-called tax havens first landed as an item on the international policy agenda and in the context of the Financial Action Task Force (FATF) formed by the G7 in 1989 to combat money laundering. The issue was further problematized by the OECD in 1998 in its report *Harmful Tax Competition: An Emerging Global Issue*. Here, the organization launched a new phase of multilateral efforts at fighting tax avoidance and tax evasion, among other things through public listing of countries contributing to harmful tax competition (OECD, 1998). To undertake this project, The Forum on Harmful Tax Practices was established and tasked to identify, report and eliminate the harmful features of preferential (tax) regimes (OECD, 2000). This involved the identification of jurisdictions meeting preestablished criteria for being '*tax havens*', including tax level, exchange of information, transparency and substantial activities. The project was framed as building on a cooperative framework, with interested parties willing to 'make positive change and contribute to emerging international principles of transparency, fairness, and disclosure' (OECD, 2000, p. 7). Thus, reporting and the listing of countries was not intended to be 'condemnatory or final', but rather 'open and dynamic, aiming to move forward cooperatively so long as a co-operative approach bears fruit' (OECD, 2000, p. 6).

Initially, 47 jurisdictions were identified and listed, which had the potential for satisfying the tax haven criteria to be subjected to further review (OECD, 2000, p. 17). The listed jurisdictions were mostly small and, in most cases, island states (see Table 3.1):

After review, six jurisdictions were found not to meet the tax haven criteria. Another six jurisdictions—Bermuda, Cayman Islands, Cyprus, Malta, Mauritius

TABLE 3.1 Jurisdictions Identified as Tax Havens by OECD

Andorra	The Republic of the Maldives
Anguilla—Overseas Territory of the United Kingdom	The Republic of the Marshall Islands
Antigua and Barbuda	The Principality of Monaco
Aruba—Kingdom of the Netherlands	Montserrat—Overseas Territory of the United Kingdom
Commonwealth of the Bahamas	The Republic of Nauru
Bahrain	Netherland Antilles—Kingdom of the Netherlands
Barbados	Niue—New Zealand
Belize	Panama
British Virgin Islands—Overseas Territory of the United Kingdom	Samoa
Cook Islands—New Zealand	The Republic of the Seychelles
The Commonwealth of Dominica	St. Lucia
Gibraltar—Overseas Territory of the United Kingdom	The Federation of St. Christopher & Nevis
Grenada	St. Vincent and the Grenadines
Guernsey/Sark/Alderney—Dependency of the British Crown	Tonga
Isle of Man—Dependency of the British Crown	Turks & Caicos—Overseas Territory of the United Kingdom
Jersey—Dependency of the British Crown	US Virgin Islands—External Territory of the United States
Liberia	The Republic of Vanuatu
The Principality of Liechtenstein	

and San Marino made advance commitments—public political commitment at the highest level—to comply with the principles of the 1998 report. These jurisdictions were required to fulfill their commitment within 7 years. Because of this commitment, these jurisdictions were excluded from the tax haven list in spite of meeting the criteria.

The extent of willingness to cooperate with the OECD to end harmful tax practices led to the adoption of a process by which tax haven jurisdictions were invited to make commitments to eliminate harmful tax practices. Those that would fail to make this commitment would be listed as '*uncooperative tax havens*'. Cooperative tax havens, on the other hand, were required to follow a timetable including a fixed set of milestones in order to stay off the list (OECD, 2000). By 2001, another five jurisdictions—Aruba, Bahrain, the Isle of Man, the Netherlands Antilles and the Seychelles had made commitments to eliminate harmful tax practices. In addition, Tonga had made satisfactory legislative changes. These six jurisdictions were thus no longer candidates for the uncooperative tax havens list (OECD, 2001). By the time the list of uncooperative tax havens was first published in 2002, 31 jurisdictions had committed to adopt while seven were blacklisted. By 2003, five jurisdictions remained on OECDs list, namely Andorra, Liberia, Liechtenstein, the Marshall Islands and Monaco. Finally, by 2009, all jurisdictions had made commitments to comply, and the list was effectively closed (OECD, 2009).

In summary, the scrutiny and classification of the activities of the listed entities on the basis of preestablished criteria created the OECD lists. The lists did not present a clearly ascending or descending order, but what they indeed did was to mark out boundaries for the inclusion or exclusion of mostly small island tax havens from a much larger community of countries in the global economy, spurring processes of adaptation to OECD requirements, including those for getting off the lists. At the same time, the term '*Tax Haven*' and the subsequent boundary drawing between havens and non-havens also helped to shift attention away from the responsibility of core OECD states by implicitly endorsing the normative position that 'Swiss private banking is acceptable, while shell companies in the Caymans are not' (Seabrooke & Wigan, 2015, p. 900).

Unlike the OECD list of tax havens, which listed countries without establishing a hierarchical order, the Financial Secrecy Index (FSI) has all the classical characteristics of a hierarchical ranking. The FSI was launched for the first time in 2009 by the Tax Justice Network (TJN), an NGO formed in 2003 with the aims of raising the level of public awareness about the scale of tax avoidance and evasion, the role and dynamics of tax havens and the resulting impact on human rights and development. TJN works to stimulate research and debate, encouraging national and international campaign activity and promoting tax justice issues in international organizations such as the EU, OECD, UN, World Bank and IMF. Active in TJN is a network of expert-activists, including lawyers, economists, accountants and political scientists, many of whom have professional experiences from academic research, public policy and campaign activism.

The FSI is an example of transnational statactivism, as it contests all traditional lists of tax havens and offshore financial centers. While these lists build on binary distinctions between tax havens and non-havens, or between onshore and offshore, the FSI shows a spectrum of secrecy to tell a slightly different story about tax havens, one that contests the official and largely hegemonic one as expressed in the lists promoted by international organizations such as the OECD and EU. In the FSI, data based on laws, regulations, cooperation with information exchange processes and other sources are combined to prepare a so-called *secrecy score*, which then forms the basis for the creation of a global scale weighting for each country, according to its share of offshore financial services globally.

What characterizes countries with high scores is that they are "secrecy jurisdictions," and as such, 'more opaque in the operations they host, less engaged in information sharing with other national authorities and less compliant with international norms relating to combating money-laundering'. It is this lack of transparency and exchange of information that 'makes a secrecy jurisdiction a more attractive location for routing illicit financial flows and for concealing criminal and corrupt activities' (all quotes from FSI - Tax Justice Network, 2015, p. 2). In this way, the FSI also implies a broadening of the scope from the narrow focus on tax onto wider financial secrecy and transparency issues.

What comes out of the calculation and numerical assessment of country performances with regard to secrecy is the ordering of the classified entities into a hierarchy taking a rather different shape from the lists originally developed by the OECD. The FSI 2015 is the fourth edition after releases in 2013, 2011 and 2009. In the FSI 2015, Switzerland is ranked first, the United States third, Germany eighth, Japan twelfth and the United Kingdom thirteenth. The United Kingdom would top the list if British overseas territories or crown dependencies like Jersey and Cayman Islands were included under its umbrella (see Table 3.2 for complete list).

Suffice it to say here that the FSI obviously conveys an entirely different picture of the matter at hand by using slightly different classification schemes and categories. The world's most significant providers of secrecy are generally not small, palm-fringed islands as the term '*Tax Haven*' has commonly come to denote, but rather some of the world's largest and wealthiest countries: member countries

TABLE 3.2 FSI 2015—Final Results

Rank	Jurisdiction	FSI Value	Secrecy Score	Global Scale Weight
1	Switzerland	1,466.1	73	5.625
2	Hong Kong	1,259.4	72	3.842
3	USA	1,254.8	60	19.603
4	Singapore	1,147.1	69	4.280
5	Cayman Islands	1,013.2	65	4.857
6	Luxembourg	817.0	55	11.630
7	Lebanon	760.2	79	0.377
8	Germany	701.9	56	6.026
9	Bahrain	471.4	74	0.164
10	United Arab Emirates (Dubai)	440.8	77	0.085
11	Macao	420.2	70	0.188
12	Japan	418.4	58	1.062
13	Panama	415.7	72	0.132
14	Marshall Islands	405.6	79	0.053
15	United Kingdom	380.2	41	17.394
16	Jersey	354.0	65	0.216
17	Guernsey	339.4	64	0.231
18	Malaysia (Labuan)	338.7	75	0.050
19	Turkey	320.9	64	0.182
20	China	312.2	54	0.743

Note: www.financialsecrecyindex.com/introduction/fsi-2015-results

of the OECD but nonetheless the conduits and recipients of illicit financial flows. As Seabrooke and Wigan (2015) observe, the FSI seeks to expose the hypocrisy of the G8 and place pressure on these states to reform this, rather than seeking to displace the blame on the mainly small island economies, those more often understood to populate the offshore world. It sheds light on the role of major economies in supplying secrecy, and thus alters the parameters of the debate. In this way, it actualizes discussions about the significance that lists can have in changing and disciplining the conduct of states, corporations and citizens as regards taxation, tax avoidance and tax evasion, and their implications for human rights and development.

Discussion and Concluding Remarks

The contest of the lists discussed earlier began well in advance of the ready-made lists that have come to circulate in public. It is useful to recall here the broad distinction made previously between first- and second-order surveillance. Both orders are present in the creation and operation of the lists analyzed, as these come to form part of wider knowledge circuits. First-order surveillance relates to the mostly implicit and tacit schemes of classification and conventions that inform the particular observations of items and judge them to be '*listable*'. First-order surveillance is commonly back-stage work. It involves the architects of assessment, processes of narrative framing, classificatory and measurement work, data processing and the configuration of artefacts such as computer software and hardware. Previously, we have seen examples of how differently the classificatory schemes used for first-order surveillance can be constructed as regards tax havens and secrecy jurisdictions, and what this can mean in terms of the imagined geographies of taxation presented on the public lists. It goes without saying that in this arena the classificatory schemes are to a wide extent malleable, suggesting at least two different ways of approaching the problem. By implication, how taxation problems are to be resolved all depends on the criteria used to establish the hierarchy of tax avoider and evaders and, ultimately, the parameters for whom to blame and from whom to require practical policy and legislative changes. Should we point our finger at the West and its rich allies elsewhere, or rather at a bunch of mostly minor tropical islands? That said, it is also clear that there are strong discursive limitations to the imagination of alternative classification schemes. We are essentially dealing with jurisdictions discursively categorized within a largely Westphalian inter-state system and world order, in which the link between taxation and sovereignty is pre-fixed.

Nonetheless, these fundamental schemes provide publics with the possibility for exercising second-order surveillance of the politicized arena of taxation. Second-order surveillance rests on the aggregation of items into visualized lists that enter public life as communication packages. This is front stage and involves the publicized lists at press conferences, circulating on the web, in media reports or official documents. In this way, the lists may seem as largely autonomous artefacts. The audiences comprise not only those who are targeted by the lists but also those who are not directly related to the lists but engaged in the work of interpretation and use for some particular purpose. They are referred to and mobilized with a specific view to conveying or contesting how things '*really are*', often anticipating expectations as to how things '*should be*'.

At a first glance, the second-order surveillance afforded by the circulating public list resembles the panoptic model and its ensuing disciplinary system so famous in discussions about surveillance and transparency in modern society (Foucault, 1977; Hansen & Flyverbom, 2015). Like the image of the prison, in which one guard would monitor the prisoners via a specially designed architecture, lists provide a lens through which the expectation of centralized observations enacted on the part of a power holder can subsequently become translated into self-regulatory modes of behavior by the observed. However, boiling down the dynamics of second-order surveillance to a unidirectional process is far too simplistic. Surveillance is used in a plethora of domains and sites, and for varying purposes, none of which necessarily lend themselves to a notion of centralized societal control (e.g., the surveillance of consumption and entertainment patterns is used for research and commercial purposes, and is commonly transformed into indices of various sorts). Moreover, '*synoptic*' processes that overlap and even challenge panoptic processes have always existed, and some would argue, possibly multiplied with the advent of new media technologies (Mathiesen, 1997; Brivot & Gendron, 2011; Gillespie, Oczkowski, & Foot, 2014). Media and communication technologies have come to make it possible for the ordinary citizen to achieve a wealth of information about political and economic institutions and the people who inhabit them. Some of this information comes from public lists, of course. What is more important here is that the material of second-order surveillance, the list, although it is in principle traceable to first-order surveillance, often acquires a life on its own. The public list turns into a relatively autonomous communication package, which condenses complex information (economies of quantification and simplification), travels easily (economies of distance) and is digestible (economies of persuasion and aesthetics), potentially shaping political, social and economic actors and their relations (Hansen & Porter, 2012). Lists can become aligned to institutional agendas and serve as important reference points for action and political struggles.

Crucially, however, it is also here that lists become implicated in narratives and visualized standards and scripts for action. While it may be the case that organizational decisions seem to be increasingly taken with reference to lists such as rankings and blacklists, these alone are too abstract. They resonate most powerfully if there is an accompanying narrative. Such narratives always rest on the identification (or invention) of a problem or need of sorts that should be remedied or alleviated. What should a low-ranked country do to perform better? Is the tax matter really something we should care about? Questions like these typically underpin lists as subtexts, reflecting a much wider discursive field in which what constitutes appropriate and legitimate practice in a specific political arena is partially predetermined and taken for granted, partially politicized. Perhaps it is also here that we need to be aware of this risk of ascribing to the list too much autonomy as a governing and ordering technology across fields or issues: the list is an ordering, but it is also being (re)ordered and (re)contextualized as it travels through the knowledge circuits that constitute the matter at hand.

This chapter has demonstrated how lists operate in the fuzzy zones between '*hard*' and '*soft*' law, the '*public*' and '*private*', and the '*local*' and '*global*'. Rankings of education and research quality launched by private institutions and international organizations are important technologies mobilized by authorities to steer, prioritize and allocate economic and human resources in national educational systems. Lists can extend into the transnational realm and connect individual or organizational conduct to the proliferating ideals about the optimization of performance and competitiveness. In this regard, lists also involve complex processes of politicization and serve as tools for international organizations, civil society and market actors to exert pressure on not only states, but also market and civil society actors themselves. Lists are often contested. Individuals and social movements can denounce them and use them as a tool for struggle, often by devising alternative lists.

Lists come to have '*objective*' appearance in that they integrate ever-larger amounts of increasingly complex narratives in what appears to be a simple, straightforward manner. Because lists both separate between items listed and allow them to be moved around, they also make possible new combinations and, importantly, serve as strong means for making comparisons. In the age of algorithmic '*datafication*', which refers to the increasing tendency to put almost any phenomenon 'in a quantified format so it can be tabulated and analyzed' (Mayer-Schönberger & Cukier, 2013, p. 78; cf. Hansen, 2015), such combinatory and comparative work increasingly happens by means of highly advanced computer-driven software. Datafication, and its popular offspring '*big data analytics*' (Andrejevic, 2014), are linked to the move among state and non-state actors toward anticipatory approaches to risk, that is, attempts at predicting and preempting future developments including specifically transborder threats, such as transnational organized crime, environmental and health threats and financial crises, which involve narratives, numbers and technical artifacts (Anderson, 2010; Amoore, 2011).

Note

1. For further investigations of numbers and lists in transnational spaces, see Larner & Le Heron, 2004; Espeland & Sauder, 2007; Heng & McDonagh, 2008; Fougner, 2008; Sauder & Espeland, 2009; Sharman, 2009; Andreas & Greenhill, 2010; Hansen & Porter, 2012; Day, Lury, & Wakeford, 2014; Erkkilä & Piironen, 2014; Hansen, 2015.

References

Amoore, L. (2011). Data derivatives: On the emergence of a security risk calculus for our times, theory. *Culture & Society, 28*(6), 24–43.

Anderson, B. (2010). Preemption, precaution, preparedness: Anticipatory action and future geographies. *Progress in Human Geography, 34*(6), 777–798.

Andreas, P., & Greenhill, K. M. (2010). *Sex, drugs, and body counts: The politics of numbers in global crime and conflict.* Ithaca, NY: Cornell University Press.

Andrejevic, M. (2014). Surveillance in the big data era. In K. D. Pimple (Ed.), *Emerging pervasive information and communication technologies (PICT): Ethical challenges, opportunities, and safeguards* (pp. 55–69). Dordrecht, The Netherlands: Springer.

Bowker, G., & Star, S. L. (2000). *Sorting things out: Classification and its consequences.* Cambridge, MA: MIT Press.

Brivot, M., & Gendron, Y. (2011). Beyond panopticism: On the ramifications of surveillance in a contemporary professional setting. *Accounting, Organizations, and Society, 36*, 135–155.

Bruno, I., Didier, E., & Vitale, T. (2014). Statactivism: Forms of action between disclosure and affirmation. *Patecipazione e Conflitto, 7*(2), 198–220.

Cobham, A., Janský, P., & Meinzer, M. (2015). The financial secrecy index: Shedding new light on the geography of secrecy. *Economic Geography, 91*(3), 281–303.

Day, S., Lury, C., & Wakeford, N. (2014). Number ecologies: Numbers and numbering practices. *Distinktion: Scandinavian Journal of Social Theory, 15*(2), 123–154.

de Goede, M., Leander, A., & Sullivan, G. (2016). Introduction: The politics of the list. *Environment and Planning D: Society and Space, 34*(1), 3–13.

Desrosières, A. (2014). Statistics and social critique. *Patecipazione e Conflitto, 7*(2), 348–359.

Eco, U. (2009). *The infinity of lists: From Homer to Joyce.* London: MacLehose Press.

Erkkilä, T., & Piironen, O. (2014). (De)politicizing good governance: The World Bank Institute, the OECD, and the politics of governance indicators. *Innovation: The European Journal of Social Science Research, 27*(4), 344–360.

Espeland, W. E., & Sauder, M. (2007). Rankings and reactivity: How public measures recreate social worlds. *American Journal of Sociology, 113*(1), 1–40.

"EU Hypocrites" (2015, August 20), EU Hypocrites. The naming and shaming of tax havens is fraught with folly. *The Economist.* Retrieved from https://www.economist.com/news/finance-and-economics/21661674-naming-and-shaming-tax-havens-fraught-folly-eu-hypocrites

Foucault, M. (1977). *Discipline and punish: The birth of the prison.* London: Penguin Books.

Fougner, T. (2008). Neoliberal governance of states: The role of competitiveness indexing and benchmarking, millennium. *Journal of International Studies, 37*(2), 303–326.

Gillespie, T, Oczkowski, P. J., & Foot, K. A. (Eds.). (2014). *Media technologies: Essays on communication, materiality, and society.* Cambridge, MA: MIT Press.

Hansen, H. K. (2012). The power of performance indices in the global politics of anti-corruption. *Journal of International Relations and Development, 15*(4), 1–26.

Hansen, H. K. (2015). Numerical operations, transparency illusions, and the datafication of governance. *European Journal of Social Theory, 18*(2), 203–220.

Hansen, H. K., & Flyverbom, M. (2015). The politics of transparency and the calibration of knowledge in the digital age. *Organization, 22*(6), 872–889.

Hansen, H. K., & Porter, T. (2012). What do numbers do in transnational governance? *International Political Sociology, 6*(4), 409–426.

Hardoon, D., Fuentes-Nieva, R., & Ayele, S. (2016). An Economy For the 1%: How privilege and power in the economy drive extreme inequality and how this can be stopped. Oxfam. Retrieved from https://policy-practice.oxfam.org.uk/publications/an-economy-for-the-1-how-privilege-and-power-in-the-economy-drive-extreme-inequ-592643.

Heng, Y-K., & McDonagh, K. (2008). The other war on terror revealed: Global governmentality and the financial action task force's campaigning against terrorist financing. *Review of International Studies*, *34*(3), 553–573.

Hirschman, A. O. (1970). *Exit, voice, and loyalty: Responses to decline in firms, organizations, and states* (Vol. 25). Harvard university press.

Johns, F. (2016). Global governance through the pairing of list and algorithm. *Environment and Planning D: Society and Space*, *34*(1), 126–149.

Kelley, J. G., & Simmons, B. A. (2014). Politics by number: Indicators as social pressure in international relations. *American Journal of Political Science*, *59*(1), 55–70.

Larner, W., & Le Heron, R. (2004). Global benchmarking: Participating 'at a distance' in the globalizing economy. In W. Larner & W. Walters (Eds.), *Global governmentality: Governing international spaces* (pp. 212–232). London: Routledge.

Lindblad, S. (2008). Navigating the field of university positioning: On international ranking lists, quality indicators, and higher education governing. *European Educational Research Journal*, *7*(4), 438–450.

Löwenheim, O. (2008). Examining the state: A Foucauldian perspective on international 'governance indicators'. *Third World Quarterly*, *29*(2), 255–274.

Martens, K., & Niemann, D. (2013). What do numbers count? The differential impact of the PISA rating and ranking on education policy in Germany and the US. *German Politics*, *22*(3), 314–332.

Mathiesen, T. (1997). The viewer society: Michel Foucault's 'panopticon' revisited. *Theoretical Criminology*, *1*(2), 215–234.

Mayer-Schönberger, V., & Cukier, K. (2013). *Big data: A revolution that will transform how we live, work, and think*. Boston, MA: Eamon Dolan/Houghton Mifflin Harcourt.

Mingers, J., & Willmott, H. (2013). Taylorizing business school research: On the 'one best way' performative effects of journal ranking lists. *Human Relations*, *66*(8), 1051–1073.

OECD. (1998). *Harmful tax competition: An emerging global issue*. Paris: OECD.

OECD. (2000). *Towards global tax co-operation*. Paris: OECD.

OECD. (2001). *The OECD's project on harmful tax practices: The 2001 progress report*. Paris: OECD.

OECD. (2009). *Countering offshore tax evasion*. Paris: OECD.

Palan, R. (2009). Crime, sovereignty, and the offshore world. *Crime and the Global Political Economy*. London: Lynne Rienner, 35–48.

Sauder, M., & Espeland, W. (2009). The discipline of rankings: Tight coupling and organizational change. *American Sociological Review*, *74*, 63–82.

Scott, P. (2013). Ranking higher education institutions: a critical perspective. In Marope, P. T. M., Wells, P. J., & Hazelkorn, E. (Eds) *Rankings and accountability in higher education: Uses and misuses*. Unesco.

Seabrooke, L., & Wigan, D. (2015). How activists use benchmarks: Reformists and revolutionary benchmarks for global economic justice. *Review of International Studies*, *41*(4), 887–904.

Sharman, J. C. (2009). The bark is the bite: International organizations and blacklisting. *Review of International Political Economy*, *16*(4), 573–596.

Stäheli, U. (2016). Indexing—the politics of invisibility. *Environment and Planning D: Society and Space*, *34*(1), 14–29.

Tax Justice Network. (2015). *Financial secrecy index 2015 methodology* (PDF Version dated 16.10.2015). Tax Justice Network. Retrieved from June 20, 2016, from www.financialsecrecyindex.com/PDF/FSI-Methodology.pdf

Wedlin, L. (2010). Going global: Rankings as rhetorical devices to construct an international field of management education. *Management Learning*, *42*(2), 199–218.

4

TIME, DRAWING, TESTING

The Making Up of the Developmental Child and the Measuring of the Nation's Development

Catarina S. Martins

Introduction

Contemporary international research on student performance takes for granted the idea that both children and nations develop and grow, and that this development can be aided by careful planning and assessments on problem solving and global competencies. This chapter explores historically how the idea of the child's development becomes a stabilized part of thinking about children and the measurement and assessment of institutional performance.

I will look at different types of documents, more than a century apart, as '*facts*' that are made to make sense of the world. These facts began to be thought of as data that represented what we could know about the objects being inquired. First, I will focus on the ways the notion of development is attached to a specific form of conceiving childhood in which time plays a central role. The notion of development as a path to an end, when inscribed within the social conceptualization of the linearity of time, transforms the child's becoming into a field of government of the present. Then, I will observe the second half of the 19th century's study of children's drawings to analyze how the idea of development in childhood was conceived in terms of universal stages of growth defined by the child's performance. This was embedded within a culture of objectivity in which differences were thought as variations of degree among certain traits, being these variations both qualitative and quantitative. Numbers acquired a different status as representing knowledge about the world and as anticipating a desired future and, simultaneously, comparison became an instrument to position each one according to the others in relation to that fiction. From the 19th century, I will jump into the 21st century. I will make an incursion into the present OECD's Programme for International Student Assessment (PISA), looking into the technologies of comparison in the making up of the creative problem solver and global competent child, the ways in which students are ordered and classified through the construction of equivalences and how that results in a picture of the nation's performance, potentiality and development. My aim is to make evident what these documents share in terms of their grids of thought and how they give intelligibility to, and assume, a certain kind of person (Hacking, 2002): the developmental child.

If it seems that I am mixing different things (Arts, Mathematics and Science), in fact what is at stake is not the specific curricular content within each school subject, but the ingredients that make specific contents possible as school subjects open to be taught, learned and assessed and how children and nations are made intelligible through these different layers that are forgotten when we see the final result. Popkewitz (2007) calls this the alchemy of school subjects. I will try to make evident that there is something more about contemporary national and international large-scale measurements, such as PISA, than just the child's capacities, at a certain age, to solve problems in mathematics or science.

Three movements are rehearsed in this chapter: (1) the notion of development is not a natural way of reasoning about the child or the adolescent; (2) the developmental child, or adolescent, inscribes the hopes and the fears of the future; and (3) the rationalization of development according to time and performance, which is part of the grammars of schooling and testing since the 19th century, provides ways of governing the present. It is not only an empirical problem open to quantification, but also political and epistemological goals that are at stake in this global space of policymaking through children's problem solving in tests and through anticipating the future. In this, I want to highlight that development and numbers are not only development and numbers; there are cultural thesis embodied in them that act in the making of the normal and the pathological, and the ways we relate to them.

Throughout the chapter, my intention is to make evident that, as any style of reasoning, the style of reasoning inscribed in contemporary large-scale assessments on children's development and problem solving, be it national or international, is a particular historical episteme that frames what is (im)possible to think, to see, to talk about and to act on in contemporary educational debates.

Making Time Matter: The 'Scientifization' of the Child and the Government of Childhood Through Development

It might seem odd to think about international students' assessments through traveling to the 19th century, but it provides a way of framing how particular epistemic principles of the child as developing and time as a measure to assess how that governing is possible. During the 19th century, the child acquired a different status in terms of her existence as an object of inquiry by the pedagogical sciences. The question itself of how pedagogy was being thought of is part of this interest in childhood as a specific stage of life that needed a conduction by the educator. This doesn't mean that the child was not, before, an object of thought. Jean-Jacques Rousseau invented Émile to talk about the education of childhood, Johann Heinrich Pestalozzi observed his son as an inspiration for his writings on childhood and education, even Charles Darwin constructed a *Biographical Sketch of an Infant* as the result of the observation of his son's expressions, gestures, emotions and language development. However, when the French pedagogue Gabriel Compayré (1897) asked if there were a science of education, his answer revealed a new grid to think about the child in a scientific way.

There was a science of education, a practical science, that was no more and no less than an applied psychology. This science was 'Pedagogy' and the rules of pedagogy were the laws of an applied psychology, according to Compayré: 'Just as the physician ought to know the organs and function of the body he treats, the farmer the nature of the soil which he cultivates, and the sculptor the qualities of the marble which he chisels', wrote Compayré, 'so the teacher cannot do without knowledge of the laws of the mental organization—that is, the study of psychology' (Compayré, 1889/1887, p. 7). It was not anymore a gaze, as the 18th-century philosophers developed, but rather a way of seeing through observation and description with the aim of attaining objectivity as part of a new rationality of government, intrinsic both to the new psychological sciences and to the modern state, in their individualizing and totalizing procedures.

The new gaze directed to childhood is both a cause and an effect of a perception that traverses different areas, from madness to criminality or genius. Exceptional manifestations of behavior in adulthood were due to certain events that could be understood going back to childhood. The child becomes then a nucleus to be known in detail in order to govern childhood and prevent future degeneracy. During the first half of the 19th century, from the French psychiatrist Jean-Étienne Esquirol to the French physician and educationist Édouard Séguin, abnormality started to be diagnosed not so much as an illness but rather as a state in which the intellectual functions did not develop in a proper way. Although the concept of development being used was very simplistic, it already involved a detection of a slowness in evolution that could be seen from a very early age. There were important differences between the types of abnormalities, the idiot being different from the retarded child, but these were regarded within an idea of a chronological development.

The ways in which the child's development was rationalized by science made childhood a spot to be explored, as it was a fiction governing the present in anticipation of what should be as the future. 'To an impartial observer', argued Compayré, 'it is evident that the mind is developed and formed with certain laws of growth which definitely constitute the psychology of the child' (1889/1887, p. 8). Chronological development was constructed as an objective and impartial way of reasoning that instantiated a consensus over a group that otherwise would be uncertain. The indexation of the social construction of time to this development, and its inscription as the way to look, talk and act on childhood made the linearity of development an unquestionable thesis about life.

Change and growth started to be described over time. The descriptions being made embodied moral principles that ordered and organized what was made into the object 'seen' and the data given as facts available for governmental purposes. Scientific objectivity, as put by Porter, 'provides an answer to a moral demand for impartiality and fairness' (Porter, 1996, p. 8). One of the battles of the Enlightenment was the creation of a common space of measurement through claiming unified systems of weights and measures. The notion of development through a chronological line, allowing comparison, was one of the materializations of this idea. The periodization of life into phases, and the partition of the phases into different stages, fell into the rhetoric of equality and progress.

Development became equivalent with a positive feature of life, be it the inevitable and necessary development of an organic body through change or the development of social metaphors like '*growth*', '*progress*' and '*civilization*'. The inscription of time into the idea of development gives rise to a '*competitive ethic*' (Jenks, 1996). There are not only the 'mental and manual skills' that, being evaluated, hierarchically shape different biological strata that classify the 'natural' development of the child and ranks it, but also the 'social stratification within the culture' that appears 'to be a justified merit that stems from development' (Jenks, 1996, p. 39). However, neither the child's development, nor the change in time that it implies, are neutral concepts. Equivalences are made to make comparison possible as a way of reasoning and governing. These equivalences embody scientific knowledges that answer specific governmental purposes for the rationalization and control of the risks inherent in a random development of the social body (Foucault, 2002/1997).

Narratives of childhood as a stage of life provided not only a representation of the present, but also the possibility to control what was yet to come. This control embodied a particular comparative thought in which time played the role of regularizing all domains and stages of life portending the future as the hope of progress and, simultaneously, the fear of decay if the present were not properly governed. The hope and the fear were about not only the conditions of living but also the normalcy and pathologies of kinds of people placed in a continuum of development from the savage to the civilized and cosmopolitan. The abnormal child, be it the retarded, the idiot or simply the son of drunks, poor parents, prostitutes, criminals or imbeciles, was dangerous for society. A series of perversions of the instincts, which were perceived as being savage, could result in thieves, liars, masturbators, murderers or destroyers. It was the potentiality of these behaviors that had to be detected in order to be corrected within the family or the school or confined in the asylum. The biologization of development became a political and moral concern for the modern state and its institutional devices.

In Séguin's *Idiocy: And Its Treatment by the Physiological Method*, for example, the isolation of the abnormal childhood acted as a rationality of government. There were differences among children that had to be studied and signaled, and these differences were not only between a norm and abnormality, but also between kinds of tones and traits within each one. Séguin affirmed that since idiocy took place in such different periods of the formation of the child, it was not:

> to be expected that it should assume an identical appearance; in fact, on entering a school, the idea of similarity is soon dispelled by the heterogeneous features of the inmates; therefore the same drawing cannot represent them but as a type, after a practical study of the varieties.
> *(Séguin, 1866, p. 43)*

The study of a human type, and the variations that could be detected within the typology, is part of the construction of a knowledge that opens up the objects of inquiry for intervention, correction and administration. It was not so much the average, but rather the inter-individual differences that existed between persons that configured the device to manage several measurements and their statistical regularities and correlations. This use of categories translated into numbers (or quantitative variations) makes the categories '*actors*' (Popkewitz, 2013) that construct things as facts, and was soon used on the government of education and childhood. Pettersson, Popkewitz, and Lindblad (2016) talk about the '*empirical turn*' in education as the emergence of the new scientific branch of statistics, giving an appearance of neutrality to the depiction of reality. Ways of observing and registering the child's attitudes, behaviors and development became more systematic in their processes and methods, being first institutionalized in hospital registers (Turmel, 2008) and, by the end of the 19th century, within schools.

The notion of development as a normativity and pathology that is encoded in clinical, psychological or pedagogical stages made time matter as an instrument to regulate the progression of the child and its different stages. Making time matter made everything be a matter of time and, more importantly, the objectivity and unquestionability of this rhetoric of time and development is also part of a narrative of equality and fairness that is explained by nature. The quest for the origin that emerged in the natural sciences with Lamarck's evolutionary family tree, and that gave rise to Darwin's theories on the *Origin of Species*, is part of the movement of a normalized temporalization of Western experiences. The stages of development through childhood are part of this machinery of time and were not only generalizations made through the description of empirical data but also principles that ordered certain ways of being.

It was not only childhood that was being regulated but also most intensively what it meant to be a person. From the roman legacy of a person within a legal framework to the moral view of the person as an immortal soul, specific psychological conceptions of personhood emerged by the end of the 19th century. The social construction of time as a linear narrative of past, present and future gave reasonability to early memories in life as the explanation of the development of some diseases in adulthood (Danziger, 1997). The developing child, as a specific kind of person, was a subject of government in the managing of life in all its regularities and irregularities.

In this section, I observed how the evolutionary child, embodying a movement in time—development—was discursively constructed as part of a production of knowledge and as a technology to govern childhood. Development was a conceptual tool to order who the child was and should be, but also who was the pathological child. I will now analyze how the idea of development in childhood was conceived in terms of universal stages of growth defined by the child's performance in drawing. My attention will be on the notion of drawing developmental stages in the fabrication of the child as an object of inquiry and research and as a new target for technologies of administration through statistics. I will also focus on how the stages of development (that cannot be seen apart from the naturalization of the notion of development and from the new techniques of government) created categories that make up the child who develops. The naturalization of development as part of childhood made comparison of each and all possible both to measure and to examine. This way of seeing and knowing became part of all pedagogical practices. From a micro scale in the development of each child's mind to a macro scale of the nation, such as the current PISA test assessments, what is at stake is always the governing of the conduct as a procedure which is based on a perpetual comparison through the construction of equivalences.

Statistical Reasoning and Drawing as a Tool for Conceptualizing the Child's Development

One cannot think about school without thinking in numbers, stages of development, partition of curricular knowledge according to those stages of development, children's ages, classes and grades. Numbers and development are part of an epistemology about the world that represents and acts in that world. By this, I mean not only that there are the lenses through which we see 'things' but also that they make those things as such, including the making of certain kinds of persons. The variable of slowness was identified according to a kind of childhood average that constituted the norm in relation to which the pathological child would be situated in school. The notion of a normal and pathological childhood was based on statistical technologies seeking large-scale regularities from which a child's growth and development acquired objectivity in terms of administration and intervention, such as the chronological timeline, along which a child's development would be normal, retarded or advanced. This rationality, which had been worked mainly by differential psychology, has acquired other dimensions and territories and, in the middle of the 20th century, the continuum of normality, pathology and exceptionality ties the theories of probability of the national populations.

The statistical technologies implied a style of reasoning (Hacking, 1992) that allowed, simultaneously, a picture of the individual and of the group. In the 19th century, statistic was called the moral science of the State, and it theorized, codified and empirically observed the world in order to contribute to the prosperity of the State and to the happiness of its citizens. Statistic was dependent from ways of representing what counted as '*empirical*' and as an object of government. The Child Study Movement in Europe and North America was one of the fields in which those techniques to depict and to provide portraits of the reality were explored relating to the investigation of child development. The American psychologist G. Stanley Hall was one of the first leaders of the Child Study Movement, initiating extensive surveys on childhood stages. His child studies provide an exemplar of new ways of registration and of visualizing and interpreting collected data about child growth and development or, in other words, of inventing empirical data to be seen and analyzed as a representation of that evolution. Under Hall's guidance, the Boston schools applied a study to know what children knew when they entered school. Hall underlined that it was important 'to make out a list of questions suitable for obtaining an inventory of the contents of the minds of children of average intelligence' (Hall, 1893, p. 13). Data were organized along an axis of time in which the child's development was inscribed. The conclusions outlined by Hall made evident the use of statistical technologies to frame the construction of reality. Hall was aware that the results of large-scale inquiries were 'in some degree the first opening of a field' asserting it needed to be, 'and in which single concept-groups should be subjected to more detailed study with large numbers of children' (Hall, 1893, p. 24).

A statistical reasoning, that Hall applied, was in the making as the way to frame and shape a reality of childhood. In Europe, James Sully also conducted large inquiries in order to enhance a theory of children's drawing through a stage approach and, in the beginning of the 20th century, to count, measure and find patterns and laws in the child's development through drawing was a demand for this scientification of the child (Martins, 2017). The impersonality and impartiality of statistical numbers were part of a culture of objectivity that allowed the descriptors of each stage of development. Within this culture of objectivity, drawing was used as an instrument to measure each child's performance through her evolution in time. The notion of the developmental child embodied specific power-knowledge relations that saw the design of the mind as having drawing stages of development in childhood.

G. Stanley Hall's previously mentioned study provided one of the first conceptualizations of the child's stages of development in drawing through this linearity of time and, in doing so, it also provided a 'map' that ordered, through psychological lenses, the well-developed child and her staircase progress. To G. Stanley Hall, the earliest and simplest representation made by the child was:

> a round head, two eyes and legs. Later comes mouth, then nose, then hair, then ears. Arms like legs first grow directly from the head, rarely from the

> legs, and are seldom fingerless, though sometimes it is doubtful whether several arms or fingers from head and legs without arms are meant. Of 44 human heads only 9 are in profile. This is one of the main analogies with the rock and cave drawings. [. . .] Last, as least mobile and thus attracting least attention, comes the body; first round like the head, then elongated, sometimes prodigiously, and sometimes articulated into several compartments, and in three cases divided, the upper part of the figure being in one place and the lower in another. The mind, and not the eye alone, is addressed, for the body is drawn and then the clothes are drawn on it (as the child dresses), diaphanous and only in outline. Most draw living objects except the kindergarten children, who draw their patterns. [. . .] The very earliest pencillings, commonly of three-year-old children, are mere marks to and fro, often nearly in the same line.
>
> *(Hall, 1893, pp. 44–45)*

I used Hall's aforementioned example to illustrate how the stage theories on child's development, in and through drawing, informed and created certain images for the child that were assumed as reasonable about the child and her performance. The child that started in the simplicity and, through the course of childhood, arrived to a more representative and complex visual description of reality and, with that, acquiring a sense of Western perspective, was seen as normal. The child was being made up from her graphical marks. The notion of time within the idea of development inscribed the morality of a path from a primitive mode toward progress and civilization. A reenactment of human race was present in the ways of conceiving the developmental child through the evolutionary stages in drawing.

Several theories about the child's development through the analysis of stages in drawing emerged, ordering who the child should be but also its other. There was the most feared period of childhood: adolescence. Earl Barnes stated that 'at thirteen, or the period of puberty, the children experience a change of ideals, and it may be that after this they realize more fully their inability to execute what they see' (Barnes, 1892, p. 459). The principles used to divide created not only a norm, but also the abject places outside the norm. The study of the child made it possible to predict her behavior and to govern ways of being, anchoring it to the barometer of normality. Children were seen to draw in predictable ways, going through specific and step-by-step stages, with an increase in terms of graphic complexity and a decrease of imagination during adolescence. However, as noticed by the English psychologist James Sully:

> One notices, too, curious divergences with respect to the mixture of incompatible features. Differences in the degree of intelligence show themselves here also. Thus in one case a child, throughout whose drawings a certain feeble-mindedness seems to betray itself, actually went so far as to introduce the double nose without having the excuse of the two eyes.
>
> *(Sully, 1900/1896, p. 360)*

The statistical reasoning worked also with the theory of probabilities and, as Sully admitted, while it was probably true that children at a certain age would share common capacities, there were those outside the norm. Taking imagination as an example, the author of *Studies of Childhood* argued that some children were decidedly unimaginative. It was about these variations that more scientific knowledge was needed. Numbers were there as units of a system of knowledge to make certain kinds of persons, to trace equivalences and to allow differentiations. 'What will best help us', Sully affirmed, "is a number of careful records of infant progress, embracing examples not only of different sexes and temperaments, but also of different social conditions and nationalities" (Sully, 1900/1896, p. 23). At one level, differences and divisions in kinds of persons were being made through the naturalization of the notion of growth and time according to certain predefined stages; at another level, these differentiations were being inscribed through social issues and inequities as the cause of that child who was not the average child. These descriptions were based on the average behaviors, and they materialized gestures that differentiated and divided who was the well-developed child from the pathological child. The distinctions were not about drawing as an artistic practice but about the making of a moral and well-behaved citizen in which development meant progression. In terms of its effects, it is important to acknowledge that the child was not only made visible through the descriptors of her development, but also she was *made*.

Developing the Child as the Development of the Nation: The OECD's PISA Rationalities

The ways of classifying the child's developmental stages in drawing were ways of dividing and differentiating the normal and desirable universal child and its other, the pathological child. A certain way of seeing and relating to childhood was in the making. During the second half of the 19th century, development emerged as a normativity that played with stages along certain scales and speed in terms of how the child crossed a specific dimension in time.

I will now turn to the 21st century in order to observe how this particular episteme of objectivity and quantification of development are being expressed in the international large-scale assessments. The culture of objectivity and assessment of the child's development will be analyzed through the rationalities of PISA's testing about what a creative child as a problem solver is and has to be in the 21st century. Today's PISA has the goal of knowing to what extent 15-year-old students can apply their knowledge to real-life situations and be equipped for full participation in society. However, what is unproblematically seen is the idea of testing at a certain age and to read the results as a portrait of a certain development, and also, what is defined as 'practical knowledge' that is not about a particular kind of knowledge but about principles that order and classify certain kinds of persons, as in the 19th century's description of each drawing stage was not drawing itself that was being evaluated, but rather principles that ordered the government of childhood.

The Construction of Equivalences and Its Differences

Comparisons between people and nations are possible only through the construction of equivalences. The equivalences being constructed in PISA are the categories that are being mobilized not only as the evidence of a target group and a way of reasoning through the notion of development, but also the categories that define both those students who will be able to fully participate in society and the pathological others. The notion of objectivity guides the propositions of PISA tests and the reading of its results as a strategy that goes beyond the distances that separate the different nations. The equivalences are constructed as universals that surpass, capture and tame any singularity.

It is not by chance that PISA elects 15-year-old students as the group to be tested. Such as childhood was seen as the period in which abnormalities could be diagnosed and, if not corrected, at least could be controlled, adolescence is here seen as the period in which particular actions and behaviors can be dangerous to the normal course of life. The concept of adolescence became as natural as childhood, however, when G. Stanley Hall (1911/1904) coined this period of time in his book *Adolescence: Its Psychology and Its Relations to Physiology, Anthropology, Sociology, Sex, Crime, Religion, and Education* and attached to it several domains including sex, crime and education. Adolescence was constructed as a turbulent time that was explained biologically and could be controlled through the organization and ordering of time in adolescence toward a civilized becoming. Developmentally speaking, adolescence precedes adulthood and the latter is the time of production. In fact, in the anticipation of the future, PISA is acting as a factory of citizens. Popkewitz, in his chapter of this book, argues that the future that is being told about the development of nations is about the hope of kinds of desired people and society. The categories and the distinctions being made act as the transcendent ordering of what the nations need for development, growth and equity. The narrative of development through time, as a path to an end, is part of today's large-scale assessments and is used as its legitimate goal.

In 2018, PISA will be assessing the global competencies of students. In OECD's saying, global competencies are divided into '*dimensions*' and '*components*' that can be measured. The OECD traces what the future should look like and what kinds of persons should live in that future landscape. The launching of the Educational Agenda for 2030 is just another example of how the '*edu-fiction*' is working. However, this futuristic educational science is making the present! Educational systems should then move and mobilize their actors around these imagined paths. The global competent person is the one that 'brings his/her knowledge, understanding, skills, attitudes and values together in order to work with others to solve globally-relevant problems and to improve the collective well-being of current and future generations' (OECD, 2016b, p. 4). What this seems to be describing is only, in fact, making up kinds of people! The images of the adolescent being played at PISA are as moral as Hall's images of the adolescent marking the boundary between the civilized and the savage, regarding the ways they order and govern the well-behaved problem solver youth and his attachment to the future of society. In PISA testing, to do well in problem solving is defined as being a 'constructive' and 'reflective citizen', which means to be a certain kind of person. In classifying the good student of the present and the future as the one who needs 'to be open to novelty, tolerate doubt and uncertainty, and dare to use intuition to initiate a solution' (OECD, 2014, p. 3), there are specific conceptual spaces in the making to be inhabited by different kinds of persons. Simultaneously, the pathological inhabitant of the present is being signaled.

The style of reasoning of large-scale assessments departs from the possibility of measuring development according to certain indicators that are shared between those being the object of testing (the age, the test, problem solving), allowing for comparison between the young and the nations, and to the formulation of a truth speech. Indicators embody the notion of the right direction. However, the categories being fabricated as universal to measure differences, such as the creative person, are neither natural nor neutral ingredients. It defines a certain way of being a person and also creates its abject (the person who is not creative). The ways in which creativity is being used contains a psychological meaning in its currency as it is related to some expected and well-defined behavior. The idea of creativity applied to a person's attributes is recent, and it appears as a product of the Enlightenment and its new arrangement of knowledge in which man replaces God as a creator. In post-war American discourses, it acquires a new breath as a natural attribute of the child as a moral being (Ogata, 2013), and the values attached to creativity are today part of that moral agenda (Osborne, 2003). Creativity and its correlates, as '*problem solving*', is becoming a soft mode of being governed and a regime for governing ourselves. In today's educational discourses and large-scale assessments, creativity is being taken as a granted, desirable and wholly positive idea that governs the creative person of the present as the creative worker and citizen of tomorrow.

A recent OECD study states that 'low performers could also benefit from developing a "growth mindset", which assumes that intelligence, character and creativity are not given traits, but qualities that can be learned and trained' (OECD, 2016c, p. 6). The identification of low performers and the correction of their state through remedial support, tailored strategies or supportive learning environments creates a space in which the rationality of development is understood as a natural common space which allows for the distinction of the low performers from the high performers. The proficiency level of students in mathematics or science, for instance, are reported according to scales. From the lower to the higher level, the developmental style of reasoning is applied through the staircase biological notion of progress and growth. PISA-D, the recent strategy for development, breaks down the lowest levels of performance in mathematics into sublevels. These stages incorporate a more detailed spectrum to 'describe' the youth from the middle- and low-income countries. The commonality (the development) and the difference (in performing into the scale) entail a double gesture. On one hand, there is the problem-solving youth who is the lifelong learner of the 21st century; on the other hand, there is the adolescent who threatens the future. Certain variables and categories are being mobilized in universalistic terms that is part of the statistical style of reasoning.

Numbers as Fictions and Development as a Way of Reasoning

PISA (OECD, 2016c) allowed worldwide nations to know that 13 million 15-year-old students in 64 countries were low performers in, at least, one disciplinary field. The numbers are used as truth facts that make proof and give evidence of an existing reality. However, numbers are not just numbers. Numbers create 'fictive spaces', as argued by Nikolas Rose, 'for the operation of government, and establish a "*plane of reality*", marked out by a grid of norms, on which government can operate' (Rose, 1991, p. 676). Numbers embody several cultural and moral theses on governing social life and establishing statistical realities organized across classifications by which people come to think about themselves and their actions, and, as such, they are important in the making up of citizens.

Numbers, under the flag of objectivity, provide terrains for comparison according to the marker of development. Development becomes then a way of reasoning about kinds of people and government. The hopes for a governable present and the fear of governmental failure makes comparison an instrument for the regulation of the nation's behavior and, at the same time, of educational actors and individuals within each nation. There is an interweaving between the micro scale of individuals and the macro scale of the nations, the space between both being justified by the principles of progress, failure and development.

The differences on results are not explained not because of specific contexts but rather because of a certain performance within a space constructed through equivalences. Thus, multiple dimensions are pointed out to save those demotivated students (the ones who do not perform well). The solutions embrace several zones of government that are about not only the youth's performance but also the embodiment of the hopes and the fears of government. The family, the community, the immigrant, the minority language and the rural students are there to explain why inequalities take place in comparing the performance of students within and among countries. As such, motivation, as a problem that is identified by PISA results, is easily seen as something that is not about the youth but about the order, administration and management of conduct and life.

The rationality embodied in PISA testing (measuring development through categories constructed as universal) is the same as the rationality embodied in knowing how the 19th-century child developed. It is clear that PISA is more about ranking nations than to position individuals. Nevertheless, these rankings are produced through the individual's performance, and they are meant to conduct the life of the nation and its citizens through the displaying of the top performers and its others. In the words of OECD, one of the goals is to 'encourage a *"race to the top"* for better and more coherent policies that can help deliver the SDGs' (OECD, 2016a, p. 3). The results of PISA could not be read in ontological terms but through a certain epistemology of governing since modernity. Objectivity and transparency come hand-in-hand with the rhetoric of applicability, fairness and impersonality. On the one hand, objectivity relates to the numbers being generated through the tests' results; on the other hand, transparency gives a sense of democracy in the application of the test and to the composition of the final *'picture of the nation'*. Like a window glass that allows one to see the outside, the transparency of the results is assumed as describing what counts as reality. However, the outside is always a landscape, a cityscape or whatever multiple layered categories that give meaning and reasonability to that seeing. The construction of equivalences that are applied to all nations allow for the emergence of the quantitative differences that will categorize those that are above the norm and make the space of governance governable.

The threats of the future are incubating within the present. Large-scale assessments are an attempt to anticipate the future through a series of calculations. These techniques of measuring the world make present specific futures (Anderson, 2010). Such as the 19th-century child about whom I have been talking, PISA is also about development through the identification of slowness in a linear path with political and moral intentions. PISA provides an image that is also an act of imagination (a fiction) in which future landscapes 'act' in the present. It seems odd to have what is not yet governing the present but, as argued by Anderson, 'making the future present becomes a question of creating affectively imbued representations that move and mobilize' (2010, p. 785). These representations affect what is possible to see and to think about what it means to be a contemporary citizen prepared for the future.

The developmental way of reasoning about children informs the knowledge that is being produced about schooling and future reforms. Even if differentiations are being made among different kinds of children creating inclusionary and exclusionary spaces, this arena of testing, measuring and a plane of reality, is not being questioned. It is not the individuality of each child that is being examined but kinds of people that are on the making.

Final Words

Throughout the chapter, there is a link between testing and accountability in which numbers are not only the result of something that is given an ontological existence, as being the child's capacities to solve a specific problem, but also the possibility of a smooth space of equivalences of the categories that organize what is being tested and then compared.

I tried to depict the historical articulation between the practices of measurement and quantification of development through the linearity of time and the government of childhood. The growth of the child, before the 19th century, was recognized, but not for governmental purposes. I focused on the 19th-century notion of child's development through the analysis of drawing. There was a style of reasoning that was emerging that also impacted education and pedagogy. If one thinks about today's assessments in arts, mathematics or sciences, it is clear how this culture of objectivity as part of equality, in calculating through equivalences the development of students and nations, goes unquestioned. The arts, mathematics or sciences are only the label under which the developmental child is made able to emerge.

The empirical turn in education was embedded within a culture of objectivity in which large amounts of data would be analyzed in order to depict the world. From these observations, the child's mental development was formulated as being equivalent with the child's performance in drawing, giving rise to different stages that ordered and divided who was the well-developed child from who was the pathological child. What was at stake was not drawing but rather principles that ordered action and ways of being. Today's PISA seeks to assess the practical knowledge and the global competencies of the young, but again, this practical knowledge and global competencies are not about a specific disciplinary knowledge nor about the young's capacities, but about the government of the young's conduct and, at the same time, this '*edu-fictions*', as I called it, provides road maps for the conduct of nations. The normal and the pathological find their places in these. The developmental child who was invented more than one century ago became naturalized and colonized the ways of relating to the times of childhood and to childhood in time. And the fiction goes on!

References

Anderson, B. (2010). Preemption, precaution, preparedness: Antecipatory action and future geographies. *Progress in Human Geography*, *34*(6), 777–798.
Barnes, E. (1892). A study of children's drawings. *The Pedagogical Seminary*, *2*(3), 455–463.
Compayré, G. (1889/1887). *Lectures on pedagogy: Theoretical and practical*. Boston, MA: D. C. Heath & Co.
Compayré, G. (1897). *Cours de pédagogie théorique et pratique*. Paris: Libraire Classique Paul Delaplane.
Danziger, K. (1997). *Naming the mind: How psychology found its language*. Thousand Oakes, CA & New Delhi: SAGE Publications.
Foucault, M. (2002/1997). *Em Defesa da Sociedade. Curso no Collège de France (1975–1976)*. São Paulo: Martins Fontes.
Hacking, I. (1992). Statistical language, statistical truth, and statistical reason: The self-authentification of a style of scientific reasoning. In E. McMullin (Ed.), *The social dimensions of science* (pp. 130–157). Notre Dame: University of Notre Dame Press.
Hacking, I. (2002). Inaugural lecture: Chair of philosophy and history of scientific concepts at the Collège de France, 16 January 2001. *Economy and Society*, *31*(1), 1–14.

Hall, G. S. (1893). *The contents of children's minds on entering school*. New York & Chicago: E. L. Kellogg & Co.

Hall, G. S. (1911/1904). *Adolescence, its psychology, and its relations to physiology, anthropology, sociology, sex, crime, religion, and education*. New York & London: D. Appleton and Company.

Jenks, C. (1996). *Childhood*. London & New York: Routledge.

Martins, C. S. (2017). From scribbles to details: The invention of stages of development in drawing and the government of the child. In T. S. Popkewitz, J. Diaz, & C. Kirchgasler (Eds.), *A political sociology of educational knowledge. Studies of exclusions and difference* (pp. 105–118). New York & London: Routledge.

OECD. (2014). *PISA in Focus 38*. Paris: OECD Publishing.

OECD. (2016a). *Better policies for 2030: An OECD action plan on the sustainable development goals*. Paris: OECD Publishing.

OECD. (2016b). *Global competency for an inclusive world, PISA*. Paris: OECD Publishing.

OECD. (2016c). *Low performing students: Why they fall behind and how to help them succeed, PISA*. Paris: OECD Publishing.

Ogata, A. (2013). *Designing the creative child. Playthings and places in midcentury America*. Minneapolis & London: University of Minnesota Press.

Osborne, T. (2003). Against 'creativity': A philistine rant. *Economy and Society, 32*(4), 507–525.

Pettersson, D., Popkewitz, T. S., & Lindblad, S. (2016). On the use of educational numbers: Comparative constructions of hierarchies by means of large-scale assessments. *Espacio, Tiempo y Educación, 3*(1), 177–202.

Popkewitz, T. S. (2007). Alchemies and governing: Or, questions about the questions we ask. *Educational Philosophy and Theory, 39*(1), 64–83.

Popkewitz, T. S. (2013). The sociology of education as the history of the present: Fabrication, difference, and abjection. *Discourse: Studies in Cultural Politics of Education, 34*(3), 439–456.

Porter, T. (1996). *Trust in numbers. The pursuit of objectivity in science and public life*. Princeton, NJ: Princeton University Press.

Rose, N. (1991). Governing by numbers: Figuring out democracy. *Accounting Organizations and Societies, 16*(7), 673–692.

Seguin, E. (1866). *Idiocy: And its treatment by the physiological method*. New York: William Wood & Co.

Sully, J. (1900/1896). *Studies of childhood*. New York: D. Appleton and Company.

Turmel, A. (2008). *A historical sociology of childhood. Developmental thinking, categorization, and graphic visualization*. Cambridge: Cambridge University Press.

5
AND THE WORLD HAS FINALLY BEEN MADE TO MEASURE

Barbara Czarniawska

The title of this commentary is a quote from Steven Shapin's (2012) review of a book by Robert Crease (2011), *World in the Balance: The Historic Quest for an Absolute System of Measurement*. Both the book and the review concentrate mostly on the domains where measurement was always an obvious element: area, currency, energy, length, power, pressure, speed, temperature, time, volume, weight (yes, I am quoting from a Converter app). In other words, finance, technology, infrastructure—but education? And yet, says Shapin at the end of his review:

> During the 1914–18 war, the Fabian socialist Leonard Woolf spoke in praise of the largely voluntary international organizations that had given the world standards of length, weight, color, electrical resistance and agricultural produce; he celebrated an 'international commission for unifying the nomenclature of apples', and he looked forward to a bright future in which 'even our chickens will be internationalized'. The worlds of science and commerce had shown the way to a harmonious international order in which voluntarily arrived at standards would embody reason, enhance productivity, eliminate confusing and unfair local customs, ensure peace and co-operation, and be guided by the wise counsel of technical expertise. A pattern of rational international governance had been established; modern metrology virtuously modelled modern political order, and the world had finally been made to measure.
>
> *(Shapin, 2012, p. 8)*

Several aspects are worth emphasizing here. Long-term perspective is necessary: as the historical anthropologist Thomas Crump reminded his readers, '[t]he origins of mathematics are in measuring and accounting, and it is notable that the earliest extant written records are largely about these things, rather than literature' (Crump, 1978, p. 507). As Theodore Porter has shown in many of his writings, the attempts to '*make the world to measure*' are very old indeed. But what happened now that finally permits achievement of this noble goal? The '*worlds of science and commerce*' met, not for the first time, but with exceptionally satisfying results.

Researchers working at the Australian National University (ANU) have conducted an experiment that has shown that reality does not exist until it is measured (at quantum level, though; Jeffrey, 2015; the original article by Manning et al., 2015). Social sciences, always eager to imitate the '*real sciences*', reacted with gratitude to technical possibilities offered by Big Data, and the dictum '*what can't be measured does not exist*' has apparently reached doctoral programs in social sciences—or so the doctoral students claim.

One element of science where measurement certainly established itself well is bibliometrics. As Hicks et al. (2015) have put it:

> Data are increasingly used to govern science. Research evaluations that were once bespoke and performed by peers are now routine and reliant on metrics. The problem is that evaluation is now led by the data rather than by judgement. Metrics have proliferated: usually well intentioned, not always well informed, often ill applied.
>
> *(p. 429)*

If researchers are evaluated by numbers, obviously, students and pupils can be so evaluated as well. It is here that the world of science meets the world of commerce. Using the vocabulary of Boltanski and Thévenot (2006), these two worlds of worth reach here an extremely successful compromise—one supplying the numbers of evaluation, the other turning those into monetary value of tuition fees and the like. This compromise, however, is achieved at costs. One is the cost of preparing the numbers: researchers and teachers on all levels spend more and more time on evaluation and self-evaluation (Morgan, 2010); there is no doubt that we are living in '*audit societies*' (Power, 1997). The other is the cost of that which has vanished (if it ever existed)—the value of that which cannot be measured by numbers.

Naturally, teachers and researchers do not produce all the numbers themselves, even if they produce more and more of those. My colleagues, organization scholars, speak of a multiplication of what they call '*meta-organizations*' (see, e.g., Ahrne & Brunsson, 2008). These are organizations that regulate the activities of other organizations, and many of them are standard-setters (Brunsson & Jacobsson, 2000). Here, again, different worlds meet: public sector and the market, education and industry—producing tools such as PISA and TIMSS, thoroughly analyzed in this volume. An interesting question arises: who are the experts who know how to produce such things; who are the employees or members of such meta-organizations? Certainly, academics, but for the most part not the academics who are moaning about, as Morgan (2010) put it, the exceedingly heavy burden of evaluation and audit distracting them from teaching and research.

Of special interest to me as an organization scholar are organizations called '*think tanks*' (a term launched in 1959, though it could be applied retrospectively to such bodies as The Fabian Society or Carnegie and later RAND). Utterly hybrid, mostly politico-scientific, they realize researchers' dream: they do research that has impact on politics. While economic sociologists have paid much effort into studies of performativity of economics (see, e.g., Muniesa, 2014), the members of think tanks are not only economists: they can be political scientists, sociologists or even anthropologists. The number of think tanks in the world goes above 6,000, according to a report from 2013 (McGann, 2014).

What are they? If Niklas Luhmann's perspective is to be taken, they are, like all communicative units, autopoietic systems: they re-create their own initial assumptions and are unable to communicate either with science or with politics. The other two worlds take from them only that which they wanted in the first place. In this sense, they will most resemble management consultants: according to Luhmann (2005), such consultants are supposed to offer their clients an applied science. A successful communication would mean, however, either that science is completely understandable (and thus there is no need for consultants) or that consultants speak exactly the same language as their clients (which means there is no difference between them and they are not needed):

> That a group of consultants [. . .] cannot communicate itself completely (but is nonetheless capable of communicating internally about this impossibility of external communication) is due to the fact that communication is the operation by means of which the group carries its own autopoiesis, and thus the means by which it regenerates its own unity, as well as the difference between this unity and its environment.
>
> *(Luhmann, 2005, p. 355)*

Luhmann added, however, that consultants (and, by the same token, think tanks) can act as '*external irritants*', which produce changes not by directly relating to clients, but by stimulating (from outside) the client's social system. Consultants thus explore the space between order and chaos, both disrupting and reconstructing the existing practices. Do think tanks do it, too?

At present, not enough is known about think tanks in relation to education policies. There are great many interesting questions to ask, even if Luhmann's perspective is seen as too radical. For example, what role are think tanks playing in establishing the numerical value of education? Are they the second important agent collaborating with Big Data advocates, or do some of them oppose the trend? Certainly at least one of them, the Council for Big Data, Ethics, and Society (http://bdes.datasociety.net) has some qualms about the world made to measure.

Further, if think tanks are composed of academics, they cannot be the same academics who are complaining about the burden of numerical reporting—even the greatest thinkers have only 24/7 at their disposal. Are they members of an elite, who interpret numbers collected by those under them? Are they ex-academics, who are basically political advisors, in the best Kissinger style? Most likely, think tanks themselves will be resistant to the attempts to study them too close, yet their role in shaping education policies is, in my opinion, difficult to overestimate. One thing is certain, though; as pointed out by Porter, no amount of data, numerical or not, will remove ambiguity—for the world and from education.

References

Ahrne, G., & Brunsson, N. (2008). *Meta-organizations*. Cheltenham: Edward Elgar.

Boltanski, L., & Thévenot, L. (2006). *On justification: Economies of worth*. Princeton, NJ: Princeton University Press.

Brunsson, N., & Jacobsson, B. (Eds.). (2000). *A world of standards*. Oxford: Oxford University Press.

Crease, R. (2011). *World in the balance: The historic quest for an absolute system of measurement*. New York: Norton.

Crump, T. (1978). Money and number: The Trojan horse of language. *MAN, 13*(4), 503–518.

Hicks, D., Wouters, P., Waltman, L., de Rijcke, S., & Rafols, I. (2015). Bibliometrics: The Leiden Manifesto for research metrics. *Nature, 520*, 429–431.

Jeffrey, C. (2015). *Experiment suggests that reality does not exist until it is measured*. Retrieved January 16, 2016, from www.gizmag.com/quantum-theory-reality-anu/37866/

Luhmann, N. (2005). Communication barriers in management consulting. In D. Seidl & K. H. Becker (Eds.), *Niklas Luhmann and organization studies* (pp. 351–364). Malmö & Copenhagen: Liber/ CBS Press.

Manning, A. G., Khakimov, R. I., Dall, R. G., & Truscott, A. G. (2015). Wheeler's delayed-choice gedanken experiment with a single atom. *Nature Physics, 11*, 539–542.

McGann, J. G. (2014). *Think tanks and civil societies program*. Philadelphia, PA: University of Pennsylvania. Retrieved January 16, 2016, from http://gotothinktank.com/dev1/wp-content/uploads/2014/01/ GoToReport2013.pdf

Morgan, J. (2010, March 4). Audit overload. *Times Higher Education*.

Muniesa, F. (2014). *The provoked economy: Economic reality and the performative turn*. London: Routledge.

Power, M. (1997). *The audit society: The rituals of verification*. Oxford: Oxford University Press.

Shapin, S. (2012). Plus or minus one ear. *London Review of Books, 34*(16), 8–10.

SECTION II
The Field of Making of Data
Problematics of Assessment

Within the second section, the development of assessments is problematized from different angles for investigating what kind of knowledge is gained and what is the reasoning behind these assessments. These chapters help us to better understand what international achievement tests are about, what reasoning lies behind them, what are the problematics framing them and how can this be understood in the making of society and its citizens. In the chapter by Regula Bürgi and Daniel Tröhler—*Producing the 'Right Kind of People': The OECD Education Indicators in the 1960s*—we are given the opportunity to understand how the OECD already in the 1960s was inspired by how education was compared within the reasoning in the IEA and how this was interpreted within the OECD sphere constituting an effort to create indicators for not only understanding, but also managing education. Creating indicators on education have a lot in common with the struggle to standardize, which is the focus in Radhika Gorur's chapter—*Standards: Normative, Interpretative and Performative*—where the author elaborates on some of the reasoning behind standardization within education. Organizations like the IEA and the OECD developed into important agencies attracting scientists and other kinds of experts. Within this milieu of knowledge-intensive activities based on specific reasoning, a specific kind of expertise is created, with a special focus on policy change. Luis Miguel Carvalho's chapter—*International Assessments and Its Expertise Fabricating Expert Knowledge for Policy*—makes an argument on how this functions and what the results are of this activity. Finally, in David Berliner's chapter—*The Implications of Understanding That PISA Is Simply Another Standardized Achievement Test*—we are given the opportunity to better understand in what ways PISA, as an example of an international large-scale assessment, is simply another standardized achievement test, which, if true, cannot as much be used for comparing nations as testing kids.

6

PRODUCING THE 'RIGHT KIND OF PEOPLE'

The OECD Education Indicators in the 1960s

Regula Bürgi and Daniel Tröhler

In general, research findings on the emergence of international assessments focus on the time period after 1990. Indeed, after the fall of the Iron Curtain in 1989, the internationalization of education policies and particularly the inclination for assessment by so-called international experts became dominant, symbolized not least by the OECD's publication of the first issue of *Education at a Glance 1992: OECD Indicators* (OECD, 1992). This is an indication of a 'comparative turn', based on international indicators that allow evaluation of the individual educational systems (Martens, 2007). However, this chapter argues that what becomes visible after the end of the Cold War is less the emergence of something new—brainchild of a neoliberal ideology of globalization, for instance—but more a materialized expression of a Cold War grid of thinking. In support of this thesis, after providing some contextual information, the chapter identifies three stages in the development of international education indicators in the 1960s—namely, first, the idea and vision of *forecasting* (largely quantitative description), then, under the catchwords of *development* and *growth*, the commitment to *planning* with regard to defined (quantitative) *benchmarks*, and, last, the idea of *management*, meaning fundamentally changing the whole school systems on all levels, foremost its quality, leading eventually to a quantification of school quality, and by that contributing to overall attempts at *social engineering*, based upon defined indicators.[1]

Cold War Aspirations as Context

To destroy German submarines while improving planning and decision making during World War II, British scientists developed a system of statistical probability calculation that was called Operational Research (Thomas, 2015).[2]

England's ally the United States implemented this mode of calculating in 1942 (Elichirigoity, 1999), where it rose to prominence under the name of Operations Research. Later it was applied to localization and identification of airplanes and to flight planning and was used subsequently as the major instrument of military planning (Rocco, 2011). In the post-war period, it was mainly the think tank Project RAND (a contraction of the term *research* and *development*; later named the RAND Corporation) that served as a vehicle for veterans to apply Operations Research to civil realms; it promised higher efficiency and effectiveness of social structures (Waring, 1995; Solovey, 2013). The world, men and matter equally, was formulated in a universal and quantified language of intervening variables, allowing communication between different academic disciplines—foremost mathematics, economics, technology and social psychology (Waring, 1995; Elichirigoity, 1999).

Operations Research was tightly linked to a method called systems analysis, which required the integration of even more variables. In contrast to Operations Research, which worked with politically given or prescribed aims from which the intervening variables were deducted, systems analysis developed hypothetical models and anticipated different aims and futures (Rocco, 2011). This difference between Operations Research and systems analysis was far reaching in three ways. First, the amount of data to be processed was increased significantly: whereas Operations Research had worked with a given number of variables, systems analysis aimed at a comprehensive number of possibilities, opening the door to massive sets of data to be analyzed and evaluated only by computers, which were being developed at this very time (Elichirigoity, 1999; Pircher, 2008). Second, systems analysis served as an instrument for switching from consultation to education (Rocco, 2011) or from tactics to strategy (Waring, 1995), since it created policy from scratch rather than just calculating with given and agreed-upon policy measures: Policy *consultation* became, in fact, policy*making* by virtue of scientific analysis. Third, this expertise in policy*making* was legitimated by the fact that hypothetical models were believed to be able to calculate, plan and create the future (Steinmüller, 2000). With that, planning the future was no longer seen in a historical continuity but in the logic of a computed and thereby predictable future (Hahn, 2006).

It is obvious that Operations Research and systems analysis were in step with the times. From 1958 to 1977, the share of US companies implementing Operations Research and systems analysis grew from 11 percent to 58 percent (Waring, 1995), and even universities established departments for Operations Research and systems analysis and produced corresponding textbooks (Heyck, 2015). In the context of the 'educationalization' of the Cold War (Tröhler, 2013), this new epistemology affected education. For example, at the Woods Hole Conference in 1959, which aimed at reforming the American school system after Sputnik, Jerome Bruner noted that in reforming education the focus was on 'the entire array of possible alternatives that might be created by using existing or newly developed technologies [...] from scratch' (as cited in Rudolph, 2002, p. 94).

Within this new epistemology, goal-oriented research in need of large-scale data became dominant (Rudolph, 2002). This had effects on education with regard to both curriculum/classroom and governance. Not only the RAND Corporation or the Air Force supported this new epistemology by sponsoring the Woods Hole Conference but also the Ford Foundation. By the end of 1950, the Ford Foundation, established in 1936 on a small scale, rose to become one of the most important US philanthropies because of a large sum of money provided by the Ford family.

The idea of maximizing '*output*' of the educational system had been at the forefront of the discussion on the National Defense Education Act of 1958. Philip H. Coombs, who had become head of the education program of the Ford Foundation (and later played a crucial role in OECD activities in education research and headed the International Institute for Educational Planning (IIEP), said before the United States Congress:

> By honoring excellence of performance in education and by honoring quality in education the Federal Government can do much to help expand the Nation's total supply of well-developed talent for all uses, not merely scientists and engineers. This is vital because a major key to our Nation's future development and progress, whether in relation to peace or to defense, is our supply of well-educated manpower.
>
> *(Coombs, 1958, as cited in Buss, 1980, p. 339)*

Development and progress in a predictable and forecasted way had become the fetish of this new epistemology. In this epistemology's perception, education was conceptualized as one of the central keys for development and progress and therewith as a panacea for solving social problems and challenges. By the end of the 1950s, Coombs was in touch with Joseph Kershaw, head of the economics department of the RAND Corporation. Kershaw, as he complained to Coombs, was tired of working with weapons systems, and he appreciated Coombs' suggestion that he should 'take a colleague and go sit in a local school system for a couple of months and see if "systems analysis" could be applied to a public-school system' (RAC, Oral Histories, 1973, p. 6). The result was the publication of *Systems Analysis and Education* (Kershaw & McKean, 1959), which had the 'aim to assess the possibilities of making quantitative comparison of education systems' (Kershaw & McKean, 1959, p. iii), as 'almost the only hope of providing systematically a better basis for intelligent choices in education' (Kershaw & McKean, 1959, p. 56). Around 10 years later, this study became very important for the OECD education programs, which were largely sponsored by the Ford Foundation (see the section on management or social engineering, later in this chapter).

Forecasting

In contrast to the United States, where technology has never been viewed as a contradiction to or even a threat to nature and democracy but rather as something sublime (Nye, 1996; Tröhler, 2010a), Europe shared at least latently a fear of apparatus (Etzemüller, 2005), as is evident in Fritz Lang's film, *Metropolis* (1927), for instance, or in Aldous Huxley's novel, *Brave New World* (1932). Europe's refraining from technological euphoria made it difficult for the new epistemology—according to which research did not *serve* political goals but *defined them* on the basis of computed scenarios of the future—to cross the Atlantic. However, even if Europe was much more reserved with regard to this epistemology, there were some technology-oriented and science-driven potential partners that supported this transfer by erecting new platforms for its dissemination in Europe.

One of the main platforms and catalysts was the Committee for Scientific and Technical Personnel (CSTP) within the Organisation for European Economic Co-operation (OEEC), which emerged from the Marshall Plan. The CSTP was founded in 1958, after Sputnik,[3] with financial support of half a million US dollars provided by the United States Department of Defense, to foster the sciences and at the same time to cultivate scientific instruments of governance (Bürgi, in print). Following the overall *educationalization* of the Cold War and in accordance with the developments in the United States, education—or a particular understanding of education—became more and more important to the committee. Europe's reluctance to embrace a vision of a harmonized world based on technological progress started to fade against the background of the substantial financial promises made by the US partners and the fear of a technological gap between Europe and both the Soviets and the Americans. Up to 1972, the CSTP was directed by the Scottish chemist Alexander King, who also became the director of the newly established Directorate for Scientific Affairs within the OECD, of which the CSTP became part after the transition from OEEC to OECD in 1961. The Directorate for Scientific Affairs, and its CSTP, opened the doors for this specific goal-oriented, science- and technology-driven, and allegedly universal epistemology to enter the European realm of policy. The epistemology combined the vision of scientific-technological productivity with the idea of education reform: in Europe, scientific-technological productivity now became *educationalized*.

It is via the fetish of scientific-technological productivity that education was able to enter the realm of the OEEC; a genuine committee of education would not have been possible at this time, as the former director, Alexander King, reported (King, 2006). Education and curricula on the whole were still seen as completely within the realm of each nation, serving the nation and its idiosyncrasy and prosperity since the beginning of the 19th century (Tröhler, 2016). Interestingly, it was not so much the developments in the United States that were seen as a model but rather (similar!) developments in the Soviet Union. Right from the beginning, the prevailing idea was to align the CSTP program with the experiences in the Soviet

Union (C(58)52 p. 18),[4] and in the 1960s, a delegation was sent to the Soviet Union to learn from Soviet experiences (STP/GC/M(60)1; STP/GC/M(60)2).

The activities of the CSTP were divided into two areas: educational expansion and statistically based information about the different school systems, including country reviews, comparisons and forecasts; and training of respective experts as well as teacher education and curriculum development, whereby the American experiences in curriculum reform were deemed as important (Eide, 1990). In this context, several initiatives for improving school education were launched,[5] most prominently perhaps the initiative for implementing New Mathematics (OECD, 1961a), and the CSTP became the 'clearing house' for the statistical data of the OEEC member countries, as we will show in the following (OEEC, 1960, p. 111).

With regard to educational expansion, the CSTP focused on generating statistical data, methods and analysis. At the first conference on statistics organized by the CSTP, *Techniques for Forecasting Future Requirements of Scientific and Technical Personnel*, held in Den Haag in 1959, the fundaments for the new epistemology in Europe were built; later on, the OECD asserted that this conference was truly groundbreaking (OECD, 1983). The proceedings and discussions were published in 1960 (OEEC, 1960); they testify visions of a 'world of tomorrow' based on scientific and technological productivity expressed in the leitmotif on the front page: 'Vigorous economic growth in the *world of tomorrow* [emphasis added] will depend largely upon an adequate supply of trained scientists, engineers and technicians' (OEEC, 1960, front page). The world of tomorrow was in need of a certain number or percentage of scientists and engineers; this percentage had to be forecast, and to conduct this forecasting, techniques had to be developed and experts created.

Indeed, the conference on *Techniques for Forecasting Future Requirements of Scientific and Technical Personnel* proved to be pathbreaking for the developments of the OECD (to be founded in 1961). The focus of the conference was on the development of technologies and methods able to predict the supply and demand of scientific personal and engineers as a basis of education policy (RAC, reel 1343, June 12, 1959). Existing data were criticized, for they had proved to be not comparable, and because even the notion of the 'engineer' had been used in different ways in the individual OEEC countries (OEEC, 1957). Accordingly, the Den Haag conference aimed not only at forecasting and prognosis but also and possibly primarily at comparison: Comparative statistics were seen as prerequisite to understanding the different education policies and their efficiencies. Only comparable data would show whether the individual countries would benefit from their human resources. These comparisons were based on quantitative factors, such as the participation of the population in the different levels of schooling or the ratio of teachers or professors to number of students (OEEC, 1960).

The conference participants agreed that a 'common language' was imperative (OEEC, 1960, p. 106), whereby the US expert on statistics and labor, Harold Goldstein, had suggested earlier that the OEEC act as a central administration or 'clearing house' (OEEC, 1960, p. 111) for the data. The CSTP was—from its very inception—encouraged to train experts in statistical analysis of the scientific and technical manpower needs or, rather, the threatening shortages (C(58)52 p. 1). The committee was open to this suggestion and had organized training seminars (STP/GC(59)1 p. 29). At the conference, Goldstein argued successfully for focusing on statistical data that allowed both comparison and forecasting:

> Improvement of the methodology on which statistical forecasting of scientific and technical manpower needs is based, with particular regard to forecasting techniques, the *acceptance of common definitions and establishing the equivalence* of scientific and technical qualifications between countries.
>
> *(STP/GC(59)1 p. 27, emphasis added)*

The common language expressed the new epistemology and the discourse related to it deliberately bypassed political taboo themes and, for strategic reasons, used a disguising rhetoric (Tröhler, 2014).

The implementation of this program drew on the country reviews that had been written since the beginnings of the OEEC, and they were to be continued after the foundation of the OECD (Kallo, 2009; Woodward, 2009). To the participants at the Den Haag conference, it was evident that this strategy would build bridges—politicians and experts together as responsible for generating statistical data. On the other hand, the participating countries would develop organizational structures assigned to prepare the country reviews, containing the desired data (OEEC, 1960). These country reviews were to become the interface to create in the individual countries a *common language* and corresponding organizational structures to be coordinated and controlled by the *clearing house* OEEC/OECD.

Planning Development and Growth to Reach Benchmarks

National delegates working in education policy made up only one half of the CSTP; the other half were scientists and engineers defined as or at least designated to become *experts*. When chemist Alexander King became the head of the Directorate for Scientific Affairs and the CSTP, he was far from being an expert in education (King, 2006). Yet he did not hire an education expert to compensate his deficit but instead his former colleague from the British Ministry of production, the social scientist James Ronald Gass. Like King, Gass was not familiar with educational issues, as noted by the Norwegian consultant and head of one of the CSTP educational planning programs, Kjell Eide (Eide, 1990).

The leading role that scientists were playing is reflected, for instance, in the mentioned Den Haag conference. Of the 32 participants, only four represented education policy, and a third of them came from engineering, followed closely by statisticians, mathematicians and economists. Sociology was represented by one person, and education was not represented at all. In contrast, the economist Philip H. Coombs, head of the education program of the Ford Foundation (and, later, head of the IIEP) was invited to talk on the notion of *planning*. His talk was pioneering for the CSTP and its activities, which changed in the 1960s from *forecasting* to *planning*, while intensifying its relationship with the Ford Foundation. Alexander King and Ronald Gass became the central pillars of the CSTP and were in close contact with as well as strongly supported by the Ford Foundation.

The optimism about the future did not include the idea of an open and undefined future. On the contrary, the future had to be planned and organized, as Albert Henry Halsey noted in a OECD conference report that was published in the first year of the new transatlantic organization's existence, and thereby education should play a crucial role:

> The direction of change is seen towards what may be called the *technological society*—a society in which human material welfare is continuously increased by the application of science to the productive process—a society, therefore, which places education in a central institutional position as *both* a source of *technological and cultural change* and as a vast training apparatus for the highly diversified manpower requirements of a *technological economy*.
> *(OECD, 1961b, p. 21, emphasis added)*

Development was the ordering idea behind progress and was understood as proceeding in stages:

> Development, as the term came to be used after 1945, was based on a familiar explanatory mechanism, a theory of stages. Those who used this concept were assuming that the separate units—'national societies'—all developed in the same fundamental way [...] but at distinct paces.
> *(Wallerstein, 2004, p. 10)*

Here, the United States was seen as unique but, at the same time, as the most advanced and, therefore, as the model to be imitated (Tröhler, 2010b). This expressed a style of reasoning according to which all societies followed a universal pathway to maturity and, therefore, notwithstanding their cultural idiosyncrasies, a predefined plan, whereby it nourished the technocratic aspirations that science could govern and accelerate this process (Heyck, 2011). It was, therefore, possible to assess and compare the various societies' progress, expressed in the notion of *growth*. Growth would happen in any case, as Walter Heller, a consultant to the US government, told the OECD, but the crucial question would be, 'Will we grow fast enough to meet the economic needs of a free, but threatened society?' (as quoted in Schmelzer, 2016, p. 196).

To guarantee the economic growth of the *free world* (and not only of Europe), the OEEC was dissolved in 1961 and the OECD founded, bearing not coincidentally the notion of *development* in its name. Accordingly, the CSTP recruited even more economists to work at the intersection of policy, planning and research, and it identified education as key for economic growth. Here, the OECD was not alone, for it was supplemented by the UNESCO-based IIEP, founded in 1963 and directed by Philip H. Coombs, the former head of the education program of the Ford Foundation and advisor to the CSTP. The IIEP had been founded to coordinate the regional UNESCO planning centers and provide them with the necessary scientific bases (Coombs, 1970). Very similar to the activities in the OECD, the courses were designed to bring economists and educators to speak the 'same language' (Coombs, 1970, p. 6). However, this language was not so much a synthesis; instead, it followed the economic rationale.

This paved the way for *planning* to become a core element in European policy, as the Standing Conference of European Ministers of Education planned a resolution on planning and investment in education (Europarat, 1964). It recommended that the investments in education of the individual European countries should be integrated in the economic plans. However, this endeavor required organizational structures that employed statistics experts and socio-economic research that was able to generate quantitative and qualitative data. To implement this kind of expertise, the Standing Conference asked the OECD to help—namely,

> that OECD, whose work in this field is greatly appreciated, be invited to formulate clearly in a model handbook the various factors involved in effective educational investment planning, so that the countries represented may have a basis for the compilation of comparable statistics.
> *(Europarat, 1964)*

It was no coincidence that the OECD was commissioned to erect a system for collection and analysis of statistical data for comparison, for the OECD was not accountable to any parliament, in contrast to the Council of Europe (the institutional umbrella of the Standing Conference of European Ministers of Education), and it is very unlikely that the parliaments of the individual member countries would have ever accepted an endeavor of this kind (Bürgi, in print). But attempts were already on their way within the CSTP; Ronald Gass pressured the delegates already in 1963 to intervene in their countries in order to provide the structures, the 'appropriate national machinery': 'He [Gass] suggested that the Committee [CSTP], basing itself on this Resolution, should make known the importance it attaches to the creation of the appropriate national machinery where this does not already exist' (STP/M(63)1 p. 9). These measures were gaining weight and legitimacy with the demand of the European Ministers of Education, and the CSTP secretariat did not hesitate to take advantage of this window of opportunity: it immediately published a note titled *The Need for Improved Statistics* (STP(64)24) that would allow solid statistically based comparisons between the member countries (STP(64)24 p. 1). The secretariat of the committee subsequently worked on a handbook to aid the national machineries in generating the desired data, the *Green Book*. The *Green Book* was published in 1967 only; it was based on inadequate data and, therefore, had no success (OECD, 1983, p. 11).

Management or Social Engineering: Producing the 'Right Kind of People'

In 1963, the aim of the CSTP policy was 'to promote adequate investment in and planning of educational resources so as to meet future growth needs' (STP(63)5 p. 2), and the Committee was proud to state: 'Gradually, a coherent O.E.C.D. policy approach has emerged' (STP(63)5 p. 1) that allowed planning for the future, or at least the next decade. These common measures were possible due in particular to the adoption of a common growth rate of 50 percent of the combined GDP within a decade by the OECD Council shortly after the establishment of the organization (Schmelzer, 2016): 'The adoption of the specific growth targets for 1970 will provide us with a more precise *benchmark* [emphasis added] against which these policies [education policies of the member countries] can be measured' (STP(62)5 p. 3). What had first been more descriptive was now decisively normative, allowing the comparative measurement of the education policies of the individual member countries and the computing of necessary investment: 'Science may well be a good thing but to be a national investment, it has to be *planned and managed* [emphasis added] like other investments' (King, 2006, p. 175). Accordingly, in 1964, educational planning was explicitly mentioned as a task for the CSTP, and with that, its targeted focus on the shortages of scientific and technical personnel faded more and more in favor of a much more comprehensive education policy (Bürgi, 2016).

However, by the middle of the 1960s, the success of planning encountered severe turbulence. The linear, partial and quantitative variables focusing only on quantitative growth became questionable—and by that the very fundament of the OECD—regarding the social damage that the rigid desire for quantitative growth caused and that had become more and more visible. This was the time when the mechanistic world view was being slowly replaced by an organic, managerial, biological and medical system of reasoning, whose governance depended, according to the stakeholders, not so much on public or democratic deliberation but on data and on scientific methods such as systems analysis (Tröhler, 2015). This fundamental epistemological shift was supported by the fact that, contrary to predictions, the data had proved that expansion of the education system had brought about neither more social justice nor more economic growth. And, last but not least, since the forecasts had not been able to include social change and its numbers proved to be wrong, the question was 'how the planner should behave in a situation in which the one thing he knows about any forecast he makes of the likely future course of events is that it will prove to be wrong' (Williams, 1972, p. 57). Accordingly, it became a high priority for the planners to erase or to nip in the bud the dangerous opinion that 'education is too complicated to trust to the planners' (Williams, 1972, p. 65).

The OECD itself was at the front line to accuse and at the same time to rehabilitate the planners. At an OECD conference on Perspectives of Planning in Bellagio, Italy, in 1968, the participants declared in an alarming language:

> We take it upon ourselves therefore to issue this collective warning that social and technological developments already *clearly foreseen* can exacerbate matters beyond any hope of peaceful relief. In doing so we express the belief that a basis of remedy already exists to help man to define and create his own *future*.
>
> *(Jantsch & OECD, 1969, p. 9, emphasis added)*

The remedy was total planning of the 'system as a whole' with all its elements: 'The need is to plan systems as a whole, to understand the totality of factors involved and to intervene in the structural design to achieve more integrated operation' (Jantsch & OECD, 1969, p. 8). According to the conference participants, mere mechanisms of self-adaptation were too slow and dangerous, since they could cause 'grave social disturbances' (Jantsch & OECD, 1969, p. 8) if the present was not ready for the future. Hence, adaptation should be 'deliberately planned' according to the 'clearly foreseen' future and 'not merely allowed to happen' (Jantsch & OECD, 1969, p. 8). Paradoxically, the solution for the difficulty with planning was seen in even more planning, or rather in total and comprehensive planning of the *system* as a whole, including not only quantitative but even more qualitative aspects. Accordingly, in the late 1960s, the OECD put more emphasis on quality (Schmelzer, 2012). The *new* planning method became known under the catchword 'prospective systems planning' and was applied to education, giving the education system a very particular identity as a *system*.

This idea of systems analysis was propagated by Philip H. Coombs, the former head of the education programs of the Ford Foundation, which in 1959 published the study *Systems Analysis and Education* (Kershaw & McKean, 1959) together with RAND. After a short engagement at the State Secretary in Washington, Philip H. Coombs was appointed director of the IIEP in 1963. It was within this function that Coombs stated at a groundbreaking conference on the World Educational Crisis in Williamsburg in 1967:

> A 'systems analysis' resembles, in some respects, what a doctor does when he examines the most complicated and awe-inspiring of all—a human being. It is never possible, nor is it necessary, for the doctor to have complete knowledge of every detail of a human being's system and its functional processes. The strategy of the diagnosis is to concentrate upon selected *critical indicators* and relationships within the system and between the system and its environment.
>
> *(Coombs, 1968, p. 8, emphasis added)*

Coombs obviously knew the difference between a body and a school, but he insisted that as an '*organic whole*' they functioned in the same ways: 'Yet, in common with all other productive undertakings, it [the education system] has a set of *inputs*, which are subject to a *process* designed to attain certain *outputs*, which are intended to satisfy the system's *objectives*' (Coombs, 1968, p. 9, emphasis added).

Crucial for the managerial turn is not only the medical comparison but also the focus on 'selected critical indicators and relationships within the system and between the system and its environment' (Coombs, 1968, p. 8). By identifying the education system as an organic system that interacts with other social systems, the planners believed that they could perceive change and thereby achieve an optimum fit between these different systems. Use of these methods was supposed to erase the shortcomings of the orthodox first-generation planning methods, and planning could be rehabilitated in the form of systemic management (Bürgi, 2016). To this end, new methods had to be developed. OECD relied explicitly on Operations Research and systems analysis, and the RAND study of 1959 served as a reference.

The new methods had to surpass the quantitative collection of quantitative data, such as numbers of students, had to quantify quality, such as learning and teaching or the curriculum, and had to set them in relation to broader social and economic goals and future developments. By focusing on 'selected critical indicators', interest became centered more on qualitative criteria of education, such as organizational structures, curricula, education research and policy. In other words, with the total and comprehensive management approach, put forward to solve the problems of planning, the planners legitimized their penetration of the inner system—the qualitative aspects of schooling that previously had been well protected based on the argument of national sovereignty. The planners' platform became the OECD Centre for Educational Research and Innovation (CERI), which was newly established in 1968 with the substantial financial support of 1 million dollars from the Ford Foundation (and later the same amount from the Royal Dutch Shell Foundation). CERI aimed at a closer interconnection between research, planning and policy; in contrast to the macro planning of the CSTP, CERI was concerned with the micro planning of schooling, its organization, administration, curricula and instruction.

The planning or management of *the system* required large-scale data (STP/M(69)1) to be computed with regard to the development of the future, providing the basis for policy in a world dependent on technology. All that this ideology needed was the 'right kind of people' to be produced by the reformed education systems. Ian Cox, a collaborator at the Shell Foundation, reported with regard to the motives of the foundation of CERI:

> King [head of the OECD Directorate for Scientific Affairs] and others recognized that the educational system produced the people needed to carry

out technological and scientific development and that the education system needed substantial revision if the *right kind of people* were to be produced

(RAC, unpublished reports, Nr. 2537, 1976, p. 14; cf. Bürgi, in print, emphasis added)

The production of the right kind of people to fit into the large-scale data-driven technocratic world as a major aim of the education system included a critique of traditional education: 'Education has long ignored and even rejected the technological society which is developing in the industrialized countries. It has persisted in preparing children for a world viewed from an inherited, traditionally cultural, outlook' (OECD, 1966, p. 32). In contrast, it was argued—and this shows the futuristic impetus—that the school curricula of a 'modern society' ought 'to prepare the pupils for their role in the world of tomorrow' (OECD, 1966, p. 32). To guarantee this *educationalized* world of tomorrow, schools were to be controlled by assessments of their 'efficiency or productivity' (CE/M(67)16 p. 53)—in short, their output. This mechanism of control was not the least a result of the OECD's lack of legal power (Bürgi, 2016). By controlling the output, the organization could ensure policy implementation without having instruments of legal governance. It is, therefore, not surprising that the organization emphasized the importance of national R&D (Research and Development) structures quasi as correspondent and informant of CERI, located outside of the universities and following strictly empirically quantitative and goal-oriented methods and working by means of indicators—as will be shown in the following section.

The Control of the System by Means of Indicators

The idea of R&D structures within the field of education and its simultaneous link to policy triggered the need to create relevant research structures that were outside the universities but that were nevertheless, as it was claimed, provided with the freedom of research (STP(67)15). The education system was defined as a 'living laboratory' (STP(67)15 p. iii); this allowed planners/managers and politicians to view the educational process—comparable to experiments in a laboratory—as a process that could be 'scientifically planned and arranged and its results objectively evaluated' (CERI/EI(68)1 p. 7). In this perspective, the educational world should 'overcome its uneasiness [. . .] vis-à-vis a rational approach to education and educational practice' and '[t]he world of education has for centuries been on its own, pursuing its own "noble" purposes, un-contested and un-tested' (CERI/EI(68)1 p. 9).

To implement this process of rationalization, interdisciplinary research was indispensable, but it was not available at the universities, in contrast to CERI or its national counterparts like the Max Planck Institute in Berlin. Educational research, or better—research on education—was to be aligned with the principles of the social sciences, such as behavioral, communication or administrative sciences or cognitive psychology (STP(67)15 p. iii; CERI/EI(68)1 pp. 15–16). The research designs should be either aligned with laboratory experiments or based on collections of large-scale field data (STP(67)15). Despite a claim to completeness, the focus was not coincidentally on aspects of *learning* (to operationalize and analyze) but rather on an encompassing process called *education* (Biesta, 2009); education was reduced to (a particular understanding of) learning.

The controlling of performance was to be handled by indicators that today are present in the *Education at a Glance: OECD Indicators* reports, which have been published since 1992, at first biannually and now annually. The roots of these indicators are, however, to be found explicitly in the conception of planning and managing a system developed around 1970 (ED(71)18 p. 1) and, inexplicitly, as early as in 1963:

> Now it seems to me that because the education system is a 'system', it is like any other piece of social machinery which uses certain processes to achieve given ends, and it is possible to analyze it and say whether, even on its own terms, it is working effectively or not.
> *(Vaizey, 1963, p. 42)*

Ends and performance (outputs) and their actual relation can be monitored and, with this, the plans (or models) permanently controlled. This was to provide rational decision making by virtue of indicators. 'Result-oriented' became, according to Kjell Eide (head of one of the CSTP planning programs), the watchword of the second generation of planners or managers (Eide, 1990, p. 34). At the 1970 OECD conference that was devoted to educational growth of the coming decade (see the previous section on management or social engineering), the assessment of performance by 'measuring the achievement and failures of the educational systems' (OECD, 1971, p. 18) was advocated. Immediately after this conference, the new Educational Committee (ED) established in 1970 published a report on 'statistical information system monitoring educational performance' that aimed at monitoring 'the performance of the educational system as a service organization' and thus transforming public schooling into a service center or system (DAS/EID/71.62).

This conversion to measure performance included a doubled claim toward the statistical data: first, qualitative aspects of schooling had to be translated into a quantitative language of numbers. Second, those numbers were not to be descriptive but were normative, carriers of meaning, indicating how good or bad an education system is performing (ED(71)1 p. 5).

CERI was already working on this in order to provide this information system of data, as sociologist Charles Arnold Anderson, founder and first director (1958–1972) of the Comparative Education Center at the University of Chicago described to the vice president of the Ford Foundation, F. Champion Ward. CERI produced a vast amount of data on the basis of a weak theoretical background:

'There is prodigious stimulation of new data and new analyses of data and a forcing of countries to examine their systems comparatively' (RAC, reel 1485, 18 April 1969). To generate these data properly, the OECD had to create benchmarks for the educational *thermometers*—to stay with Coombs' medical language—and to attribute meaning to them in order to assess how healthy or rather how sick the patient was. In other words, educational goals and standards had to be developed and accordingly operationalized by the OECD. Here, on the other hand, there was skepticism, and opposition was raised both in the CSTP and in the OECD council (STP/M(69)2 p. 8), in particular by the British delegate, who emphatically emphasized that 'different societies had different goals' (STP(70)32 p. 18). The definition of education goals was a matter of national sovereignty, and the role of the OECD was to be limited to helping the countries in the pursuit of *their* aims. However, this British opposition was countered by several delegates by the exigencies of 'modern societies' (STP/M(69)2, S 8–14) that were assumed to be global or at least European (Tröhler, 2010b). As the French delegate stated:

> The choice of objectives depended to large degree on the system of values accepted by society. It was with these values in mind that the Minister of National Education had at the Versailles Conference envisaged a 'new European standard of culture'.
> *(STP/M(69)2 p. 14)*

To guarantee continuous reporting and, with that, ongoing control of the member states of the OECD, uniform models of planning and analysis had to be developed (STP(68)2; STP(68)8). These new mechanisms introduced educational monitoring (the term was coined around 1970) *avant la lettre*. In the wake of this development, planning remained a priority of the CSTP. In 1969, its member countries joined a program called country educational planning, which even broadened the scope of the OECD's control over the national monitoring systems:

> It [educational planning] will necessarily become more catalytic and less prescriptive in detail more evaluative and policy-oriented and yet also more technical in that the range of its scientific considerations and investigations, particularly in the behavioral and social sciences, will be greatly expanded.
> *(STP(69)5 p. 3)*

The quantitative and comparative evaluation of performance/output was to become the major fundament of educational planning in the individual member countries. Accordingly, with the newly initiated country educational planning program in 1971, the development of indicators to analyze the national education systems had become crucial (ED(71)18 p. 1). It would take more than 20 years for these ideas to become an effective instrument of governance, as seen in "Education at a Glance" (OECD, 1992), published annually, and in the PISA study conducted every 3 years, which associated competencies with indicators and neglected contents of curricula (Labaree,

2014) in the *living world laboratories* conceiving societies worldwide as a homogenous entity—that was and is the grail for this kind of quantitative comparative research.

Notes

1. Substantial parts of this chapter have been developed in much more detail in a PhD dissertation by Regula Bürgi (Bürgi, 2017).
2. For a more detailed account, see Bürgi (2016).
3. However, the initiative was launched in 1957, shortly before Sputnik (C(58)52, p. 2), based among other events on the OEEC report, *The Problem of Scientific and Technical Manpower in Western Europe, Canada, and the United States* (OEEC, 1957).
4. Another model was the NATO Science Committee, as a letter from Alexander King to a collaborator of the Ford Foundation, Waldemar A. Nielsen, shows (RAC, reel 1231, December 20, 1957).
5. OEEC (1960b). *School Mathematics in OEEC Countries*. Paris: OEEC; OECD. (1963a). *Chemistry Today*. Paris: OECD; OECD. (1963b). *New Thinking in School Biology*. Paris: OECD; OECD. (1964). *Mathematics To-day*. Paris: OECD; OECD. (1965). *Teaching Physics Today*. Paris: OECD.

References

Biesta, G. (2009). Good education in an age of measurement: on the need to reconnect with the question of purpose in education. *Educational Assessment, Evaluation and Accountability, 21*(1), 33–46.

Bürgi, R. (2016). Systemic management of schools: The OECD's professionalization and dissemination of output governance in the 1960s. *Paedagogica Historica, 52*(4), 408–422.

Bürgi, R. (2017). *Die OECD und die Bildungsplanung der freien Welt: Denkstile und Netzwerke einer internationalen Bildungsexpertise*. Opladen: Barbara Budrich.

Bürgi, R. (in print). Engineering the free world: The emergence of the OECD as an actor in education policy, 1957–1972. In M. Leimgruber & M. Schmelzer (Eds.), *The OECD and the international political economy since 1948* (pp. 285–310). Basingstoke: Palgrave Macmillan.

Buss, D. C. (1980). The Ford Foundation in public education: Emergent patterns. In R. F. Arnove (Ed.), *Philanthropy and cultural imperialism: The foundations at home and abroad* (pp. 331–361). Boston, MA: G. K. Hall.

Coombs, P. H. (1968). *The world educational crisis: A systems analysis*. New York: Oxford University Press.

Coombs, P. H. (1970). *What is educational planning?* Paris: UNESCO/IIEP.

Eide, K. (1990). *30 Years of educational collaboration in the OECD*. Paris: UNESCO.

Elichirigoity, F. (1999). *Planet management: Limits to growth, computer simulation, and the emergence of global spaces*. Evanston: Northwestern University Press.

Etzemüller, T. (2005). *1968, ein Riss in der Geschichte? Gesellschaftlicher Umbruch und 68er-Bewegungen in Westdeutschland und Schweden*. Konstanz: UVK.

Europarat. (1964). *Resolution on planning and investment in education (No. 2)*. Retrieved from www.coe.int/t/dg4/education/Standing_Conferences/w.4thSession_london1964.asp#P42_3232

Hahn, F. (2006). *Vom Unsinn bis Untergang: Rezeption des Club of Rome und der Grenzen des Wachstums in der Bundesrepublik der frühen 1970er Jahre*. Freiburg: Albert Ludwig University of Freiburg. Retrieved from www.freidok.uni-freiburg.de/volltexte/2722/

Heyck, H. (2011). Die Moderne in der amerikanischen Sozialwissenschaft. In B. Greiner, T. B. Müller, & C. Weber (Eds.), *Macht und Geist im Kalten Krieg* (pp. 159–179). Hamburg: Hamburger Edition HIS.

Heyck, H. (2015). *Age of system: Understanding the development of modern social science*. Baltimore, MD: Johns Hopkins University Press.

Jantsch, E., & OECD. (1969). *Perspectives of planning* (Proceedings of the OECD working symposium forecasting and planning, Bellagio, Italy 27th October–2nd November 1968). Paris: OECD.

Kallo, J. (2009). *OECD education policy: A comparative and historical study focusing on the thematic reviews of tertiary education*. Jyväskylä: Jyväskylä University Press.

Kershaw, J. A., & McKean, R. N. (1959). *Systems analysis and education*. Santa Monica, CA: Rand Corporation.

King, A. (2006). *Let the cat turn round: One man's traverse of the twentieth century*. London: CPTM.

Labaree, D. (2014). Let's measure what no one teaches: PISA, NCLB, and the shrinking aims of education. *Teachers College Record, 116*. doi:116:090303

Martens, K. (2007). How to become an influential actor: The "comparative turn" in OECD education policy. In K. Martens, A. Rusconi, & K. Leuze (Eds.), *New arenas of education governance: The impact of international organizations and markets on educational policymaking* (pp. 40–56). Basingstoke: Palgrave Macmillan.

Nye, D. E. (1996). *American technological sublime*. Cambridge, MA: MIT Press.

OECD. (1961a). *New thinking in school mathematics*. Paris: OECD.

OECD. (1961b). *Ability and educational opportunity*. Paris: OECD.

OECD. (1962). *Policy conference on economic growth and investment in education* (Washington 16th–20th October 1961). Paris: OECD.

OECD. (1966). *Curriculum improvement and educational development: Modernizing our schools*. Paris: OECD.

OECD. (1971). *Educational policies for the 1970s* (Conference on policies for educational growth, Paris, 3–5 June 1970). Paris: OECD.

OECD. (1983). *Educational planning: A reappraisal*. Paris: OECD.

OECD. (1992). *Education at a glance 1992: OECD indicators*. Paris: OECD.

OEEC. (1957). *The problem of scientific and technical manpower in Western Europe, Canada, and the United States*. Paris: OEEC.

OEEC. (1960). *Forecasting manpower needs in the age of science*. Paris: OEEC.

Pircher, W. (2008). Im Schatten der Kybernetik: Rückkopplung im operativen Einsatz: Operational research. In M. Hagner & E. Hörl (Eds.), *Die Transformation des Humanen: Beiträge zur Kulturgeschichte der Kybernetik* (pp. 348–376). Frankfurt: Suhrkamp.

Rocco, P. (2011). Wissensproduktion in der RAND Corporation. In B. Greiner, T. B. Müller, & C. Weber (Eds.), *Macht und Geist im Kalten Krieg* (pp. 301–320). Hamburg: Hamburger Edition HIS.

Rudolph, J. L. (2002). *Scientists in the classroom: The Cold War reconstruction of American science education*. New York: Palgrave Macmillan.

Schmelzer, M. (2012). The crisis before the crisis: The 'problems of modern society' and the OECD, 1968–74. *European Review of History, 19*(6), 999–1020.

Schmelzer, M. (2016). *The hegemony of growth: The making and remaking of the economic growth paradigm and the OECD, 1948–1974*. Cambridge: Cambridge University Press.

Solovey, M. (2013). *Shaky foundations: The politics-patronage-social science nexus in Cold War America*. New Brunswick, NJ: Rutgers University Press.

Steinmüller, K. (2000). Zukunftsforschung in Europa: Ein Abriss der Geschichte. In K. Steinmüller, R. Kreibich, & C. Zöpel (Eds.), *Zukunftsforschung in Europa: Ergebnisse und Perspektiven* (pp. 37–54). Baden-Baden: Nomos.

Thomas, W. (2015). *Rational action: The science of policy in Britain and America, 1940–1960*. Cambridge, MA: The MIT Press.
Tröhler, D. (2010a). The technological sublime and social diversity: Chicago pragmatism as response to a cultural construction of modernity. In D. Tröhler, T. Schlag, & F. Osterwalder (Eds.), *Pragmatism and modernities* (pp. 25–44). Rotterdam: Sense Publishers.
Tröhler, D. (2010b). Harmonizing the educational globe: World polity, cultural features, and the challenges to educational research. *Studies in Philosophy and Education, 29*(1), 7–29.
Tröhler, D. (2013). The OECD and cold war culture: Thinking historically about PISA. In H.-D. Meyer & A. Benavot (Eds.), *PISA, power, and policy: The emergence of global educational governance* (pp. 141–161). Oxford: Symposium Books.
Tröhler, D. (2014). Change management in the governance of schooling: The rise of experts, planners, and statistics in the early OECD. *Teachers College Record, 116*(9), 13–26.
Tröhler, D. (2015). The medicalization of current educational research and its effects on education policy and school reforms. *Discourse: Studies in the Cultural Politics of Education, 36*(5), 749–764.
Tröhler, D. (2016). Curriculum history, or the educational construction of Europe in the long 19th century. *European Educational Research Journal, 15*(3), 279–297.
Vaizey, J. (1963). The role of education in economic development. In H. S. Parnes & OECD (Eds.), *The Mediterranean Regional Project: Planning education for economic and social development*. Paris: OECD.
Wallerstein, I. (2004). *World-systems analysis: An introduction*. Durham, NC: Duke University Press.
Waring, S. P. (1995). Cold calculus: The cold war and operations research. *Radical History Review, 63*, 28–51.
Williams, G. L. (1972). Educational policies, plans, and forecasts during the nineteen-sixties and seventies. In OECD, *The development of educational planning*. Paris: OECD.
Woodward, R. (2009). *The organisation for economic co-operation and development*. Oxford: Routledge.

Unpublished Sources

OECD Archive, Paris
Committee for Scientific and Technical Personnel (STP; STP/GC; STP/GC/M; STP/M)
Directorate for Scientific Affairs (DAS/EID)
OECD Council (C) and executive board of the council (CE; CE/M)
Educational Committee (ED)
Centre for Educational Research and Innovation (CERI/EI)
Rockefeller Archive Center (RAC), Sleepy Hollow (New York):
Reel 1231, Gen 57, Organization for European Economic Cooperation 1957 (20 December), OEEC (Alexander King) to Ford Foundation.
Reel 1343, Gen 59, Organization for European Economic Cooperation 1959 (12 June), OEEC (H. Metzgen) to Ford Foundation (Philip H. Coombs), Conference on Educational Forecasting.
Reel 1485, PA 68–361 1969 (18 April), C. Arnold Anderson (University of Chicago; Center for Comparative Education) to Ford Foundation (F. Champion Ward), CERI.
Oral Histories, Series 4, Box 1, Folder: COOMBS, Philip Hall 1973 (10 July), Interview with Philip H. Coombs. Oral History Project.
Unpublished Reports, No. 2537 (James W. Armsey) 1976 (15 March), Ford Foundation, Centre for Educational Research and Innovation. A Retrospective Review of a Ford Foundation Grant.

7
STANDARDS
Normative, Interpretative, and Performative

Radhika Gorur

Introduction

This chapter follows the development of the International Standard Classification of Education (ISCED), from the early desire for comparative information on school systems in the 1930s, through the many attempts at creating international comparative statistical tables, to the creation and adoption of ISCED by UNESCO in 1978 and its subsequent establishment and revisions. Using the theoretical and analytical resources of Science and Technology Studies, it follows the behind-the-scenes activities of ISCED-in-the-making to explore how such large-scale regulatory devices are created. Demonstrating the socio-technical nature of standardization, I show how these technologies of visibility and legibility are not merely descriptive but also interpretive. I highlight the regulatory power of classification and standardization and demonstrate that they are also performative—they bring new worlds into being. I argue that standardization is thus a deeply political practice involving highly consequential normative judgments. The recognition of the politics of these apparently technical practices is crucial if we are to recover for statisticians the moral responsibility that is effaced by the myth of '*objective*' science and the routinization of standards.

Large-scale quantification and comparison is impossible without standardization. But setting, maintaining and regulating standards is no easy task (Bowker & Star, 2000; Timmermans & Epstein, 2010). Latour and other scholars in Science and Technology Studies (STS) have empirically traced the enormous effort, the institutional support, the consensus of experts, legal agreements, conferences and meetings, trials of strength, translations of interests and the methodological agility that attends the creation and maintenance of standardized frameworks and the establishment of scientific practices (cf. Shapin & Schaffer, 1985; Latour, 1987,

1993; Knorr-Cetina, 1999; Gorur, 2013). They reveal the intimate intertwining of '*science*' and '*politics*' in what is often considered a purely '*objective*' or technical enterprise (Desrosières, 1998; Latour, 2005).

I explore the politics of quantification (Miller, 2005) using the establishment and stabilization of the International Standard Classification of Education (ISCED) as a case study. On the basis of the conceptual resources of STS and the sociology of standards and measurement (Star & Lampland, 2009; Busch, 2011; Gorur, 2013, 2015; Woolgar, 1991), I trace how the desire to establish a standardized framework that would enable international comparisons in education was born, how it struggled to find traction and how it eventually came to be established in the form of ISCED, and use this case study to explore the politics of quantification. Latour (1988, p. 228) has famously described science as '*politics by other means*'. Understanding this renders the '*technical*' history of ISCED intensely interesting for its '*politics*'.

In telling this story, I highlight the following: first, standardizations, classifications and enumerations are not merely descriptive but also interpretive (Poovey, 1998). Although ISCED has become an indispensable tool for generating systematic knowledge about education systems globally, its own interpretive role remains obscure. This history demonstrates that standardized nomenclatures, definitions, structures and formats of data gathering represent efforts to promote particular interpretations to the exclusion of others. Second, classification and standardization exert a regulatory power (Hacking, 1983; Pickering, 1993; Chia, 1998; Knorr-Cetina, 1999) and are thus normative—they promote particular ideals to which populations are expected to conform. Finally, they participate in the production of particular worlds—so they are also performative. Although statistics are often thought of as merely representing states of affairs, the exercise of translating the world into numbers requires the world to be conceptualized and ordered in particular ways to be rendered calculable in the first place. Moreover, as soon as such standards are created and comparisons made, they begin to act on the world to create new ambitions, articulate new 'matters of concern', develop new patterns of growth and deficit, create new groups and rearrange relations between different actors (Gorur, 2016b). Understood as normative, interpretive and performative, standardization becomes a deeply political practice, rather than merely 'technical' and '*objective*'. In highlighting the politics of numbers, my aim is not to debunk numbers or to denounce number makers. Rather, I seek to recover for statisticians (and not merely the policymakers who use these data) the moral responsibility that is effaced by the myth of '*objective*' science and the routinization of standards.

For tracing this history, which goes back several decades, I drew upon published accounts of those engaged in the production of these indicators. This includes accounts of the development of the ISCED provided by John Smyth, who served in UNESCO for nearly 30 years, between 1972 and 2000, using such historical data as UNESCO meeting minutes and out-of-print documents unavailable to most researchers; the firsthand accounts of Stephen Heyneman, who served with the World Bank for 22 years, between 1976 and 1998, and was involved in the development and revision of ISCED; the works of Norberto Bottani, formerly the Principal Administrator of the OECD's Centre for Educational Research and Innovation (CERI), and Head of the Project on International Indicators of Education Systems (INES) 1988–1997; and the accounts of Claude Sauvageot, who headed the task force for revising ISCED. Interweaving the historical and the theoretical (cf. Pickering, 1993), I explore how conceptual resources combined with institutional practices to enable categorizations, standardizations and formalizations in education. I trace the possibilities that became imaginable as new maps and pictures emerged through the use of quantification and measurement in education on a global scale, and follow the gradual imposition of order over messy realities to produce a world that is rendered measurable, quantifiable, comparable, comprehensible and legible in particular ways.

The Story of ISCED

Education is regarded a key to escaping poverty and as a means of participating in employment. An educated population is seen as increasing a nation's human capital and thus national prosperity. Countries try to predict '*skills shortages*' and formulate their immigration policies and education policies accordingly. Education is also internationally established as a fundamental right, and access to good education as an issue of equity and social justice. Because literacy is so critical to the fortunes of individuals and nations, there has long been an interest in mapping national and global patterns of literacy and illiteracy. Nations often included surveys of literacy as part of their census surveys. Countries were also interested in learning from each other for raising literacy levels, and indeed in conducting comparative statistical surveys.

Despite deep interest, the diversity in structures, terminologies, measurement practices and the types of statistical data gathered across the nations of the world made comparative tabulation of data extremely challenging. The need was felt for some device that could tame this diversity and restate the facts in commensurate terms. It was to satisfy this need that ISCED was born. Part of the United Nations' International Family of Economic and Social Classifications, ISCED was established through an international agreement, formally adopted by member nations of UNESCO, to collect national statistics using agreed nomenclature and definitions, and to report these data in a standardized format to IGOs for their reports and comparisons. ISCED has become the essential framework underpinning a vast range of educational data collected globally.

Although now widely used and taken for granted as indispensable, ISCED was decades in the making, and required heated debates and the mobilization of enormous resources, expertise and goodwill to come to fruition. In this section, I recount the struggles to develop ISCED. I demonstrate how the apparently '*technical*' debates and decisions that attended these early attempts and the eventual development of ISCED were at once also political. The descriptions of education systems that were sought for decades became possible only when an interpretive tool—the ISCED framework—was introduced. The framework was also, from the start, performative—it rearranged relations, redistributed attention and enabled the world to become legible in very particular ways. ISCED is the invisible infrastructure without which international comparisons in education would not be possible.

Early Attempts

Education was one of the first to be recognized as a field of statistical inquiry at the International Statistics Congress in 1853 in Brussels (Heyneman, 1999). Early attempts at comparisons were *ad hoc* compilations of national accounts produced by individual nations, rather than comparative summaries (Smyth, 2008). Countries had their own methods of collecting data about a range of social factors, and these included some aspects of education or literacy in some countries.

After World War I, the League of Nations set up the International Commission on Intellectual Cooperation in 1921 to promote cooperation among scientists, facilitate student and staff exchanges in universities, develop norms for intellectual property, promote the mutual recognition of university qualifications, and set up international bibliographies (Smyth, 2008). Smyth reports that in 1926, France set up the International Institute of Intellectual Cooperation (IIIC) as a part of the International Commission, funded by the French government, the Rockefeller Foundation and the Carnegie Endowment. The IIIC set up a Committee in collaboration with the International Statistical Institute to focus on international statistics on 'the principal manifestations of intellectual life in different countries' (Smyth, 2008, p. 8). The components of this survey provide a wonderful glimpse into how '*intellectual life*' was conceptualized: they included enumeration of 'scientific research establishments to museums and archives, historic and artistic monuments, book production and publishing, theatres, concerts, cinema, radio broadcasting, patents and inventions, and employment in the liberal professions' (Smyth, 2008, p. 8). Education, science and culture were thus intimately connected in this understanding of measures of '*intellectual life*'. Education itself was classified in six sections—as higher, secondary, primary teacher, adult and specialized education. Smyth reports that this exercise was undertaken with full awareness that these categories were not uniform across the systems included in the measures. There were wide national variations in what and how statistics were collected.

Despite the lack of standardization in the categories of education, the International Statistical Institute adopted a resolution to call for national statistics to be prepared in accordance with a model table. A trial publication was proposed, using already-available data to be fitted into this model table, 'taking into account national differences in the relevant definitions, legislation, and administrative practices' (Smyth, 2008, p. 9). This was the first attempt by any authoritative body to conceptualize a global framework for statistical comparison in education. Although the ambition was heroic, comparability was not ensured. Differences in the duration and content of, for example, a classification such as '*primary school*' confounded comparison (Smyth, 2008). Moreover, IIIC suffered from lack of funding and the lack of an authoritative mandate, and the initiative petered out. But the desire to generate internationally comparative accounts of educational progress never really went away.

The interpretive work of such a '*model table*' is immediately apparent, as is its regulatory ambition of getting all nations to collect data that was deemed important for international comparison. When nations were required to collect data that they had not previously collected, possibly new problems, gaps, solutions and matters of concern became apparent. These new patterns had the power to redirect policy attention in possibly profound ways.

Taming Disorder: Yearbooks and the Standardization of Nomenclature

Encouraged by the efforts of the IIIC and the International Statistical Institute, a variety of institutions became involved in data gathering and sharing, including the International Bureau of Education (IBE), started by the University of Geneva's School of Educational Sciences. With Jean Piaget as Director, IBE's diverse membership included the Republic and Canton of Geneva, the Governments of Ecuador, Egypt and Spain and the Ministries of Public Education of Czechoslovakia and Poland. IBE carried out a number of surveys spanning a range of topics that included school administration and teacher education. It invited member and non-member nations to present developments in their countries at the Council's annual meetings and instituted the annual International Conference on Public Education (Smyth, 2008).

With the publication of the first International Yearbook of Education in 1933, with survey information from 35 countries, the tricky issue of comparative tables reasserted itself. Should each country's data be reported separately, as self-contained chapters describing that country's situation, or should a summary table with data of all the nations be presented so they could be taken in at a glance, facilitating comparison? Smyth's accounts suggest that early discussions about creating summary comparative tables were attended by hesitations and misgivings, and the idea of summary comparisons was seen as both impractical and undesirable by Piaget. However, Smyth reports, the lure of such comparisons was compelling, and Yearbooks were appearing elsewhere as well. In 1925, Teachers College, Columbia, had published the Educational Yearbook of the International Institute of Teachers College, the introduction to which outlined some of the challenges facing such comparisons, including non-standard nomenclature, missing data and the instability of financial information. The Year Book of Education was published by 'a group of leading educationalists' in 1933 in the UK, containing chapters on each country, 'a set of international tables of student enrollments, numbers of teachers and educational expenditures, and a chapter entitled "Comparative Statistics" prepared by the comparative educationist Nicholas Hans' (all quotes from Smyth, 2008, p. 11).

Hans was well aware of the challenges of such comparisons, including differences in terminology, and the fact that the same term, such as '*secondary school*', may mean very different things in different countries. For this, he proposed the antidote of developing an artificial, standardized framework that all countries would adopt. Even this, however, would not solve the problem, since organizing data in accordance with this framework required considerable expertise and knowledge, and often data were simply not available (Hans, 1933, cited in Smyth, 2008). To get around this, Hans' classification focused on the functions of educational institutions to establish equivalences and make comparisons, an approach ISCED would eventually adopt.

Notwithstanding Piaget's misgivings, IBE's 1937 edition of the International Yearbook presented summarized international comparative tables, representing 'the world's first successful attempt to overcome the natural reluctance to compromise on each nation's different definition of a "school", a "teacher" and a "pupil"' (Heyneman, 1999, p. 66). Data in the Comparative Statistics chapter of the 1937 Yearbook included information on education budgets, and numbers of schools, pupils and teachers (Smyth, 2008). Curiously, Smyth reports, despite the vexatious variations in the meanings of terms such as primary school, secondary school and so on, no attempt was made to provide explanation or detail. Budgets were presented in the currencies of each country, making comparison difficult, and placing the burden of interpretation on the reader. In part this may have been because the limitations of such comparisons were well recognized (Heyneman, 1999).

But such comparisons only whetted the appetite. Merely having a common framework was not enough to report data comparatively. Some method of calculating equivalences was required. Meaningful comparison required speaking in a common language. And for any systematic and standardized data collection to be enforced, an international organization capable of collecting and interpreting such statistics was needed (Smyth, 2008). UNESCO, formed in 1946, was precisely such an organization.

Mapping Illiteracy: UNESCO's Crucial Role of Coordination

After World War II, UNESCO assumed leadership for international cooperation in reducing illiteracy. The world, previously categorized as communist and non-communist, was now remapped as '*developed*' or '*underdeveloped*'. Educating the masses, particularly in the underdeveloped nations, became a moral and economic priority. But to do this, it was important to understand the size and location of the problem of illiteracy. Statistics about literacy and illiteracy were needed. The international statistical service on education was proposed and adopted at the first session of UNESCO's General Conference, and a statistical office was established in 1950 (Heyneman, 1999), with two purposes: building up a database of available national statistics and mobilizing and facilitating experts to enable standardization and thus international comparability.

Pursuing the first goal, in 1952, UNESCO published the *World Handbook of Educational Organization and Statistics*, which contained data on 57 countries. A year later, *Progress of Literacy in Various Countries*—a preliminary statistical study of available census data since 1900, a detailed international comparative account of literacy statistics based on census data from 1900s to the 1950s, was published. Not all countries had such a long history of census records, so only 26 countries appeared in the document.

If the earlier efforts were motivated by curiosity about other nations and focused mainly on the cultural aspects of education, UNESCO's efforts at this stage were focused on providing the statistics that would help promote equity and human rights, claiming that, '[i]n particular, the public administrator, the educator, the social scientist, and even the economic planner will want to know the number and proportion of men and women who cannot read and write among the inhabitants of their area' (UNESCO, 1953, p. 9).

Illiteracy was thus cast as a matter of global concern and an object of remediation. UNESCO's statistics were no longer merely interested in description—there was a clear interventionist agenda. The '*mapping*' project highlighted the power of standardization as a technology of visibility. It is worth noting that '*economic planners*' were mentioned almost as an afterthought in connection with those who might find comparative education statistics useful. That education today is routinely seen in economic terms as return on yield and human capital attests to the performativity of such comparisons (Gorur, 2016a, b).

The *Progress of Literacy* report also underscored the limitations of these comparisons. The methodology for collecting data was not defined prior to collection. UNESCO simply used national census data that had been collected within each of the 26 nations. It thus had little control over who was included in the analysis and how '*literacy*' and '*illiteracy*' were defined in different nations over those 50 years of surveys, and indeed how information about literacy levels was elicited. The sources of these data (marriage registers, military records and population censuses) were also problematic (UNESCO, 1953). In many cases, data were just missing—not all countries collected the same types of data. Censuses were conducted at different times and at different frequencies.

But most challenging and frustrating were the wide differences in the definitions of literacy and illiteracy. In 1948, the United Nations Population Commission had recommended a definition of literacy for census purposes as 'the ability both to read and write a simple message in any language' (UNESCO, 1953, p. 13). But the data in this report predated that instruction. In any case, countries used their own criteria despite the recommendation:

> Definitions of literacy and illiteracy are widely divergent, ranging from 'can read' or 'cannot read' to 'can or cannot write a short letter to a friend and

read the answer'. Ability to sign one's name is in some cases considered sufficient evidence of literacy, while in others it is not.

(UNESCO, 1953, p. 11)

The questions used to elicit information about literacy also varied widely from one country to the next, and from one census to the next.

Despite these challenges, the historical publication of the first-ever international comparisons of literacy and illiteracy was seen as useful in producing pictures of progress in improving literacy and indeed in developing better methodologies for generating education statistics.

Fifty nations had adopted UNESCO's Universal Declaration of Human Rights in 1948, which cast education as a fundamental right, with at least elementary education being free and compulsory. The World Education Survey (1955), was to produce a situation report 'to reveal the size of the task ahead' (UNESCO, 1955, p. 13). The '*situation*' was thus being mapped for the purpose of changing it. The Survey embedded and anticipated an ideal future (cf. Poovey, 1998) and provided the impetus to mobilize international political action to realize this future.

Simultaneously, UNESCO's Expert Committee on Standardisation of Educational Statistics, established in 1951, started working toward a common framework against which data might be collected. It developed 'a set of definitions and rules for classifying education' to facilitate international comparability, including definitions for terms such as 'compulsory school age population, school age population, government-financed school, government-aided school, independent school, school, class, grade, student, and teacher and for 'defining the distinctions between general and vocational education'. Most significantly, four crucial terms—school, class, student and teacher—came to be defined. Four categories or levels of education were identified (all quotes from Smyth, 2008, p. 17).

The Slipperiness of Standards in Practice

UNESCO members adopted a set of definitions and principles of classification that were designed for international reporting, in which literacy was defined as: a person is literate who can with understanding both read and write a short simple statement on his (her) everyday life.

National data gatherers had to determine, case by case, whether someone was literate or not. What did it mean to read with understanding? What constituted a simple statement? Smyth (2005) reports that UNESCO advised member states about the methods of measurement to be used:

(a) Ask a question or questions pertinent to the definitions given above, in a complete census or sample survey of the population.
(b) Use a standardized test of literacy in a special survey. This method could be used to verify data obtained by other means or to correct bias in other returns.

(c) When none of the above is possible, prepare estimates based on (1) special censuses or sample surveys on the extent of school enrollment, (2) regular school statistics in relation to demographic data, (3) data on educational attainment of the population.

Even this was not failsafe. For instance, infants who could not even speak as yet were part of the census—and in some cases, they were included in the count of illiterates. Despite all its efforts at standardization, variations persisted (UNESCO, 1955). The creation of definitions and classifications, apparently, was not enough to achieve standardization. However bitterly a small committee of experts might fight to stabilize nomenclatures and methodologies, the scale of the project, the enormous geographical distribution and the number of actors involved meant that uniformity and standardization were difficult to maintain.

Interested in identifying and eradicating illiteracy, early UNESCO surveys sought only to distinguish between literacy and illiteracy and did not include much qualifying information. As a result, the literate category was quite wide—including, according to the definition assigned, those who could write their name to those with high academic qualifications. Enrollment data indicated only if people were enrolled in an institution but not about the quality of education provided, since the priority was universal primary (or *'fundamental'*) education.

In 1957, World Illiteracy at Mid-Century, using data from 73 national surveys (Smyth, 2005), highlighted the serious issue of adult illiteracy, particularly in Asia, Africa and Central and South America. The population of adult illiterates was estimated at 700 million. This spurred many countries into focusing on addressing the issue of adult illiteracy, requiring more specific information on literacy.

And, Finally, ISCED

Although the desire for an artificial framework to enable education statistics to be gathered in a standardized way globally was expressed as early as the 1930s, it was only in the latter part of the 1960s that ISCED finally began to be drafted. Between 1966 and 1974, regular meetings and international consultations were held for this purpose, and a draft was submitted to the International Conference on Education in 1975, where it was approved and later incorporated in a revised version at UNESCO's General Assembly in 1978. The new classification system was to compare education statistics and to continue to link them with economic statistics. This link shaped how ISCED was conceptualized: 'ISCED should facilitate the use of education statistics in manpower planning and encourage the use of manpower statistics in educational planning' (UNESCO, 1976, p. 1).

A *'universe of education'* was defined as organized and sustained communication designed to bring about learning. Each of the terms—'organized', 'sustained', 'communication' and 'learning'—also then needed to be defined. The definitional work was quite elaborate, ensuring appropriate inclusions and, just as importantly, exclusions (UNESCO, 1976). The universe of activity was divided into four segments: regular school and university education, adult education, formal education and non-formal education. All education was conceptualized as classifiable in terms of 'levels', designated by a number (UNESCO, 1976).

The 'much sought-after link' between education and 'manpower planning' (Smyth, 2008, p. 31) was achieved through another set of categorizations and nomenclatures: education was conceptualized as '*units*' comprising courses and programs, which could be linked to occupations or groups of occupations (Smyth, 2008). Courses were linked to subject matter and skills, and programs by subject matter content. Program groups with related content constituted '*fields*'. Taking a combination of level, field and program, a five-digit coding system was developed to classify education offering. The framework, the categories, the sources of information and the methods of data collection were designed to maximize statistical mapping, so that they articulated with national census exercises and other data collection processes. This multipurpose system assembled data to different levels of detail on the different units, such as students, teachers, financial information and so forth (UNESCO, 1976).

The ISCED classification system became a powerful technology of visibility. As a framework, ISCED 'offers itself as a technical grid which has to be projected on the world according to preconceived goals, categories and modes of enactment' (Sotto, 1998, p. 72) and reflects and mediates the way those with the expertise, regulatory authority and necessary resources conceptualized the world. Member states now had a template for data collation, and by collecting data about the same phenomena, they could all '*see*' the same way (Law, 2009; Gorur, 2016b). Increasingly, it became a critical tool for national policymakers in setting their goals and priorities: these grids embedded anticipations of the future and were oriented to collecting data to enable future projections. They connected the past and the future into a modernistic continuum—a linear anticipation of steady improvement.

However, despite standardizing the definitions of categories, opportunities for breaking rules were many and needed to be constantly countered with increasingly specific rules and instructions. The *Manual of Educational Statistics* provided protocols for data collection to aid standardization.

The Synthetic and Normative Purposes of Education Surveys

Drawing from UNESCO documents, Smyth argues that the World Surveys of literacy were the result of not only synthetic ambitions but also normative ones. The surveys were not simply to reveal the current state of affairs; assembling these statistics itself became a normative act in the service of providing basic education as a human right. The frameworks that were employed played a critical role in the '*state of affairs*' that came to be '*revealed*'.

In the early 1960s, as newly independent former colonies embarked on development programs, education planning became deeply intertwined with '*manpower*' [*sic*] planning. New institutions such as UNESCO's International Institute for Educational Planning (IIEP) came up, linking education with economics, industry and labor. With donors keen to provide assistance to education that was linked to the economy and '*manpower needs*', these imperatives began to inform the kind of statistics that were needed. At the meeting of the Experts on Relevant Data in Comparative Education, the Statistical Division expressed the 'need for work on an educational classification system capable of cross-classification with occupational and industrial classifications, one outcome of which would be the provision of a scheme helpful to manpower and educational planners' (UNESCO, 1963, cited in UNESCO, 1994).

This linking of statistics in one area with statistics elsewhere in the UN system was, at this time, quite widespread, with improvements occurring in statistics related to income, trade, industrial activity, health, labor and other fields, including revisions to the International Standard Industrial Classification (ISIC) and the International Standard Classification of Occupations (ISCO), which were completed in 1968 (UNESCO, 1994). This articulation across different sectors has the crucial effect of stabilizing practices—when practices become widely networked, they are much harder to change, even if they are found wanting in some way. At the same time, some mutual accommodation is often required to ensure that the methodologies and frameworks articulate with each other.

The original ambition of developing internationally comparable education statistics was translated into the desire 'to enable national educational planners to derive educational development plans from employment projections broken down by occupation' (UNESCO, 1994, p. 4). In particular, specifying the tertiary '*field of study*' was seen as a way to link to manpower needs, though the interpretation of '*field*' was left unspecified. Not only were new purposes determining what data were collected, but the generation of data also made new purposes imaginable.

As major an achievement it was, ISCED was outdated even as it emerged. Crucially, the 'manpower' rationale began to weaken by the time ISCED came to be adopted, replaced by a global focus on the market economy rather than state planning (Smyth, 2008). Interest grew in the link between education and earnings, rather than that between education and occupations. Complex categories with stages and fields and program groups became less important than information about return on investment in education.

A New Focus on Outcomes and Quality

The focus on return on investment meant an interest in the efficiency of systems and outcomes of education. ISCED came to be used in pragmatic ways to strengthen the governance of education, which had become a major national budget item. The OECD's Indicators of Education Systems (INES) project focused on developing international comparative indicators of system inputs, processes and outcomes. UNESCO began to focus on the Education for All initiative. These major events meant that international comparisons of education quality became a compelling concern (UNESCO, 1994).

But ISCED was not designed to support the quality comparisons that were now sought; it operated on an ordinal logic, based on *levels* of study rather than *quality* of study, and 'education standards at any given ISCED level in one country are not necessarily equivalent to those at the same ISCED level in another country. In other words, only the educational structures can be assessed as comparable or equivalent' (UNESCO, 1994, p. 7). This created a significant issue methodologically as focus shifted to quality and human capital.

The 1994 Meeting of Experts on ISCED was called specifically to consider if and how ISCED could serve the new need for calculations of human capital. Human capital was based on '*amount of education*' in a country's population, which, in turn, requires a cardinal, or weighted, metric (rather than an ordinal one like ISCED). The experts concluded that the principles underpinning ISCED were fundamentally incapable of supporting calculations of human capital and suggested ISCED could not merely be updated but needed fundamental revision:

> ISCED cannot be expected to support international statistics of a type which it was never designed to support. Its original purposes and scope were quite limited. This should be kept in mind during the current exercise of updating and revision.
>
> *(UNESCO, 1994, p. 9)*

In 1995, a restricted team of education specialists was set up to refine ISCED to accommodate various types of education programs, including new post-compulsory options such as distance education. But developing ISCED 97 was no easy task, and the Committee failed to make any headway despite 2 years of trying (Sauvageot, 2008). Following this, a restricted task force was set up, with Claude Sauvageot at the helm. Well aware of the fraught nature of such a task, Sauvageot observed: "It took a lot of persuasion and a great deal of friendship to convince me to take part in this adventure" (Sauvageot, 2008, p. 213). John Smyth, whose publications form much of the basis for the history I have assembled here, was also part of this task force, as was OECD's Andreas Schleicher.

Description, Interpretation and Performativity

Sauvageot (2008) reflects on a range of challenges involved in the development, implementation and revision of ISCED. Some of these are detailed ahead.

The Politics of Nomenclature

One of the most important and challenging aspects of ISCED was the nomenclature assigned to various levels and categories of education. Ideally, nomenclature must be specific enough to be meaningful and descriptive, plastic enough to accommodate variations and restrictive enough to prevent wrong attributions. The pre-primary and the post-secondary categories were particularly problematic, as the programs differed widely among countries. The definitions accommodated varied interpretations. At the same time, the framework did not provide the scope to recognize certain important practices. For example, cases where work and study overlapped, such as apprenticeships, could not be represented in the older version of ISCED. It was difficult to distinguish between preschool and childcare. The classification system thus not only facilitated making some parts of the systems visible, but also equally made invisible some types of education provision. The effects this could have on funding, recognition and policy can only be speculated upon. Importantly, instead of the actual system dictating the representational framework, the framework had begun to influence the system (Gorur, 2016a, b).

Sauvageot points out the importance of nomenclature being understood uniformly for comparisons to be effected. However, an obvious challenge is the plurality of languages, which confounds this ambition. Securing definitions even in one language was not easy, and the meetings of the Expert Group tasked with revising ISCED found that "discussions on definitions were lively and passionate, with every member trying to use or validate the opinions or organization of their own country" (Sauvageot, 2008, p. 214). Differences in understandings and interpretations of nomenclatures can dramatically alter the policy pictures that come to be painted. For instance, teacher qualifications are regarded in some countries as vocational diplomas, and in others are university degrees. Depending on which definitions are taken into the reckoning, the number of '*qualified teachers*' reported in surveys might vary significantly.

When the all-important nomenclature is changed or the description or definition altered, another major headache is created for statisticians. Previously collated data must now be recast retrospectively into the new categories to ensure coherence across time series. Thus, each new iteration would retrospectively influence the understandings of education systems and comparisons.

Distortion in Usage

One of the dimensions along which ISCED classifications are done is the type of orientation (academic, vocational, etc.) of a program. This classification has proven difficult to maintain because, irrespective of the intended orientation by the program, those enrolled might end up orientating themselves quite differently. Patterns of usage have revealed that some level categories are used in ways that are inconsistent with their original intention. Someone doing a vocational diploma might use it not to join a trade, but as a bridge to a university degree program. However clearly and restrictively a level is defined, it still does not guarantee uniform use and application:

> Level 4 is seldom used [...] Despite the instructions given by the OECD, several countries have continued to classify some of their programs under level 3 or level 5 although several experts were expecting these programs to be classified under level 4.
> *(Sauvageot, 2008, p. 219)*

One reason classification evokes such passion is that it affects how nations look in international comparisons. Sauvageot talks about the tendency of many countries to classify courses with a research component into a higher level because having more people attaining the highest level would make the nation look better on these comparative tables. This tendency to put national pride ahead of getting useful data for policymaking is starkly reflected in headlines that accompany announcements of contemporary league tables in education.

The Illusion of Comparability

Using compelling examples, Sauvageot explains that the comparability gained by the imposition of such frameworks is an illusion. For example, Level 1 in ISCED is specified as generally 6 years in duration, but:

> nobody is actually capable of comparing the content of a school year in a given country with that of another. Should we consider the total number of teaching hours, teachers' qualification, the educational equipment available to the pupils (books for example)? Many other elements such as Internet access can now be added to this list. In short, a school year is never identical within the same country, let alone from one country to the next.
> *(Sauvageot, 2008, pp. 219–220)*

Sauvageot suggests that comparisons should be based on the purposes and objectives of systems rather than the duration of courses. The latter could mislead—for example, programs designed to provide more time for students with learning difficulties may tend to get classified as higher level programs because they are longer. Sauvageot concludes: "The existence of a nomenclature accepted by all is a necessary condition but it is not sufficient" (Sauvageot, 2008, p. 220). The making of standards is an ongoing activity.

Maintaining Classification

Ongoing revisions are critical to the ambition of maintaining comparability. The UNESCO Institute of Statistics (UIS) has now formally been bestowed a '*custodian*' role and charged with the authority and the responsibility for maintaining ISCED. The specified responsibilities include maintaining links with other relevant classifications, providing proper descriptions of the structures and classifications, promoting the use of ISCED, developing and providing materials to guide its implementation and use and 'establishing monitoring mechanisms for proper feedback from ISCED users about problems in its use' (Sauvageot, 2008, p. 23). Making changes—even when they are improvements—is as tricky as devising the original categories, and requires extensive cooperation and the clout of strong institutions. Revisions to ISCED involve gathering a global technical advisory panel of international experts, and ministerial offices and policymakers are also consulted. Every revision is accompanied by detailed training manuals and programs to ensure the new version is properly used. Retrospective reclassification is done to ensure continuity.

Often left out of official accounts of these exercises are the reliance on personal connections and friendships to get things done, the trust in colleagues to whom work can be safely delegated, the critical behind-the-scenes role of assistants, the many glasses of wine and fine dinners that would have cemented relationships and secured cooperation and dissolved the deadlocks and bitter controversies that might have frustrated the Committee on some occasions.

Conclusion

The tortuous history of ISCED serves to illustrate the normative, interpretive and performative nature of standards and classifications. When the project of developing devices to facilitate international comparison of education statistics began in the early 1930s, with fewer countries, more informal processes and a tolerance for imprecision, a range of features could be included, such as cultural and social indicators (number of museums, for example). As the scope and scale of the project expanded, and the tolerance for imprecision reduced, the description of an education system came to be more narrowly defined in terms of enrollment, levels, fields and finances. The focus shifted—first to the extent of literacy and illiteracy, and later to manpower planning and human capital. But such '*precision*' came at the price of describing education itself in, we might argue, a narrow and imprecise way.

These changes in description have not only mirrored changing ambitions and changing concerns, they have also shaped the ways education systems were understood, how certain problems came to be seen as '*matters of concern*' (Latour, 2004) and how and where international attention came to be directed. As an interpretive tool, ISCED could translate nations' statistics to create global patterns of deficit. The linking of enrollment with attainment shaped the ambitions to measure quality—a project that was also taken up by the OECD and has resulted in the very influential Programme for International Student Assessment (PISA). This project of quality and outcomes measurement has now gained renewed attention under UNESCO's Sustainable Development Goals, with a range of agencies and organizations looking to develop global comparative metrics of education quality.

Despite the huge machinery of regulation and the detailed manuals and the regular training programs, the slipperiness in the implementation of standards is hard to tame. Experts sigh in exasperation as their most carefully constructed classifications are misunderstood and misused. Nevertheless, ISCED remains a powerful regulatory mechanism—it is imposed on member nations by formal agreement. Compliance is insisted upon. Its use is guaranteed through formal agreement, but it also imposes a subtler influence. Comparisons inevitably lead to competitiveness, with countries setting new goals and developing new ambitions based on the relative performance of other nations. Comparisons may lead to the borrowing of policies and practices. Thus, standards embed normativity.

ISCED classifications can impact the recognition of programs and institutions, with consequences both for how a nation's educational progress is understood, and for the value assigned to institutions. Frequently, non-formal education, programs in early childhood and vocational programs struggle to be counted within such classificatory schemes. This recognition could impact their funding prospects and their continuance and viability.

Despite their contingent and messy provenance, numbers based on this classification scheme take on the impersonal tone of objective and calculations and measurements. The passion and emotion of experts is exhausted in committee meetings, and it is only the cool agreements that get translated and consolidated into classifications and calculations. But 'science' is intricately intertwined with 'politics' as experts grapple to mobilize and stabilize such mechanisms. Their continued viability depends on regulating their users. Every now and again, the evolving changes in education exceed the range of variations permitted within the classification, so that definitions and categories are called into question and need to be revised. Each revision entails more work to create as seamless an articulation as possible between the old and the new schemes.

If the international community invests so heavily in such classifications, it is because they are such powerful regulatory tools. With advances in statistical methodologies and analytical software, the collection and use of international comparative data is now routine in a range of fields. Publications such as OECD's *Education at a Glance* report a breathtaking array of education data annually about a range of countries in a comparative format (Gorur, 2015). The synoptic view afforded by such comparisons is powerfully seductive.

Such systems are very difficult to dismantle. For statisticians, the task often seems to be one of defending the scheme they have established—their focus is often on regulating its use to enforce fidelity. Even where there is recognition of a theoretical vacuum or a contradiction underpinning these standards, a sense of pragmatism appears to override any hesitation in using them. For example, using ISCED for purposes for which it is clearly not intended is simply seen as a mere technicality. But understood as performative, interpretive and normative, the work of standardization becomes much more than an issue of statistical validity or mathematical precision or pragmatism; it becomes an issue of responsibility and ethics. Such an understanding places an obligation on those engaged in such work to look beyond statistical validity and other technical aspects and to engage with greater awareness and responsibility with the politics and consequences of standardization.

References

Bowker, G. C., & Star, S. L. (2000). *Sorting things out: Classification and its consequences.* Cambridge, MA & London: MIT Press.
Busch, L. (2011). *Standards recipes for reality.* Cambridge, MA & London: MIT Press.
Chia, R. C. H. (1998). Introduction—Exploring the expanded realm of technology, organization and modernity. In R. C. H. Chia (Ed.), *Organized worlds—Explorations in technology and organization with Robert Cooper* (pp. 1–17). London & New York: Routledge.
Desrosières, A. (1998). *The politics of large numbers: A history of statistical reasoning.* Cambridge, MA & London: Harvard University Press.
Gorur, R. (2013). The invisible infrastructure of standards. *Critical Studies in Education, 54*(2), 132–142. doi:10.1080/17508487.2012.736871
Gorur, R. (2015). Producing calculable worlds: Education at a glance. *Discourse-Studies in the Cultural Politics of Education, 36*(4), 578–595. doi:10.1080/01596306.2015.974942
Gorur, R. (2016a). The performative politrics of NAPLAN and MySchool. In B. Lingard, G. Thompson & S. Sellar (Eds.), *National testing in schools: An Australian assessment* (pp. 30-43). London & New York: Routledge
Gorur, R. (2016b). Seeing like PISA: A cautionary tale about the performativity of international assessments. *European Educational Research Journal, 15*(5), 598–616. (Article first published on-line: July 14, 2016; Issue published: September 1, 2016). https://doi.org/10.1177/1474904116658299
Hacking, I. (1983). *Representing and intervening: Introductory topics in the philosophy of natural science.* Cambridge: Cambridge University Press.
Heyneman, S. P. (1999). The sad story of UNESCO's education statistics. *International Journal of Educational Development, 19*(1): 65–74.
Knorr-Cetina, K. (1999). *Epistemic cultures: How the sciences make knowledge.* Cambridge, MA: Harvard University Press.
Latour, B. (1987). *Science in action—How to follow scientists and engineers through society.* Cambridge, MA: Harvard University Press.
Latour, B. (1993). *The pasteurization of France.* Cambridge, MA: Harvard University Press.
Latour, B. (2004). Why has critique run out of steam? From matters of fact to matters of concern. *Critical Inquiry, 30*, 225–248.
Latour, B. (2005). *Reassembling the social: An introduction to actor-network theory.* Oxford: Oxford University Press.
Law, J. (2009). Seeing like a survey. *Cultural Sociology, 3*(2): 239–256.
Miller, C. A. (2005). New civic epistemologies of quantification: Making sense of indicators of local and global sustainability. *Science, Technology and Human Values, 30*(3), 403–432.
Pickering, A. (1993). The mangle of practice—Agency and emergence in the sociology of science. *American Journal of Sociology, 99*(3), 559–589. doi:0.1086/230316
Poovey, M. (1998). *A history of the modern fact—Problems of knowledge in the science of wealth and society.* Chicago & London: The University of Chicago Press.

Sauvageot, C. (2008). A tool for international comparison: The international standard classification of education (ISCED). In A. Charras & C. Sauvageot (Eds.), *Education and formations: International comparisons*. Paris: Ministry of Higher Education and Research Evaluation, Forecasting and Performance Directorate.

Shapin, S., & Schaffer, S. (1985). *Leviathan and the air pump—Hobbes, Boyle, and the experimental life*. Princeton, NJ: Princeton University Press.

Smyth, J. A. (2005). *UNESCO's international literacy statistics, 1950–2000 (Background paper prepared for the Education for All Global Monitoring Report 2006—Literacy for life)*. Paris: UNESCO.

Smyth, J. A. (2008). The origins of the international standard classification of education. *Peabody Journal of Education, 83*, 5–40.

Sotto, R. (1998). The virtualization of the organizational subject. In R.C.H. Chia (Ed.), *Organized worlds: Explorations in technology and organization with Robert Cooper*. London & New York: Routledge.

Star, S. L., & Lampland, M. (2009). Reckoning with standards. In M. Lampland & S. L. Star (Eds.), *Standards and their stories* (pp. 3–24). Ithaca, NY & London: Cornell University Press.

Timmermans, S., & Epstein, S. (2010). A world of standards but not a standard world: Toward a sociology of standards and standardization. *Annual Review of Sociology, 36*, 69–89.

UNESCO. (1953). *Progress of literacy in various countries: A preliminary statistical study of available census data since 1900*. Paris: UNESCO.

UNESCO. (1955). *World survey of education: Handbook of educational organization and statistics*. Paris: UNESCO.

UNESCO. (1976). *International Standard Classification of Education (ISCED)*. Paris: UNESCO Division of Statistics on Education, Office of Statistics.

UNESCO. (1994). *Meeting of experts on the International Standard Classification of Education (ISCED)*. Paris: UNESCO.

8

INTERNATIONAL ASSESSMENTS AND ITS EXPERTISE FABRICATING EXPERT KNOWLEDGE FOR POLICY

Luis Miguel Carvalho

Introduction

Over the last decade, the Programme for International Student Assessment (PISA) has become a major tool for the intervention of the Organisation for Economic Co-operation and Development (OECD) in the education sector. Since its beginnings, PISA has been constantly presented as an expert-based knowledge answer to the government's needs of trustworthy data about the performance of their education systems (e.g., OECD, 2001, 2007, 2014). This self-presentation has been pointed out again recently in *Beyond PISA 2015: A Longer-Term Strategy of PISA*, where the future of the program is equated:

> PISA [...] aims to provide reliable information on how well education systems prepare students for further study, careers and life. PISA also provides a basis for international collaboration in order to define and implement effective educational policies. [...] PISA is policy-oriented. It focuses on providing data and analysis that can help guide decisions on education policy. [...] is a collaborative effort. Decisions about the scope and nature of the PISA assessments and the background information collected are undertaken by leading experts in participating countries. Governments oversee these decisions based on shared, policy-driven interests.
>
> *(OECD, n. d.: 1–2)*

Thus, PISA may well be represented as large-scale international assessment oriented by the desideratum of creating knowledge for policy—briefly, a knowledge generated in order to assist policymaking and to provide policymakers with steering tools. From the perspective I adopt in this chapter, PISA is more than a new (or a developed) type of international comparative assessment created in order to provide '*robust*' data/information to policymakers or, even more, to enhance evidence-based policymaking. I approach it here as an exemplary case of the noticeable presence, in contemporary policy processes, of social administration modes that favor persuasion through knowledge and act through the actors' reflexivity: it is a knowledge-policy instrument that combines inquiry procedures and sophisticated methods of calculation and data analysis with interpretations and rules about/for the steering of education (Lascoumes & Le Galès, 2007; Carvalho, 2012). From this point of view, PISA displays a particular way of challenging education systems though continuous mutual surveillance practices and, concomitantly, bears principles and practices for policymaking and also for the production of educational knowledge. Hence, my interest here is to contribute to a discussion about the reconfiguration of the interdependencies between policy and knowledge, by focusing the fabrication and diffusion of PISA's expert knowledge for policy.

Therefore, I address the making of expert knowledge for policy as a complex of interdependent practices—following Latour (1989), this encompasses the construction of a subject of inquiry and the building of a monopoly of competence about it, but also the intéressement of different social worlds, in order to guarantee informational, financial and human resources, and the production of public confidence. This means that the credibility and 'sense of usefulness' achieved by PISA depends on interesting and attracting diverse actors around a complex flow of activities and products that, concurrently, guarantee that it may be accepted as an appropriate instrument for the understanding and the governing of education system. I clarify this analytical approach in the first section of the chapter.

I develop my main analysis about the making of expert knowledge for policy within the PISA project by focusing two collections of practices that support (a) the making and legitimation of PISA knowledge, and (b) the continued and lasting exchanges with selected actors—ultimately, the creation and increase of symbolic and functional dependences of PISA in various social worlds. Thus, in the second section of the chapter, I describe and analyze practices that support the making and legitimation of PISA knowledge, regarding what counts as knowledge for policy and what this entails in terms of social processes and contents.

Finally, in the third section, I turn to OECD's interventions related with the enlargement of symbolic and functional (inter)dependencies with diverse social worlds, by means of proliferation and sophistication PISA's data/information/knowledge deliverables, as well as by means of connecting PISA products with other types of governance practices developed by the OECD beyond the formal spaces of PISA.

Contextualizing and Framing the Analysis

The current credibility and '*sense of usefulness*' achieved by PISA is traceable in the variety of sociopolitical mobilizations of PISA in national and supranational contexts and also in its capacity to keep different social worlds (policymakers, experts, high-administration agencies, media), with their diverse interests and ideas, committed with its use for the imagination and/or scrutiny of educational systems, policies and practices.

The Aggregation Effect

These trends are identifiable in a quite extensive literature on the PISA receptions and effects in European contexts published in English language academic journals between 2000 and 2014. From a recent review of this literature (Carvalho & Costa, 2015), I highlight three main ideas: the multiple purposes ascribed to PISA in the processes of active reception and use; the selective presence of PISA data/information/knowledge in many European contexts; nonetheless, along with such variability, a few commonalities are patent in national receptions, such as the legitimation of new governing modes, the naturalization of mutual surveillance as a way of governing, and the redefinition of reference societies.

The first two ideas may be summarized as follows: there is an assignation of multiple purposes to PISA texts and objects, particularly of legitimation (of reforms, of specific policies, of regulatory instruments), information (for the steering of education systems, either as a complementary or as a compensating/substitutive source) and idealization (supporting the construction of diverse educational ideals, projections or narratives, about education and educational reform); PISA objects/texts are ubiquitously present in national contexts, by the hands of different users—politicians, and other players involved in public educational debates, national experts and researchers prolifically using it for secondary analysis, but they are re-interpreted, made acceptable and efficient for each sociocognitive context, thus, subject to diverse selections (e.g., regarding the information displayed in the reports or the policy domains addressed by PISA recommendations).

Finally, the third idea rests on the perception that, despite the persistent existence of critical voices, PISA is usually perceived in several worlds—and not only in policy milieus, it is important to keep always this in mind along this chapter—as capable of raising public awareness about education systems, and capable of helping to identify problems and provide good examples, and as accurately portraying the performance of education systems, their weaknesses and strengths. Furthermore, such naturalization of PISA is associated with the adoption of evidence-based approaches (even if 'only' a phony adoption or a kind of a 'categorical' script for policymaking), the creation of new assessment structures and the development of instruments for the monitoring of education systems.

The Ecologies of a 'Knowledge for Policy' Project

Considering the aforementioned trends, one might consider that the power of PISA lies, largely, in keeping actors referring to it or using it for the imagination and/or the scrutiny of educational systems, policies and practices. But why is PISA reaching and interesting so many social worlds?

Certainly, the current consecration of PISA is not understandable without an historical approach. As a 'knowledge for policy' project, PISA has a trajectory and an institutional environment in which it draws and operates.

PISA is part of a knowledge tradition. It is part of a comparative project that Nóvoa (1998) characterized as steered by pragmatic reasoning, committed to the building of indicators for decision making, and driven by the purposes of finding the factors explaining the performances of education systems, and the best systems and solutions related with. It is also part of a particular stream of comparative education knowledge materialized in the form of international large-scale assessments, gradually emergent after World War II (Lindblad, Pettersson, & Popkewitz, 2015). Looking at more large and deep institutional factors, the success of PISA may well need to be related to the '*the emerging age of accountability*' (Hopmann, 2007) or to the centrality of the cybernetic paradigm in the imagination of the knowledge society and its government (Breton, 2005). Finally, trust in PISA is inextricably linked to the 'privileging of numbers as a way of telling the truth about social life and people' (Popkewitz, 2011, p. 33; cf. Porter, 1995), as part of a historically rooted struggle in which the qualification of objectivity goes hand in hand with the disqualification of subjectivity.

The success of PISA lies in capitalizing on an institutional environment and following an appropriate course of action. But the picture will be incomplete if one forgets to keep under analysis the collection of practices that keep PISA facing successfully other monitoring tools, either on an international, regional or national scale. In other words, one must keep under examination the OECD's participation in the making of an organized space for the imagination and exchange of the data/information/knowledge it engenders and disseminates.

History counts here, too, surely: PISA has a course that is inseparable of the trajectory taken by OECD on education governance. Germinated in the context of OECD's International Indicators of Educational Systems project (Morgan, 2011), PISA is a materialization of an educational agenda marked, since the 1990s, by the idea of monitoring quality, and the continuous fabrication of educational problems and solutions to face the needs of the so-called knowledge economy (Rinne, Kallo, & Hokka, 2004). It is also the most fruitful example of the OECD's '*comparative turn*' (Martens, 2007) and of this infrastructural and epistemic governance that, as mentioned by Sellar and Lingard (2013, pp. 13–14), generates a 'self-perpetuating dynamic, though which the OECD both prescribes education policy approaches and assesses the performances of national education systems in these terms'. Moreover, the OECD's credibility precedes and fosters the recognition of PISA—in other words, the current trustworthiness gave to PISA surely cannot be separated from the status achieved by the OECD as an '*expert organization*', that is and following Noaksson and Jacobsson (2003), an organization that responds to the (self)perception according to which generates specialized knowledge, simultaneously sensitive to politicians' needs and free from political considerations and particularisms, based on empirical studies and grounded in knowledge about which there is a relative scientific consensus.

Although I accept that the confidence placed in OECD precedes and promotes the judgment of PISA as a valid and useful tool, I also want to highlight something else: the success of PISA depends also on the creation of lasting connections between heterogeneous actors. Thus, the success depends on connecting these actors to PISAs' inquiry, exchange and publication activities and on having them sharing the vision of PISA as a proper data/information/knowledge provider.

Consequently, it is important to consider the ecology created by PISA, that is to say—adapting Everett Hughes' notion of '*ecology of institutions*', as quoted by Star and Griesemer (1989)—the choices taken within the Program about its material, informational and human sources, and also the actions carried out to establish continued and lasting exchanges with selected actors. These exchanges depend on several interdependent activities (Carvalho, 2012): together with the inquiry, relevant face-to-face activities occur (taking place in meetings, workshops, seminars, etc.), and multiple publications and other products have a worldwide flow. Besides, these activities are set up to enroll and engage heterogeneous actors, ideas and interests, in the production, dissemination and use of PISA texts and technologies.

I develop my main analysis about the fabrication of (expert) knowledge for policy within the PISA project as the making of an ecology by focusing, sequentially, practices that support the making and legitimation of PISA knowledge and practices that support the making of continued and lasting exchanges with selected actors in various social worlds.

Making and Legitimizing Expert Knowledge for Policy

Data/information/knowledge by diverse forms generated under the PISA label, within a '*collaborative effort*' between OECD officials and staff, experts, policymakers and their representatives, is generated under certain conventions regrading what is knowledge for policy and how it should be fabricated:

> In a ground level, we have expert groups of mathematics, reading, science and so on, they are the scientists. Then, we have the PISA Governing Board (PGB) who puts all of this together and then negotiate the conflict and interests among countries; they decide what way we want to give to this competence, how many multiple-choice questions do we have, how many open questions. The PGB is the body that actually strategically manages the project [. . .] The Consortium is a contractor who basically does what the PGB decides.

> [. . .] you need to distinguish very carefully between two things: one is the generation of the evidence, that's the PISA study, and the other is our role in communicating the results and we actually have physically separated the two. So, the second part is clear when the knowledge broker should come in, clearly remedied the reports, we try to communicate the policy making, and so on, but that fight has hardly influence the generation of information. [. . .] we at the OECD prepare the draft, the text is discussed with the countries, with the experts.
> *(Interview with OECD official, January 2009)*

In this collection of quotations, one might depict a few conventions close to those portrayed in literature analyzing the narratives of contemporary experts about the knowledge they produce (see Nowotny, Scott, & Gibbons, 2001), particularly the characteristics of a transgressive, collective, self-organized and self-authorizing knowledge: the starting point of PISA surveys is partly defined by the national representatives (representatives of OECD members and PISA associates) at the PGB, and the results of the scientific/technical work are open to their scrutiny; surveys, analyses and publications are developed by experts and OECD professionals, who collectively validate the data/information/knowledge that they generate.

What is more, the configuration of the interdependencies between the social worlds involved in the making of the surveys, analyses and deliverables, enacts specific patterns for their relations and about the relations between knowledge and policy: the public authorities grant the status of experts to certain social actors and simultaneously accept them as key partners in the processes that support the construction of cognitions and rules for the mutual surveillance of their education systems.

On the corollary, all these players are bonded to—and committed with—a '*knowledge for policy*' project that legitimizes OECD as the provider of an expert-based independent framework and method for the monitoring and steering of school systems. Significantly, for OECD actors, their practices prove the advantages of the existence of the forum of supranational deliberation that accommodates experts and countries, and that generates knowledges and consensus independent of national parochialisms and interests:

> Actually, you would be very impressed because many things that are very controversial in your own country or in my own country [. . .] You can bring three mathematicians from your country on a table and they will not agree about geometries. Very different views because they are various narrow interest groups, they're various most sort of strong lobbies in countries on different scenes. And we assemble people across countries and suddenly you see how small minded is your own debate, my own debate and you will

see suddenly 'Oh, this is the bigger picture, people are actually willing to do things they would never do nationally.

(Interview with OECD official, January 2009)

Differentiating a New Subject of Inquiry/Policy

PISA was created and developed under a particular claim of singularity, regarding other (and previous) large-scale assessments: 'Rather than examine mastery of specific school curricula, PISA looks at students' ability to apply knowledge and skills in key subject areas and to analyze, reason and communicate effectively as they examine, interpret and solve problems' (PISA Website FAQ).

This claim marks a differentiation from the rationale of previous comparative studies of student performances and their dependency on national curricula, namely from those developed by the International Association for the Evaluation of Educational Achievement since the 1960s. Though, it introduces another shift: from the conventional self-reflection of national school systems (based on their own categories and outputs, with assessments relying on tests and examinations based on national curriculum goals and content) and toward the territory of outcomes, thus directly connecting the contexts, practices and results of teaching/learning with the so-called demands of the school system environment. This shift aligns with the recurrent OECD script about the regulation of schools systems, reframing the old problem of preparing the young generations to the future in a much broader issue—the issue of international competitiveness: school systems have to adapt to changes in the economy and society from industrialization to post-industrialization knowledge economies and societies, and PISA is the supplier of rigorous comparative data, which allows policymakers to learn about the place of each educational system in the worldwide competitive space, to identify their country's relative positioning vis-à-vis the 'knowledge society' and/or 'knowledge economy' and, consequently, to 'move' their education systems to the (physical and symbolic) time of 'tomorrow's world'.

In sum, it can be said that around the PISA project the OECD circumscribes a precise area of knowledge, around a single object—and, thus, builds a monopoly of expertise on a specific subject of assessment—the so-called competencies of literacy. The success of this project is also the success of the performance of the OECD as a 'creator, purveyor, and legitimator of ideas' (Mahon & McBride, 2009, p. 84). This means to be able to produce innovative subjects and objects, to break away from the stereotypes, to differentiate in relation to existing knowledge and policy ideas:

[Interviewer: What are the main challenges you think that PISA have faced all along the years?] I think that challenges would be to transfer the debate that is focused on the input of education in the past, 'how much do you spend', 'how many chairs', 'do you have how many teachers', to transform that debate into a debate that looks at the results achieved and to compare those results. Every education system can say that we have improved, every education system is doing better today than it was yesterday, but the real question today is the pace of change quickly enough to keep up a front in a global war.

[. . .] Education is a field that in my view has been dominated by ideas, ideologies, and opinions and so on. It's not a field very rich in data and what PISA has done it has made it more difficult for politicians to just come up with their own opinions. So, I think that's the first impact that PISA had from the beginning, basically showing policymakers which statements they can justify and which not.

(Interview with OECD official, January 2009)

Assembling and Purveying Knowledge for Policy

The '*new subject*' was generated within the OECD indicators project (Indicators of Education Systems; INES) but certainly build on the experiences and reflections on the experiences of many of the promoters in previous large-scale assessments. In fact, the OECD did not only reuse the methodological knowledge previously developed but also 'recruited' actors previously linked to comparative international studies (Morgan, 2011). Nonetheless, along the last two decades, the development of PISA knowledge, disciplined by the so-called literacy framework but also by assumptions, concepts and methods from the psychometric world, entails contributions generated by experts from very different knowledge communities: experts related to PISA core domains (mathematics, reading, science), but also with ICT and financial literacy (included in the 2012 survey); the 'hard' knowledge of statistics, psychometrics and compared assessment; knowledge of social psychology in relation to the study of attitudes; and streams of knowledge coming from policy evaluation and analysis, and from the school effectiveness tradition.

Thus, data/information/knowledge used and delivered depends on the degree of consensus between these experts, their permeability to political and cultural factors or pressures. It rests on consensus among research consortiums, groups of experts, national representatives, about what counts as usable knowledge, but is played out under then supervision of OECD Secretariat, the structure formally responsible for the management of the daily activities of PISA. When asked about the role of the Secretariat, one member presents it as a networker and a catalyst for interaction between experts and politicians:

> The success of PISA is set to establish a real international network of experts who exchange and use opinions, which struggle and fight [. . .] what is mathematics? How it should be defined? [. . .] a lot of debates about it.

> [. . .] A bureaucracy is someone who directly manages the project and we cannot do this, possibly even if we had 50 people here it wouldn't work. The image I had was the image of a catalyst. [. . .] basically, being able to get the right people to the room at a politically level, at a scientific level, at technical level, let them negotiate, let them discuss. There have been times when there was difficult to find an agreement and then we play a part. Now, countries have a lot of trust in the OECD but most of the hard negotiations are done among experts from the countries and the expert groups are checked by the country, not by us. They try and they usually find an agreement.
>
> *(Interview with OECD official, January 2009)*

Though this self-portrayed networker and catalyst—mediator when needed— also has to keep those who gather performing appropriately to OECD's canons what is expected from an organization that struggles for the status of a truth seeker and teller. Because the achievement of PISA does not depend only on bringing actors and ideas into relation; it depends also on fulfilling their informational needs and, simultaneously, on keeping them in (the project) and acting with proper scripts. Throughout, the several sequences of tasks that make PISA the manager of everyday activities ensures that certain procedural protocols are respected and ensures that interactions follow the common values and rules expected in a social space created by a putative expert organization, like consensus building and high trust in expertise, but also responsiveness to external changes and criticisms. A good example is the production of the PISA final reports (each cycle):

> There are three phases in this process. The first is the phase where we discuss [. . .] On the reporting side we developed an outline and that outline is discussed in the meeting with countries, then we collect all the tables and we send them out by emails, the countries usually send us lots of commends, like on this report the last time I counted there were 5.000 pages of comments, from the experts, from the countries and so on. We prepare the second version, read again, convene the countries, we discuss it and we incorporate the changes and then at the end we must make sure that all the countries are happy with the text and every country has to sign off on the report and then we publish it, but I must say that this report is only one product.
>
> *(Interview with OECD official, January 2009)*

This practice emerges as an effective strategy for reaching consensual decisions. The ways of producing an enormous number of documents—mobilizing people to work on successive draft versions—along the PISA flow of activities constitute a complex system of normative and functional coordination. These '*open processes of writing*' generate perceptions of membership and belonging, and (at least) of partial authorship, and they effectively conduce to the production of consensual decisions (e.g., regarding the framework or regarding the structure and writing style of the reports) and to the adoption of standardized procedures that steer the participants (e.g., the technical norms that guide the implementation of PISA inquiries).

But PISA reaches beyond PISA formal actors (OECD, national representatives and national managing structures, experts groups, consortiums). In fact, PISA establishes effective associations with other (individual or collective) actors, largely by disseminating multiple and diverse knowledge-related materials (e.g., reports, databases, videos):

> I mean the on-line database that we've put out on the web is the first step, because we have realized that many people find it too difficult to use we've now developed the manuals and I really hope that in a long term there will be a different balance in the use of the data and the interpretations that we have here. I think we now have a good evidence base, but the use of that evidence base by the research community is really something that we need to further strength because PISA is an independent evaluation instrument so it's important that there's also a real sort of high level independence in the use of that information.
> *(Interview with OECD official, January 2009)*

The variety of informational products are explicitly generated to target populations, to audiences with diverse interests and skills, and opens up—that's what is important—a multiplicity of possible uses, whether in order to reproduce, to recontextualize the data/information/knowledge or even in order to produce knowledge from it. I address this issue in the following section.

The Broadening of PISA Ecology

I move now to the consideration of the social-organizational processes that support PISA's current status of relevant resource, by focusing OECD's intervention in the structuration of a sociocultural space for the diffusion and use of knowledge for policy.

Multiplication of Deliverables

I use the expression '*multiplication of deliverables*' to identify the plurality of consumable data/information/knowledge objects generated under PISA. And I discuss them as enhancers of PISA multiple mobilizations. Indeed, these deliverables are resources for attracting diverse social worlds, and attaching multipurposes to PISA. Simultaneously, they proved to be a way to attach more policy-related and knowledge-related activities to PISA and OECD.

In 2008, after three PISA cycles, a significant variety of publications were produced under the PISA label (Carvalho & Costa, 2009): main, thematic, extensive, national and technical reports; databases; documents with assessment basics (written for teachers, parents and pupils), directed toward target populations. In 2014, after the two subsequent cycles, this picture presents a few important changes: the objects become more sophisticatedly elaborated and their variety is amplified, thus fostering the intensification of possible uses.

Exhorting Policy Emulation and Policy Learning

One of the new deliverables are the 'in-depth' reports suggestively entitled Strong Performers and Successful Reformers. These reports draw up PISA lessons for specific countries who request it. Based on the framework of the OECD's Leveraging Knowledge for Better Education Policies—GPS project, the reports are prepared by '*task forces*' of experts and members of national education bodies, from several countries, involving meetings with national stakeholders. The content of reports varies according to each 'case' but always include data on the country's performance in PISA, its positioning among the other performers, more or less detailed examples of 'best practices' from other countries, and implications for national policymakers (with different labels—as policy recommendations, next steps, policy lessons from and for). Reforms based on local adaptation of best practices are the expected outcome.

This same ethos is displayed in video series, jointly produced with Pearson Foundation. Presented as 'highlighting initiatives taken by education authorities [. . .] to help school students to do better', they are sites for the praise of betterment, with the recognition of each system's specificities and of national authorities' efforts toward the advancement of their systems.

Shortcuts to Knowledge

A different type of deliverables for a quick access is developed since 2011. The country-specific overviews summarize information about the performances of each country, regarding the OECD average; the continuities and changes of students' performances, and other system variables over the cycles; the identification of factors related with better results and, in some reports, short notes concerning areas requiring improvement. The brief *PISA in Focus* displays four or five pages of explicitly policy-oriented texts on a specific PISA theme: from student performances and attitudes toward school and learning to family background, to classroom environment to education policy. Released monthly, these briefs are based on PISA, TALIS (the Teaching and Learning International Survey program) and *Education at a Glance* and provide a selection of data about an educational problem raised by OECD (e.g., 'Does homework perpetuate inequities in education?', 'Do students have the drive to succeed?', 'Who are the strong performers and successful reformers in education?'). These briefs close with a 'bottom line'—a final statement on the issues addressed, varyingly combining conclusive judgments on data, reflection appeals and reassurance thoughts.

From FYI to DIY

But among all the new deliverables there are some that have to be pinpointed, since they foster a different type of relationship with PISA's—and other OECD's—data and analyses: the DIY products, that is, products that are set to activate a quasi-autonomous relation with PISA data. These deliverables (like the 'Interactive Data Selection' and the 'Multidimensional data request') allow users to select and compare data at school and student-level variables. What is more, these DIY products are connected to a new device—the 'Education GPS'—that allows the user to access data provided by PISA, TALIS and *Education at a Glance*, as well as to prepare 'his own' country reports, using texts and sophisticated charts provided by the tool, and to compare the countries' performances. Additionally, the device (that seems to configure a meta-tool) gives the user the imagination of conducting himself a 'rhizomatic' structure of 14 themes—and almost 50 subthemes—of education policy, powered by research and analysis supported by the OECD. These technologies support a new feature in the OECD regulatory intervention: as Williamson observes, not just as a center of calculation but as a 'center of visualization'—'their visualizations', he adds, 'act as surfaces on which millions of educational performances and measurements are inscribed and made visible for inspection, analysis, evaluation and comparison' (Williamson, 2015, p. 12).

At this point, it is important to stress the following: the success of knowledge for policy surely depends on the scientific and technical credibility that it achieves, but it also requires the fulfillment of the condition of being relevant and able to be handled by an audience, what Lindquist (1990, pp. 31–35) refers to as the criterion of '*contextuality*'. Thus, the success of knowledge for policy rests on the condition of being consumed, shared or learned by its audiences, as credible and manageable. This is a crucial to understand why and how PISA is used differently by so many diverse actors. And the ecology of PISA rests on this feature too: PISA reaches varied social worlds by means of these exchangeable packages of data/information/knowledge and assembles people to it through this '*commodification*' of data/information/knowledge practices and products. Thus, it is a resource for the structuration of a technical/functional and institutional ecology of PISA.

The Enlargement of a Social-Cultural Matrix

Herein, I draw on a variety of the enlargement of PISA presence in educational settings, considering what Grek has referred to as the construction of a 'social matrix of interrelated governing actors' (Grek, 2010, p. 401). And I do it to illustrate the representation of PISA as a platform for the mobilization of actors to create and diffuse rules about education and education governance.

The document *Beyond PISA 2015: The Longer-Term strategy for PISA* reiterates the self-portrait drawn at the foundation of the Programme and sets several objectives, one of which is relevant for the present argument: 'to aim for greater synergies between PISA and OECD and other international surveys and data collections on education in order to provide more coherent information about learning outcomes as students move through the education system' (OECD, n.d., p. 6). This objective is not utterly new. In the last 5 years, the enlargement of the PISA scope has been particularly evident in two types of moves: the creation of adapted assessment techniques, in order to expand the involved countries and to create new users at a local level, and the creation of combined effects with other OECD tools.

In the first case, OECD has launched the PISA for Development, oriented to the so-called developing countries; and the PISA-based Test for Schools, for use by schools and school networks, and envisaged to extend to the local spaces what PISA claims to achieve at a system level, which is, to foster policy and educational learning and improvement, the sharing of best practices and the identification of 'what works'. Or, from an analytical perspective, in order to move OECD's 'injunctions-knowledges' directly on the school units (see Rutkowski, 2015; Lewis, Sellar, & Lingard, 2016).

In the second case, several connections are being established with another OECD programs, by expanding the assessment of education and training-related performances to new 'populations'—adults and higher education students: the Programme for International Assessment of Adults Competencies and the Assessment of Higher Education Learning Outcomes. But connections have been developed also with a very different tool that focuses on the teachers' working conditions and practices—the TALIS program.

The 'longer-term strategy for PISA' stresses the importance of this 'synergy' with TALIS in order to improve a methodological consistence between their constructs and procedures. Furthermore, it imagines new 'alignments' regarding the survey cycles and the samples up to the coordination of surveys. But synergies between these tools are already being developed, and they occur far beyond the inquiry activities, because both are being used, since 2011, in publication activities and exchange activities about teachers and teaching, and developed in the context of the International Summit on the Teaching Profession. The Summit is, in fact, a helpful example of the 'inscription' of PISA in *'meditative'* (Jacobsson, 2006) and *'exhortative'* (Bradford, 2008) regulation practices that are being developed outside the formal activities of PISA.

The Summit started in 2011 by the joint effort of the US Department of Education and other US-based partners, the OECD and the Education International Education (EI), a 'global' federation of teachers' unions. Since then, the OECD and the IE keep up the event, though with the collaboration of other countries' authorities. The rationalizations and justifications for each party involvement may vary—'recognizing that education is the great equalizer in society, the challenge for all of us is to equip all teachers with the skills and tools they need to provide effective learning opportunities for their students', according to the OECD's Secretary-General, or 'the summits uniquely bring together governments and teacher unions to act on enhancing the quality of education', according to the General Secretary of Education International—but the ethos of the forum is clear: it is a space for a worldwide evidence-based dialogue. Within this ethos, each Summit includes presentations, roundtable discussions, questions and answers with attendees, rapporteur summaries and, finally, a short report.

More important, though, the Summit merges actors from education systems that are selected for being 'top countries' in the PISA survey, legitimated either for having higher performances or for being classified as rapidly improving systems. Plus, the activities developed in Summits are based on reports previously elaborated by the OECD: in 2012 and 2014, PISA results where the main source of reports and framers of meditative activities, but they were also used in the 2011 and 2015 reports, mainly combined with data provided by TALIS, whose numbers and categories are also an important source of legitimation and information of Summits (see Robertson, 2012).

I take as an example the 2012 preparatory report (Schleicher, 2012), which uses PISA results to collect, from the so-called best-performers and fast-improvers, a list of 'promising policies and practices' to improve teaching and teachers work. Sanctioning PISA as a provider of accurate knowledge about the education systems, the report uses PISA data as an entry to frame the debate, to identify a few '*best practices*' and to generate a collective repertoire about teachers work. In fact, the 'examples' are included in a broader argument about what to expect from teachers. It's not exactly a profile of teachers' competencies for the 21st century what is proposed, but the OECD argument has a narrative thread that defines 'the way of thinking and acting' about those competencies. And the thread is as follows: as PISA shows, today, school systems need versatile teachers who adapt, learn and constantly develop their professional knowledge; it is necessary that these versatile teachers are provided with a core of technical knowledge specific to the teaching profession; however, at present times, such technical knowledge is fragile and doesn't have a 'universally' recognized existence. Therefore, to bridge the gap, the OECD envisions a model to improve the use and dissemination of 'proven or promising practices, necessary for the accumulation and legitimation of such professional technical knowledge'.

In this narrative that frames 'the path to take' and the 'issues to deal with', one recognizes again the performance by the OECD of the creator and purveyor and of legitimator of ideas (Mahon & McBride, 2009) but also the knowledge-policy networker. In this case, OECD assumes to be the organizer of the making of standards about teachers and teaching, by selecting, joining and legitimizing diverse knowledge sources and agencies: knowledge and innovation inspired by research and evaluation, innovation inspired by the entrepreneurial development of new products and services and innovation inspired by teachers and head-teachers.

At the end of this story, PISA may be described as a part, and an important resource, of a much broader process—a process of meta-regulation in which the OECD intervenes creating discursive and organizational spaces where performs as framer and mediator. So the continuous expansion of PISA ecology is also the expansion of a cognitive matrix of governing by an 'independent' provider of a specific knowledge.

Finale: A Moralizing Instrument

The credibility of such knowledge rests largely in the objectivity of numbers. But numbers are not merely numbers, as Popkewitz recently reminded us: 'Numbers embodied in educational discourses', he adds, 'are instantiated by moral and political discourses' (Popkewitz, 2011, p. 34). Accordingly, PISA is not just a well-developed international comparative assessment created to assist policymaking with robust data or with "cold" and "crystalline" numbers. Together with inquiry procedures and sophisticated methods of calculation and data analysis, it carries values and interpretations of social realities as well as accurate conceptions about how these realities should be oriented, coordinated and controlled.

In this respect, PISA's cognitive and normative injunctions operate over several core categories of schooling and, of more interest to the present discussion, PISA introduces cultural dicta about policymakers and policymaking in contemporary times as well as about the making of knowledge to policy and the use of knowledge in policy—it introduces rules about the mutually constitutive relationship between educational knowledge and educational governance. More generally, these rules institutionalize a '*governing knowledge*' (Ozga, 2008). In fact, PISA's data and analysis are set up to be used by putative rational and moral actors who are asserting to be responsible for the course of their actions: to contemplate, to reflect and to draw lessons. As shown throughout the discussion about the new PISA deliverables, the concern is not merely to 'bridge the gap' between the expert knowledge and the layman or the policymaker knowledge, but to facilitate an imagined learning relationship between them; it is not only a matter of putting texts on the users 'language', but it is also to make them to engage in specific relationship with data/information/knowledge. Knowledge for policy is '*pedagogy for policy*'.

PISA's knowledge for policy has an implicit script for policy actors and other social actors in the education sector: with such 'reliable measurements' in hand, they are enabled to monitor their systems; to analyze their system performance, at the light of the performances of others; to compare with benchmarks and contemplate how to improve their systems and to draw policy lessons. When it does so, it drives the actors' choices about the legitimate means to make sense of their settings and actions (Mangez & Hilgers, 2012), and endorses rules about the governing of education: regular and systematic assessments are truthful practices for the improvement of national education systems; such improvement has to be analyzed hand in hand with the pace of change of other countries; international comparison of student performances is a means to capture the educational complexity and to develop the quality of education systems.

These rules situate the actors in an imagined timeline—leading from the 'industrial society' to the 'knowledge society'—while putting them in a competitive-cooperative worldwide space. This is a space where comparing through numbers technologies became 'obvious' resources to the location and orientation of actors (Lindblad, 2008) and, furthermore, exert a moralizing power, by assigning either guilt or virtue to education systems and their regulators.

References

Bradford, N. (2008). The OECD's local turn. In R. Mahon, & S. McBride (Eds.), *The OECD and transnational governance*. Vancouver: UBC Press.

Breton, L. (2005). La 'société de la connaissance': généalogie d'une double réduction. *Éducation et Sociétés*, *15*, 45–57.

Carvalho, L. M. (2012). The fabrications and travels of a knowledge-policy instrument. *European Educational Research Journal*, *11*(2), 172–188.

Carvalho, L. M., & Costa, E. (2009). Production of OECD's PISA: Final report. *Project KNOWandPOL*. Retrieved from www.knowandpol.eu/

Carvalho, L. M., & Costa, E. (2015). The praise of mutual-surveillance in Europe. In R. Normand & J.-L. Derouet (Eds.), *A European politics of education?* (pp. 53–72). London: Routledge.

Grek, S. (2010). International organisations and the shared construction of policy 'problems'. *European Educational Research Journal*, *9*(3), 396–406.

Hopmann, S. (2007). Epilogue. In S. Hopmann, G. Brinek, & M. Retzl (Eds.), *PISA according to PISA* (pp. 363–415). Wien: LitVerlag.

Jacobsson, B. (2006). Regulated regulators: Global trends of state transformation. In M.-L. Djelic & K. Sahlin-Anderson (Eds.), *Transnational governance* (pp. 205–224). Cambridge: Cambridge University Press.

Lascoumes, P., & Le Galès, P. (2007). Understanding public policy through its instruments. *Governance*, *20*(1), 1–21.

Latour, B. (1989). *La science en action*. Paris: La Découverte.

Lewis, S., Sellar, S., & Lingard, B. (2016). PISA for schools: Topological rationality and new spaces of the OECD's global educational governance. *Comparative Education Review*, *60*(1), 27–57. Retrieved from www.jstor.org/stable/10.1086/684458

Lindblad, S. (2008). Navigating in the field of university positioning. *European Educational Research Journal*, 7(4), 438–450.

Lindblad, S., Pettersson, D., & Popkewitz, T. S. (2015). *International comparisons of school results: A systematic review of research on large scale assessments in education*. Stockholm: Swedish Research Council.

Lindquist, E. A. (1990). The third community, policy inquiry, and social scientists. In S. Brooks, & A.-G. Gagnon (Eds.), *Social scientists, policy, and the state* (pp. 21–51). New York: Praeger.

Mahon, R., & McBride, S. (2009). Standardizing and disseminating knowledge: The role of the OECD in global governance. *European Political Science Review, 1*(1), 83–101.

Mangez, E., & Hilgers, M. (2012). The field of knowledge and the policy field in education. *European Educational Research Journal, 11*(2), 189–205.

Martens, K. (2007). How to become an influential actor: The 'comparative turn' in OECD education policy. In K. Martens, A. Rusconi, & K. Leuze (Eds.), *New arenas of education governance* (pp. 40–56). London: Palgrave.

Morgan, C. (2011). Constructing the OECD programme for international student assessment. In M. Pereya, H.-G. Kotthoff, & R. Crawson (Eds.), *PISA under examination* (pp. 47–60). Rotterdam: Sense Publishers.

Noaksson, N., & Jacobsson, K. (2003). *The production of ideas and expert knowledge in OECD*. Stockholm: SCORE.

Nóvoa, A. (1998). *Histoire et comparaison*. Lisbon: Educa.

Nowotny, H., Scott, P., & Gibbons, R. (2001). *Re-thinking science*. Cambridge: Polity Press.

OECD. (2001). *Knowledge and skills for life*. Paris: OECD Publishing.

OECD. (2007). *PISA 2006: Sciences competencies for tomorrow's world*. Paris: OECD Publishing.

OECD. (2014). *PISA 2012 results: What students know and can do* (Vol. I, revised ed.). Paris: OECD Publishing.

OECD. (n.d.). *Beyond PISA 2015: A longer-term strategy of PISA*. Retrieved from www.oecd.org/pisa/pisaproducts/Longer-term-strategy-of-PISA.pdf

Ozga, J. (2008). Governing knowledge: Research steering and research quality. *European Educational Research Journal, 7*(3), 261–272.

Popkewitz, T. S. (2011). PISA: Numbers, standardizing conducts, and the alchemy of school subjects. In M. Pereyra, H.-G. Kotthoff, & R. Cowen (Eds.), *PISA under examination* (pp. 31–46). Rotterdam: Sense Publishers.

Porter, D. (1995). *Trust in numbers: The pursuit of objectivity in science in public life*. Princeton, NJ: Princeton University Press.

Robertson, S. (2012). Placing' teachers in global governance agendas. *Comparative Education Review, 56*(3), 584–607.

Rinne, R., Kallo, J., & Hokka, S. (2004). Too eager to comply? OECD education policies and the Finnish response. *European Educational Research Journal, 3*(2), 454–485.

Rutkowski, D. (2015). The OECD and the local: PISA-based test for schools in the USA. *Discourse: Studies in the Cultural Politics of Education, 36*(5), 683–699.

Schleicher, A. (Ed.). (2012). *Preparing teachers and developing school leaders for the 21st century*. Paris: OECD Publishing.

Sellar, S., & Lingard, B. (2013). The OECD and global governance in education. *Journal of Education Policy, 28*(5), 710–725.

Star, S. L., & Griesemer, J. R. (1989). Institutional ecology, 'translations', and boundary objects. *Social Studies of Science, 19*(3), 387–420.

Williamson, B. (2015). Digital education governance: Data visualization, predictive analytics, and 'real-time' policy instruments. *Journal of Education Policy, 31*(2): 123–141. doi:10.1080/02680939.2015.1035758

9
THE IMPLICATIONS OF UNDERSTANDING THAT PISA IS SIMPLY ANOTHER STANDARDIZED ACHIEVEMENT TEST

David C. Berliner

Introduction

It occurred to me one day that despite all the excitement, and both the satisfaction and handwringing engaged in by some nations after scores are released, that the Programme for International Student Assessment (PISA) is merely another Standardized Achievement Test.

Almost all Standardized Achievement Tests (SATs) try to adhere to certain principles of design, have similar correlates, and have similar limits on the interpretations of the results obtained. Neither the popular press nor most politicians ordinarily understand these realities and their implications. Opinion makers are unaware that many of the Standardized Achievement Tests we commonly use do not have the powers attributed to them.

It is not far from the truth to call the scores derived from some of these assessments '*talismanic*' (Haney, Madaus, & Kreitzer, 1987). That is, for many people, test scores have special powers, particularly of prophesy, a bit like the Kabbalah of the middle ages.

Scores from SATs are a part of the metrification associated with the modern world, no doubt aided by a global marketplace in which business leaders and technologists, instead of humanists and educators, have garnered political power. Contributing to this trend toward metrification has been the ascendance of economics as an influential discipline throughout the world (Lingard et al., 2015). But, in my opinion, economists, journalists and politicians too often seek in metrics powers that are more illusionary than they are real.

What Do We Know About High-Quality SATs and PISA?

PISA is simply another SAT, so we have knowledge with which to criticize it, because over the decades we have learned what constitutes a high-quality SAT. Well-designed SATs should have items that have been written carefully, have been scrutinized well, have been tried out, demonstrate little gender or cultural bias and contribute to test reliability. The total test must also provide convincing arguments about its validity for particular purposes. Not all SATs meet such standards in an exemplary manner, and PISA is no exception.

Language and PISA Items

PISA is being used cross-nationally. Thus, every item in this SAT must have the same meaning in each country to ensure that each country has items that are not positively or negatively associated with the all-important passing rates for items. If this condition cannot be met, interpretation of this SAT may be seriously compromised. Many scholars, myself included, are not sure that these basic criteria, for this particular SAT, can be met, although PISA designers say they can do just that. Common sense and supporting research challenges PISA's claims.

For example, here, alphabetically, are just a few of the countries that take the *same* items: Argentina, Australia, Austria, Azerbaijan, Belgium, Brazil, Bulgaria, Canada, Chile, Colombia, Croatia, the Czech Republic, Denmark and so on. It is quite likely that it is quite difficult to have test items mean precisely the same thing in each of these nations, and thus be an item of equivalent difficulty in each of these nations' languages.

Some of us find it hard to believe that *item equivalence* can be ensured for the 65 nations, 65 cultures and their subcultures, 65 dialects and languages, that participated in the 2012 PISA test. My colleague Gene Glass (2012), one of the most distinguished educational researchers in the world, asks:

> How do you write a reading test in English and then translate it into Swedish (or vice versa) and end up confident that one is not intrinsically more difficult than the other? I insist that the answer to that question is that you can't. And to claim that one has done so merely sweeps under the rug a host of concerns that include grammatical structure, syntax, familiarity of vocabulary, not to mention culture of the students taking the test.
> *(http://ed2worlds.blogspot.se/2012/02/among-many-things-wrong-with.html).*

Years ago, Gerald Bracey (1991) pointed to one international test where 98 percent of Finnish students, but only 50 percent of American students, scored correctly on a vocabulary question. The students were asked to indicate whether '*pessimistic*' and '*sanguine*' were antonyms or synonyms. Because 'sanguine' does not exist in the Finnish language, the word 'optimistic' was substituted, making the question much easier to answer.

So common sense leads many of us to believe that no one can produce two non-trivial passages of text, in two different languages, and make them, and the questions derived from them, of equal cognitive difficulty. A figure from an item on the 2006 PISA reading test (Organisation for Economic Co-operation and Development, 2009) illustrates this concern. It is a passage intended to tap comprehension. It sets up the questions this way:

> A murder has been committed, but the suspect denies everything. He claims not to know the victim. He says he never knew him, never went near him, never touched him . . . The police and the judge are convinced that he is not telling the truth. But how to prove it?

The description before the items themselves then goes into genetics and genetic testing in the science labs that modern police use. It is a complex set up to a complex question, and that has its own difficulties in a cross-cultural context. But more important for me is that I do not believe that such an item is of the same cognitive and emotional character in scientifically advanced countries with appreciation for the police, and scientifically less advanced countries, with fear of the police.

Another figure from the same 2006 PISA exam (Organisation for Economic Co-operation and Development, 2009) was designed to examine the problem solving and quality of scientific thinking by 15-year-olds. The figure used for priming one set of items is a photograph of Dolly, the first cloned sheep (see Ruiz-Primo & Li, 2015). Background information about the biological and medical skill needed for that cloning experiment is presented. The prose is technical in nature, and it is followed by questions.

Although PISA developers claim otherwise, it is hard to believe that the substantial amount of reading required in these two items is likely to be interpreted the same in, say, Hungary, Denmark and Korea. Nor are the questions associated with each of these contexts likely to yield equal pass rates. Glass (2012, response to BLOG comments) says this:

> It is not a matter of the fidelity of a translation. It is a matter of producing psychometric equivalence right down to percentage points of difficulty between two items. Even small differences in item difficulty between two items in different languages accumulated across several items could produce differences between two nations of the magnitude observed for many of the nations in these international rankings. To place one's trust in the PISA

Context and PISA Items

In fact, the common sense about this issue is fully supported by the research of Ruiz-Primo and Li (2015). They point out that items on PISA are intended to tap deeper learning than do multiple-choice items. To do that requires the design of a context. The context must be read and understood before the actual questions designed to tap problem-solving skills are asked. These kinds of question are in contrast to straightforward multiple-choice questions, designed to assess memory for factual knowledge, and where text providing background contexts are usually not necessary.

Ruiz-Primo and Li believed that these context-dependent questions might be understood differently in different countries, a perfectly reasonable hypothesis that was confirmed. They found differential student performance, *by nation*, on PISA, associated with the contexts in which items were presented. They also found evidence that item contexts across countries affected male and female respondents differently.

Illustrations and PISA Items

We need also to remember that items designed to tap problem solving, not simple memory, often have illustrations associated with them, as well as contexts. But Solano-Flores and Wang (2015) discovered that items with illustrations are interpreted differently in different countries. Their research demonstrates that cultural differences in interpretation of illustrations *significantly affected the scores obtained by nations*.

One such illustration for a PISA math item shows footsteps of a man walking in sand. (Organisation for Economic Co-operation and Development, 2009). It describes that the pace length P is the distance from the rear of two consecutive footprints and gives a formula to use for a series of questions that follow. The formula to use in solving the problems is $n/p = 140$. In this case, n is the number of steps per minute and p is the pace length in meters.

Commenting on this particular figure, Sjøberg (2007) says:

> If the marked foot**step** is 80 cm (as suggested in other information that is given), then the foot**print** is 55 cm long! A regular man's foot is actually only about 26 cm long, so the figure is extremely misleading! But even worse: From the figure, we can see (or measure) the next foot**step** to be 60% longer [than the first foot**step**]. Given the formula (provided), this also

implies a more rapid pace, and the man's acceleration from the first to the second foot**step** has to be enormous!

After other criticisms, Sjøberg says:

> The situation is unrealistic and flawed from several points of view. Students who simply insert numbers in the formula without thinking will get it right. More critical students who start thinking will, however, be confused and get in trouble!
>
> *(see also Sjøberg, 2015)*

Construct Irrelevant Variance and PISA Tests

Another criterion for good SATs is to minimize construct irrelevant variance. If construct irrelevant variance affects the scores obtained, the interpretation of the test is more difficult, and the inferences that we want to make from the test may be suspect.

Test items should be related to the constructs under investigation, in this case—reading, science and mathematics knowledge. But we see that in cross-national testing, there are potential sources of construct irrelevant variance that are due to differences in languages and in the interpretations of contexts and illustrations. And how do we avoid irrelevant variance in science assessment when the United States, Libya and Myanmar continue to reject the metric system? Or because the reading load is quite heavy when illustrations and contexts are employed, it seems a sure bet that reading ability is a source of construct irrelevant variance in the assessment of both mathematics and science.

Raw Scores and Imputed Scores Derived From PISA Items

I have little doubt that PISA technicians are skilled. PISA has employed some of the best measurement people in the world. But common sense and research now suggest that even small differences in national raw scores that are due to small differences in the interpretation of items associated with language, illustrations, contexts and construct irrelevant variance make PISA interpretations quite a bit more problematic than we have been led to believe. Because of these factors, there is certainly a high likelihood of small national differences at the level of individual items. These small differences become magnified when sophisticated statistical models are used to put the national scores into a metric with a mean of about 500 and a standard deviation of about 100, from which the ranks of nations on PISA are determined. As I understand it, total scores are imputed from characteristics of each of the items passed, and we now know that these items are likely to reflect national differences in language and culture, not simply student achievement. In fact, raw scores among nations hardly differ, whereas the scaled scores and ranks used in interpreting PISA scores differ quite a bit. This situation arises because of the predictions of total scores from the small sample of items given to each student in a PISA sample. Table 9.1 illustrates this point. Here, you see PISA 2012 raw scores, scaled scores and ranks for selected countries.

As can be seen, nations with the *same raw scores*, say Slovenia and the United States, have scale scores that differ quite dramatically. Slovenia is given the scale score of 501, whereas the scale score for the United States is determined to be 481. This is hard for the common person to understand: same raw score, but scale scores that differ by 20 points, and producing a difference of 15 ranks. Note also that Finland and Israel differ by 2 raw score points but by 52 scale score points, and by 29 ranks.

If each test form of about 30 items is a purposeful sample of the 109 math items used in 2012, then many nations are performing quite similarly up until the imputation scheme, where the sampling design is used to determine the scale scores and ranks for a nation. What we get, a bit magically for most of us, is a lot of imputed (or plausible) scores for a nation's students.

The psychometric procedure used to determine these scores from samples of items, but not the whole test, uses the well-known, and quite brilliant, Rasch model. But as I understand it, this model works only if the questions PISA uses in each country have the same difficulty level. And we have just seen that because of language, the use of illustrations, and the need for descriptive contexts, equality of difficulty across nations is unlikely and perhaps impossible.

TABLE 9.1 Selected National Raw Scores, Scaled Scores and Ranks for PISA 2012

Nations	PISA Raw Score Math, 2012	PISA Scaled Score in Math	Rank of Nation
Finland	13	519	12
Poland	13	518	14
Vietnam	13	511	17
Austria	13	506	18
Ireland	13	501	20
Slovenia	12	501	21
France	12	496	25
Iceland	12	493	27
Norway	12	490	30
Spain	12	485	33
United States of America	12	481	36
Croatia	11	471	40
Israel	11	467	41

This suggests that we can expect some wide ranges of values in the scale scores determined from the forms that a nation used and the plausible or imputed values determined from those forms. And that is exactly what we get. For example, according to the 2006 reading rankings, Canada could have been positioned anywhere between the 2nd and 25th ranks, Japan between the 8th and 40th and the UK between the 14th and 30th (Kreiner, 2011). Such variation in scores and the associated ranks suggest that the reliability of PISA scores and rankings are more questionable than consumers of PISA have ever been led to believe (Kreiner & Christensen, 2014).

The number of items in mathematics in 2012 = 109. Students in each country take about 30 percent of these items on different forms of the tests. PISA scores for countries are based on the unassigned as well as the taken items, with scores on the unadministered items predicted or extrapolated from the scores on the administered items, using weights based on student samples in each nation.

PISA Reliability

Standardized Achievement Test designers pride themselves on having high reliability so that the possibility of valid inferences can be made from the scores obtained. But the PISA designers may not always meet that criterion as well as they might hope to do. For example, in two provinces of Italy (Bratti & Checchi, 2013), the opportunity arose to retest students a year later with the same forms of the PISA test that they originally took the previous year. This study was concerned with the value added by the students' schools. They chose to use PISA as the Standardized Achievement Test from which the school's added value would be calculated. In one province, tested in Italian, the year-to-year student scores were quite highly correlated, as might be expected when using a well-designed SAT. But in another province, French speaking, the correlation of the students' scores from year-to-year were quite low, in fact, near zero. This is not very reassuring. The differences, it seems, were due to different attrition rates over the single year, which meant that in the low reliability district, a slightly different cohort took the test the second time. Since PISA is given every 3 years, and different 15-year-old cohorts are used in each nation, the stability of scores over the 3 years between assessments is quite likely to be less than is desirable for the design of national education policies that depend heavily on reliable trends. The trends derived from these data may, therefore, be quite suspect.

Sampling Issues and PISA Testing

The trustworthiness of the raw scores and especially of the imputed scores clearly depends on the sampling schemes devised by PISA. That too is not perfect. Loveless (2013) has shown that the extremely high PISA scores obtained by Shanghai in 2012 were obtained, in part, by leaving out tens, if not hundreds, of thousands of children of migrants. These migrants are often rural Chinese families without government permission to work in Shanghai. The children of these illegal or undocumented families are not always permitted to go to school, or they may be purged from public school by age 14, just before the samples for the following year's PISA assessments are determined. The sampling errors were well known to PISA, though apparently ignored by them, and ignored as well by newspapers around the world that discussed how good the Shanghai schools appeared to be.

Similarly, and quite convincingly, Carnoy and Rothstein (2013) have identified PISA sampling problems in the United States. For example, the 2009 PISA sample had 40 percent of the participating US students coming from schools where half or more of the students were eligible for free and reduced lunch programs. But the percent of US students actually in schools with such high rates of poverty is much lower. Carnoy and Rothstein (2013) determined that if the 2009 sample had been correct, the rank of the United States on PISA would have gone from 14th to 6th in reading, and from 25th to 13th in mathematics.

Validity and PISA Testing

All SATs depend on convincing evidence of validity to justify both their use and their costs. To claim *Content Validity* for PISA would require evidence that the PISA assessments of 15-year-olds today be related to the real-world tasks that are required of adults in their work and home lives in, say, 10–15 years from now. PISA explicitly seeks assessment tasks that are representative of the skills needed *in the future*, making it impossible to judge PISA on the adequacy of its content validity in the way that we can judge other tests, TIMSS, for example, which attempts to assess contemporary curricula.

A *construct validity* argument would find that scores on PISA, PIRLS, TIMSS and certain national tests (NAEP and NAPLAN, for example) are moderately or strongly correlated in each of the content areas assessed. There is evidence that this is true, so the construct validity argument can be made, but not as strongly, perhaps, as might be desired. Score and rank order differences that arise as a function of taking these different tests promote the argument that the mathematics, science and reading knowledge constructs being measured in different nations may be different. This results in difficulty in test score interpretation for a particular test in a particular country. The United States, for example, does extremely well on the PIRLS test of reading. We do quite well, on the TIMSS science and mathematics tests. But we do not do as well on PISA. How shall we judge our national level of achievement when these tests of similar constructs yield such different estimates of US achievement?

The *consequential validity* argument has already been alluded to—newspapers and politicians each go mad with the PISA results, either attributing credit to national governments for things they may have had nothing to do with, or blaming institutions and people for results they do not like, even though those institutions and people may not have had much influence on the results. We know that in the United States, the variance attributable to teachers and schools from results of virtually all SATs is quite small, compared with the variance attributable to social class, income, neighborhood, educational level of the mother and so forth. So interpreting the results of PISA in ways that laud or condemn teachers and schools makes little sense. While Finland and the United States differ in scores on PISA, they also differ on childhood poverty rates. Finland's childhood poverty rate is about 4 percent, whereas the poverty rate for children in the United States is likely to be over 20 percent. Though politicians and journalists may blame schools and teachers, it is certainly the case that the social systems of the two nations have real effects on PISA scores (see Condron, 2011). Clearly, in almost all PISA countries, the tests have consequences. Results are attended to in both appropriate and highly inappropriate ways. In the United States, valid inferences drawn from PISA data are a rare experience.

One more type of validity needs to be addressed, that of *predictive validity*. PISA really is about predicting a nation's fate as a function of the test scores generated by its school systems. The economists Hanushek and Woessmann (2010), along with the OECD and many politicians, make the case that a substantial rise in PISA scores for nations would mean trillions of dollars in increased business activities. Their argument is that as nations set about to improve their curriculum, their schools and the quality of their teachers, they will soon have higher PISA scores, and that will inevitably make their national economies hum. The data used by Hanushek and Woessman (2010) to make these oft-repeated claims for predictive validity have been seriously challenged and now appear to be indefensible (Komatsu & Rappleye, 2017).

So PISA is taken quite seriously as an omen; the scores are talismanic objects. But, for me, the logic of this is closer to that of the cargo cults of the early 20th century than the realities associated with modern nation-states.

I find at least three things wrong with the economic benefits argument. The first is that Standardized Achievement Tests only weakly show any effects of curriculum, schools and teachers. Thus, improving these aspects of schooling will meet with very limited success in influencing PISA scores. Teachers and schools simply do not affect the variance in Standardized Achievement Tests by very much. Thus, all policies derived from SATs such as PISA, NAEP, TIMSS and others, that are designed to improve schools *without* improving the economic and social conditions of the children and families in those schools, are doomed to deliver tiny benefits.

PISA obtained its magical powers, becoming endowed with predictive validity, in part, because of a search for an index that assessed the potential of our globalized economies (Rizvi & Lingard, 2010). It does not do this well at all. For example, based on the results of previous administrations of PISA, at a time when Japan did especially well on PISA, theirs was the economy to watch. We did. Japan's economy failed, and after more than 10 years of strong PISA scores, it is still failing. On the other hand, the 2000 administration of PISA provided a rude shock for Germany, as it garnered a relatively low score. Their economy, however, moved on to become the strongest in the EU. In 2000, Finland also received a rude shock (Sahlberg, 2011). Because of its high PISA scores, it became the Fantasyland for Western nations. And although it has fallen off a bit in recent PISA testing, it is still acknowledged as a world leader. But what about the Finnish economy? It has not been doing well for a number of years, despite all of Finland's PISA talent (Hugh, 2015). Not long ago, the Finnish prime minister said that his high-scoring country is in a 'lost decade'. Finland's economy has fallen behind its Nordic neighbors and its European peers. Pay increases have been on hold, government debt has almost doubled from 2008 to 2014, taxes are up a few percent and the jobless rate not long ago was about 9 percent.

And at the same time that Germany worried, and Finland was surprised, the United States and Israel did relatively poorly on PISA. Yet each of their economies has thrived in the years since. The United States, in fact, with modest performance on PISA, has won the distinction of being number one on the 2014, 2016 and 2017 GEDI Index (Acs et al., 2016). The GEDI is the World Global Entrepreneurship Index. While PISA gets attention as a predictor of future economic prosperity, despite no proof that it actually has predictive validity, it might be more reasonable to expect the GEDI to be such a predictor instead. Few US pundits said anything about the release of the GEDI, though they rarely miss a chance to wring their hands over PISA scores. Yet the GEDI researchers were associated with the Imperial College Business School, the London School of Economics, the University of Pécs and George Mason University. Researchers at these institutions studied entrepreneurship in 120 nations. They have found consistently that the number one1 country in the world was the United States. It strikes me that entrepreneurship among adults is much more likely to be a predictor of a nation's future economy than is PISA. This is especially true when that test assesses 15-year-old American kids who know that the test scores count for nothing, and that the results are never seen by their teachers or their parents. Korean youth may take the PISA for the honor of their country. Youth in the United States take the test because they are ordered to. I wouldn't predict much based on that kind of sample. Contrary to the despair over PISA scores in the United States, the GEDI authors say that entrepreneurship plays a crucial role in the US economy, and as a result, policy initiatives are created to encourage entrepreneurial behavior. This, coupled with the culture of determination and motivation, makes the United States a great place to be an entrepreneur.

Moreover, the researchers say, the gulf between the United States and other countries is large and appears to be widening, not narrowing. In addition, the

2014 GEDI compared the experience of female entrepreneurs for the first time, to reflect the increasing participation and importance of women in entrepreneurship around the world. The researchers determined that the United States is also the world's leader in female entrepreneurship.

Furthermore, while the US PISA scores lead many to predict doom and gloom for our economy, there is also the Global Innovation Index. It too appears likely to predict future economic activity for nations better than would a SAT like PISA. The Global Innovation Index is put together each year by two prestigious universities and a UN committee and uses 82 different metrics to determine rankings. That 2016 index is presented as Table 9.2 (Dutta, Lanvin, & Wunsch-Vincent, 2016).

TABLE 9.2 Rank on the Global Innovation Index and Rank on PISA 2015

Country and Rank on the 2016 Global Innovation Index	Mean Rank on 2015 PISA (Based on Combined Rankings in Reading, Mathematics and Science)
1. Switzerland	18
2. Sweden	23
3. United Kingdom	21
4. United States	30
5. Finland	7
6. Singapore	1
7. Ireland	14
8. Denmark	17
9. Netherlands	14
10. Germany	14
11. South Korea	8
12. Luxembourg	34
13. Iceland	34
14. Hong Kong (China)	4
15. Canada	7

In the first column, I entered the Global Innovation Index ranking for the top 15 nations. As you can see, the United States ranks 4th, which is not bad at all. Then I entered the combined ranks of these nations on PISA 2015 and correlated the two measures. The correlation is negative. PISA seems not to predict a nation's innovativeness. I think, therefore, that claims of predictive validity for PISA remain unsubstantiated.

There is one more issue that is both a concern about reliability and validity for PISA: the number of false positives and false negatives that show up at the item level. New Zealand researchers (Harlow & Jones, 2004) studied items that students had gotten wrong and right on an international SAT of science and did a version of dynamic testing with the students. They administered the items individually to the students and probed whether the students who got the items wrong really did know the answer if probed a bit. And they probed to see whether the students who got the items correct had the knowledge required for a correct answer. Their research revealed that many of these New Zealand test takers were false negatives on the test items; that is, they did know their science but got the item wrong. Many others were false positives; that is, they did not know their science well but got the item right anyway. More work like this needs to be done, since these results suggest problems with both the reliability and validity of PISA and other SATs.

A Conclusion About PISA Quality

PISA is clearly better supported and has better personnel working on it, and its technical characteristics are better than many other Standardized Achievement Tests. But like all other SATs, it has faults and is not above criticism. I have criticized the assumption of comparability of the test across nations because of the real possibility of differences in the cognitive complexity of items and item understanding in the different languages and cultures of each nation. It is more than just translation that is of concern. The contexts and illustrations from which PISA items are derived were found *not* to be equivalent across countries. And it is likely that they can never be made equivalent until we all speak Esperanto!

The difference in scaled scores and ranks associated with identical raw scores among nations may stem from slight differences in item difficulty by country. And if that is true, then the requirements of the Rasch model are not met and imputation of PISA scores and their associated ranks is seriously flawed.

We now know as well that samples drawn in each nation are not always as accurate a representation of the entire population as they should be, and this too makes the imputation of scores from the samples problematic. Looking at reliability also revealed some rough spots for PISA. That is, sampling procedures and cohort differences from administration to administration make trends much more difficult to trust than is acknowledged. In addition, the predictive validity of PISA in the economic realm appears to be quite overstated. And, finally, the rates of false negatives and false positives, at the item level, on one PISA administration, have been found to be of considerable magnitude. Both reliability and validity depend on the magnitude of these occurrences being quite small. But that may not be the case.

Technically, I doubt if any organization can do a better job than PISA in designing a cross-national test that is an appropriate starter of conversations about education. But the national angst, joy and subsequent policies derived from either low or high sores on PISA assessments are misplaced. Because of its inherent design flaws—*not unlike every other Standardized Achievement Test I know*—PISA results at best might initiate conversations about each nation's visions for childhood, schooling and economic vitality. PISA should *not* be a catalyst for change without considerable time spent in conversations about one's own national education system in a globalized world. I would limit PISA's influence not just because of the technical problems I have just reported; it will always struggle with those. Rather I'd limit its influence in the United States because PISA's biggest flaw is unacknowledged, and that is, that the test is picking up the cruel realities of contemporary US policies about income distribution and housing, medical care, jobs, wages and so forth.

PISA is a Standardized Achievement Test and, as such, is a reflection of our society much more than it is a reflection of our curriculum, teachers, schools and students. That is, the biggest problem with all SATs is the same: in our times, too many inferences about the quality of life in our schools are being drawn while too few inferences are being drawn from these tests about the quality of life for our families and in our neighborhoods.

The Limits of PISA and Other SATs in Providing Information for Policies About Teachers and Schools

I will make a bold statement: there are no SATs—neither state, national or international—whose scores cannot be very well predicted from demographic data. The SATs are notoriously insensitive to teacher and school effects and powerfully influenced instead by cohort and neighborhood effects and by family social class, particularly level of poverty. SATs are reflective of sociological variables much more than they are reflective of instructional and educational variables. The evidence for this is overwhelming and avoided by most of those who use PISA data to design policy. Note that what I say suggests that every policy derived from PISA (and other SATs) concerned with the improvement of schools and classrooms is doomed to small effects. This is best described by Haertel (2013), who reviewed the literature on SATs and offers the analysis that is Figure 9.1:

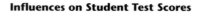

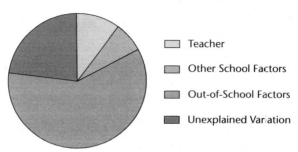

FIGURE 9.1 Variance Accounted for on SATs by Source

Teachers account for about 10 percent of the total variance; schools also account for about 10 percent of the total variance. Error (unexplained variance) accounts for about 20 percent of the total variance. The majority of the variance in scores on SATs, about 60 percent, is accounted for by out-of-school factors such as family, neighborhood, income and so forth.

Here is the most important point of this figure: policies designed to affect teachers that are derived from SATs will usually affect only about 10 percent of the variance we see in students' test scores. And policies designed to affect curriculum, leadership, scheduling, time usage, homework or other school-level factors will also affect only about 10 percent of the variance in SAT scores. It is the outside-of-school variables that affect SAT scores the most. I have identified a set of out-of-school factors known to affect the test scores produced by schools (Berliner, 2009; Wilkinson & Pickett, 2010). These all affect what occurs inside the school and inside the classroom.

- Percent of low birth-weight children in the neighborhood
- Inadequate medical, dental and vision care in family and neighborhood
- Food insecurity in the family
- Environmental pollutants in home and neighborhood
- Family relations and family stress
- Percent of mothers at the school site who are single and/or teens
- Percent of mothers at the school site who do not possess a high school degree (or have not finalized secondary education?)
- Language spoken at home
- Family income
- Neighborhood characteristics

    - Rate of violence
    - Drug use

- Mental health
- Average income
- Mobility rates of families
- Availability of positive role models
- Availability of high-quality early education
- Transportation to get to jobs.

Concern for these variables, more than PISA test scores, seems much more likely to affect student achievement. Our contemporary thinking about these out-of-school issues begins with the Coleman report (Coleman et al., 1966). That report shocked our democracy 50 years ago, as it convincingly argued that teachers and schools were not nearly as powerful as we thought in breaking the cycle of poverty. Although that fact has been understood for a long time now, it is too often ignored by policymakers and researchers alike (Powers, Fischman, & Berliner, 2016).

Borman and Dowling (2010), in their reanalysis of the Coleman data, using more modern and more powerful statistical measures, make two claims that are important for the argument being made here. First, they claim that teacher effects, compared with composition effects, *are a minor predictor of student scores*. Second, they claim that the *peer and compositional effects on achievement test scores* are about twice as strong as is the racial or social class standing of the students themselves. Who you go to school with matters a lot.

Because, in the Western world, we almost always live in socioeconomic and racially homogenous enclaves, our schools are often segregated by race and class. In terms of school achievement, the race and class of those individuals matter, but only a little, until those racial and social class characteristics influence the peer, or cohort, or composition of students at the school site. Some peer groups and cohorts promote high achievement, and some do not; what must be remembered is that the aggregate scores obtained on SATs given to those classrooms and schools is substantially independent of the teachers' and schools' effects on those students.

The point of this all is that teachers, who currently get so much blame for the outcomes of our schools, are probably accounting for only about 10 percent of the variance in those aggregate outcomes. And the schools, frequently the recipients of blame when PISA or other SAT scores are low, also account for about 10 percent of the variance in SAT outcomes.

The most recent support for this claim is from the American Statistical Association. Their position paper was on value-added models (VAM) of teacher evaluation (American Statistical Association, 2014), in which a pre- and a post-SAT is used to judge the value added to student scores by a particular teacher. They say that most VAM studies find that teachers account for about 1 percent to 14 percent of the variability in test scores and that the majority of opportunities for quality improvement are found in the system-level conditions.

Conclusions Considering the Limits of SATs for Policies

So outside-the-school factors are often three times more powerful in affecting SAT scores than are inside-the-school and inside-the-classroom factors. Put differently, outside-of-school factors are six times more powerful than are teachers and six times more powerful than are the schools when influence on SATs is analyzed. Policies dealing with teacher and school improvement that are derived from SATs like PISA can have only limited success.

A few million independent anecdotes about how teachers affect individual students are proof enough of their power to influence individuals. In my life, they made a big difference in what kind of person I became, and some of my teachers also affected the habits of mind I bring to my work and to my personal life. My children have also been positively affected by some of their teachers. And I am sure that readers of this chapter have similar stories to tell, the vast majority of which are about positive effects, although teachers have the power to negatively affect individual children as well.

This is a paradox and, like all paradoxes, a bit confusing: teachers and the schools attended by a nation's children affect the individual students in their classes enormously—teachers really do touch eternity (Barone, 2001). But teachers and schools affect the SATs ordinarily used to judge teachers and schools only a little. PISA is merely a SAT. It measures demographic characteristics quite well and is almost useless for suggesting policies that affect teachers and schools that will affect the scores on those SATs.

Summing Up

At the start of this chapter, we saw that PISA, like every other SAT, struggles with technical problems, including that most important criterion for any SAT: its meaning. What is PISA valid for? I would argue that PISA is perfectly wonderful for starting conversations about schooling; the outcomes desired for a nation's youth; the curriculum to achieve those outcomes; culture and child-rearing practices and their effects on school achievement; income distribution and its effects on youth behavior and school achievement, the design of trust relationships between educators, parents, and policymakers; discussions about whether a metric really can be created for everything that a community wants to assess; and so forth.

The distinguished British comparative educator Robin Alexander (2012) is likely to agree with a good deal of what I say in this chapter. He has some remarkable insights into the madness that attends to PISA scores because of their inappropriate use. For example, he notes how a team headed by Michael Barber wrote a report for the multibillion dollar management corporation McKinsey & Co. that is inane (my description). The report, titled *How the World's Best-Performing Education Systems Come Out on Top*, was almost universally praised by policymakers throughout the western world. Its authors concluded from PISA 2003 that

'Three things matter most: (1) getting the right people to become teachers, (2) developing them into effective instructors, and (3) ensuring that the system is able to deliver the best possible instruction for every child' (Barber & Mourshed, 2007, p. 2). Well, duh! I might have written such banality well before anyone ever heard of PISA. This really is not high-level thinking, especially given the cost of the report. But, in addition, as I have argued earlier, this report is not merely ordinary in its conclusions: it is also wrong!

Policies aimed at teachers' schools and school systems will have little effect on national school system achievement as measured by SATs, because SAT scores are reflections of other things—income inequality, housing policy, cohort effects, culture and so forth. This expensive and lauded report has no clue about what makes for an SAT score.

Alexander (2012) cites others who also would have found Barber's McKinsey report ridiculous. Ernest Boyer, an influential educator and policy analyst of the 1960s, once said: 'Schools can rise no higher than the communities that support them' (Boyer, 1983, p. 6). Not long after, in 1970, the well-respected British social scientist Basil Bernstein said 'Education cannot compensate for society' (Bernstein, 1970, p. 344). I would like to end this chapter with the insights of a scholar who works for PISA (Andreas Schleicher, 2009), and one who I believe to be much wiser, though he wrote 115 years earlier (Michael Sadler, 1900; see Alexander, 2012). Schleicher, after examining PISA data, says the ideal school might have little bits of Finland, Japan, England, Israel, Norway, Canada, Belgium and Germany in the way it develops students' individual strengths, gets teachers to cooperate, sets clear performance targets, celebrates discourse and helps students to learn from their mistakes and so forth. But Sadler says:

> In studying foreign systems of education, we should not forget that the things outside the schools matter even more than the things inside the schools, and govern and interpret the things inside . . . No other nation, by imitating a little bit of German organization, can thus hope to achieve a true reproduction of the spirit of German institutions . . . All good and true education is an expression of national life and character . . . The practical value of studying in a right spirit and with scholarly accuracy the working of foreign systems of education is that it will result in our being better fitted to study and understand our own.
>
> *(Sadler, 1900, p. 50)*

That is what PISA and other SATs are good for. They are capable of providing data for conversations about schooling in each society. PISA has no magic. Its scores are not talismanic. It is a starting place for conversations and not for the immediate design of policy (see Sellar, Thompson, & Rutkowski, 2017).

Policies about teachers and schools, like those promoted by McKinsey and company, are both misleading and useless if they are expected to produce large changes in the scores on an SAT. PISA is simply another SAT, with some added and unusual technical problems, and all the usual insensitivities to teaching and schooling that characterize all Standardized Achievement Tests.

References

Acs, Z., Szerb, L. Autio, E., & Lloyd, A. (2016). *Global entrepreneurship index, 2017*. Washington, DC: Global Entrepreneurship and Development Institute.

Alexander, R. (2012). *International evidence, national policy and classroom practice: Questions of judgement, vision and trust*. Paper given at the Third Van Leer International Conference on Education: From Regulation to Trust: Education in the 21st century. Jerusalem, May 24, 2012.

American Statistical Association. (2014, April 8). *ASA statement on using value-added models for educational assessment*. Retrieved September 1, 2017 from www.amstat.org/policy/pdfs/ASA_VAM_Statement.pdf

Barber, M., & Mourshed, M. (2007). *How the world's best performing school systems come out on top*. Chicago: McKinsey and Company.

Barone, T. (2001). *Touching eternity: The enduring outcomes of teaching*. New York: Teachers College Press.

Berliner, D. C. (2009). *Poverty and potential: Out-of-school factors and school success*. Boulder, CO and Tempe, AZ: Education and the Public Interest Center, University of Colorado/ Education Policy Research Unit, Arizona State University. Retrieved September 2, 2017, from http://nepc.colorado.edu/publication/poverty-and-potential

Bernstein, B. (1970). Education cannot compensate for society. *New Society, 26*, 344–347.

Borman, G. D., & Dowling, M. (2010). Schools and inequality: A multilevel analysis of Coleman's equality of educational opportunity data. *Teachers College Record, 112*(5), 1201–1246.

Boyer, E. L. (1983). *High school: A report on secondary education in America*. New York: Harper & Row. Quoted in H. J. Noah The use and abuse of comparative education. In P. G. Altbach & G. P. Kelly (Eds.), *New approaches to comparative education*. Chicago: University of Chicago Press.

Bracey, G. W. (1991). Why can't they be like we were? *Phi Delta Kappan, 73*(2), 104–117.

Bratti, M., & Checchi, D. (2013). *Re-testing PISA students one year later. On school value added estimation using PISA—OECD*. Retrieved September 1, 2017, from www.iwaee.org/papers%20sito%202013/Bratti.pdf.

Carnoy, M., & Rothstein, R. (2013). *What do international tests really show about U.S. student performance?* Washington, DC: Economic Policy Institute. Retrieved September 1, 2017, from www.epi.org/publication/us-student-performance-testing/

Coleman, J. S., Campbell, E. Q., Hobson, C. J., McPartland, J., Mood, A. M., Weinfeld, F. D., & York, R. L. (1966). *Equality of educational opportunity*. Washington, DC: U. S. Government Printing Office.

Condron, D. J. (2011). Egalitarianism and educational outcomes: Compatible goals for affluent societies. *Educational Researcher, 40*(2), 47–55.

Dutta, S., Lanvin, B., & Wunsch-Vincent, S. (Eds.). (2016). *The global innovation index 2016: Winning with global innovation*. Ithaca, NY: Cornell University; Fontainebleau: INSEAD; and Geneva: WIPO.

Glass, G. V. (2012). Among the many things wrong with international achievement comparisons. *Education in Two Worlds*. Retrieved September 1, 2017 from http://ed2worlds.blogspot.com/2012/02/among-many-things-wrong-with.html

Haertel, E. H. (2013). *Reliability and validity of inferences about teachers based on student test scores.* The 14th William H. Angoff Memorial Lecture. Educational Testing Service: Princeton. Retrieved September 1, 2017, from www.google.com/search?q=https%3A%2F%2Fwww.ets.org%2FMedia%2FResearch%2Fpdf%2FPICANG14.pdf&oq=https%3A%2F%2Fwww.ets.org%2FMedia%2FResearch%2Fpdf%2FPICANG14.pdf&gs_l=psyab.3 . . . 0.0.0.25241.0.0.0.0.0.0.0..0.0. . . . 0. . . 1..64.psy-ab..0.0.0.JS-vdw79OWk

Haney, W., Madaus, G., & Kreitzer, A. (1987). Charms talismanic: Testing teachers for the improvement of American education. *Review of Research in Education, 14,* 169–238.

Hanushek, E. A., & Woessmann, L. (2010). *The high cost of low educational performance: The long-run economic impact of improving PISA outcomes.* Paris: OECD. Retrieved September 1, 2017, from www.oecd.org/edu/school/programmeforinternationalstudentassessmentpisa/thehighcostofloweducationalperformance.htm

Harlow, A., & Jones, A. (2004). Why students answer TIMSS science test items the way they do. *Research in Science Education, 34,* 221–238.

Hugh, E. (2015). *Is Finland's economy suffering from secular stagnation? A fistful of dollars / European opinion.* Retrieved September 1, 2017 from http://fistfulofeuros.net/afoe/is-finlands-economy-suffering-from-secular-stagnation/

Komatsu, H., & Rappleye, J. (2017). A new global policy regime founded on invalid statistics? Hanushek, Woessmann, PISA, and economic growth. *Journal of Comparative Education, 53*(2), 166–191. Retrieved September 2, 2017 from http://dx.doi.org/10.1080/03050068.2017.1300008

Kreiner, S. (2011). *Is the foundation under PISA solid? A critical look at the scaling model underlying international comparisons of student attainment* (Research Report 11/1). Copenhagen: Department of Biostatistics, University of Copenhagen. Retrieved September 1, 2017 from https://ifsv.sund.ku.dk/biostat/annualreport/images/c/ca/ResearchReport-2011-1.pdf

Kreiner, S., & Christensen, K. B. (2014). Analyses of model fit and robustness. A new look at the PISA scaling model underlying ranking of countries according to reading literacy. *Psycometrica, 79*(2), 210–231.

Lingard, B., Martino, W., Rezai-Rashti, G., & Sellar, S. (2015). *Globalizing educational accountabilities.* New York: Routledge/Taylor & Francis.

Loveless, T. (2013). *Attention OECD-PISA: Your silence on China is wrong.* Washington, DC: Brookings Institute. Retrieved September 1, 2017 from www.brookings.edu/research/attention-oecd-pisa-your-silence-on-china-is-wrong/

Organisation for Economic Co-operation and Development. (2015). *Data base PISA 2012.* Retrieved September 2, 2017, from www.oecd.org/pisa/data/pisa2012database-downloadabledata.htm

Organisation for Economic Co-operation and Development. (2009). *Take the test: Sample questions from OECD's PISA assessments.* Paris: OECD Publishing. Retrieved September 1, 2017 from www.oecd.org/edu/school/programmeforinternationalstudentassessmentpisa/pisatakethetestsamplequestionsfromoecdspisaassessments.htm

Powers, J. M., Fischman, G. E., & Berliner, D. C. (2016). Making the visible invisible: Willful ignorance of poverty and social inequalities in the research-policy nexus. *Review of Research in Education, 40,* 744–776. doi:10.3102/0091732X16663703

Rizvi, F., & Lingard, B. (2010). *Globalizing education policy.* London: Routledge.

Ruiz-Primo, M. A., & Li, M. (2015). The relationship between item context characteristics and student performance: The case of the 2006 and 2009 PISA science items. *Teachers*

College Record, *117*(1), 1–36. Retrieved September 1, 2017 from www.tcrecord.org/content.asp?contentid=17728

Sadler, M. (1900). How can we learn anything of practical value from the study of foreign systems of education? In J. H. Higginson (Ed.), *Selections from Michael Sadler: Studies in world citizenship*. Liverpool: Dejall and Meyorre.

Sahlberg, P. (2011). *Finnish lessons: What can the world learn from educational change in Finland?* New York: Teachers College Press.

Schleicher, A. (2009). 'Wie einer auszog, das Lernen zu messen: was den PISA-Erfinder Andreas Schleicher austreibt', Geowissen 44/2009, Retrieved September 2, 2017 from www.buecherkiste.org/-epaper-geowissen-442009-die-ideale-schule.

Sellar, S., Thompson, G., & Rutkowski, D. (2017). *The global education race: Taking the measure of PISA and international testing*. Edmonton: Brush Publishing.

Sjøberg, S. (2007). PISA and "real life challenges": Mission impossible? In S. T. Hopmann, G. Brinek, & M. Retzl (Eds.), *PISA according to PISA* (pp. 203–224). Berlin: LIT Verlag.

Sjøberg, S. (2015). PISA and global educational governance—A critique of the project, its uses and implications. *Eurasia Journal of Mathematics, Science & Technology Education*, *11*(1), 111–127. Retrieved September 1, 2017, from www.academia.edu/10486753/PISA_and_Global_Educational_Governance_A_Critique_of_the_Project_its_Uses_and_Implications

Solano-Flores, G., & Wang, C. (2015). Complexity of illustrations in PISA 2009 science items and its relationship to the performance of students from Shanghai-China, the United States, and Mexico. *Teachers College Record*, *117*(1), 1–18. Retrieved September 1, 2017, from www.tcrecord.org/content.asp?contentid=17725

Wilkinson, R., & Pickett, K. (2010). *The spirit level: Why greater equality makes societies stronger*. London: Penguin.

SECTION III
Large-Scale Assessment as the Production of Numbers

This section explores international large-scale assessments as not just parts in constituting the society and its citizens by chance. For this to happen, the results from the tests have to gain or, at least claim, legitimacy. This is a central discussion in the third section. One way of doing this is to blot out the borders between the results presented in reports emanating from the organizations performing the tests, science, policymaking and media. PISAs use of the social media platform Twitter for communicating their findings is investigated by Miguel A. Pereyra, Antonio Luzón, Mónica Torres and Daniel Torres-Salinas in their chapter *PISA as a Social Media Event: Powering the 'Logics of Competition'*. They capture principles on PISA at work on Twitter such as the decoupling of policy, research and practice. Another example of how the results emanating from international large-scale assessments are traveling is done in the chapter by Christina Elde Mølstad and Daniel Pettersson—*Who Governs the Numbers? The Framing of Educational Knowledge by TIMSS Research*. In this study, the dissemination of '*facts*' from TIMSS into the field of science is investigated. By doing bibliometric research on where and by whom the data from TIMSS are used, they are in a position to present the scientific field of what they call TIMSS research. Finally, *OECD as a Site of Coproduction: The European Education Governance and the New Politics of 'Policy Mobilization'*, written by Sotiria Grek, illustrates how lines are blotted out and how a specific reasoning is gaining legitimacy. The chapter explores how the OECD invites other actors and how in that process legitimacy can be further gained.

10
PISA AS A SOCIAL MEDIA EVENT
Powering the 'Logics of Competition'

Miguel A. Pereyra, Antonio Luzón, Mónica Torres, and Daniel Torres-Salinas

> The Organisation's visibility took a number of significant steps forward again in 2013. Total dissemination of OECD content increased by more than 38% to 16.6 million instances across all publishing platforms (iLibrary, Google books, etc.). Visits to the OECD website reached 16.4 million for all of 2013. The Organisation's presence in social media channels also increased considerably through Twitter, YouTube and Facebook.
> (Secretary-General's Report to Ministers, OECD, 2014, p. 31)

Introduction—Setting the Context

For over a decade, the OECD (Organisation for Economic Co-operation and Development) has conducted a study of the skills and abilities of 15-year-old students about to complete their period of compulsory education. Better known as PISA (Programme for International Student Assessment), this study has not only influenced the educational policies in OECD member states but has also become integral to their economic and social policies. As explored in this book, PISA is used and integrated into assessment and evaluation policies and practices, reorienting the political discourses and agendas about educational reform toward questions of curriculum and standards, understandings of quality and market needs, often putting excessive emphasis on performance targets (Kotthoff & Pereyra, 2009; Martens et al., 2010; Pereyra, Kothoff, & Cowen, 2011; Breakspear, 2012; Lindblad, Pettersson, & Popkewitz, 2015).

PISA does not bring about radical changes in the governance of educational systems but rather it indirectly induces it. PISA indicates how one thinks about the discourse of excellence, results and accountability leading to the emergence of multiple discourses that legitimize certain policies, values and *'cosmovisions'* influencing political and social power (Martens & Jakobi, 2010; Pereyra, Kotthoff, &

Cowen, 2011; Meyer & Benavot, 2013; Sellar & Lingard, 2014, Vromen, 2017). The publication of the PISA results is one of the OECD's most successful products fostering what David K. Kamens (2013) calls a '*horse race mentality*' among participating countries/economies that defines the '*winners*' and '*losers*' and furthers an 'inevitable sense of crisis' (Kamens, 2013, p. 133). The classification of education systems not only creates a new and visible '*global panoptism*' but it also reorients the national education polices (Lingard, Martino, & Rezai-Rashti, 2013). In the last two decades, the OECD has acquired political authority by aligning 'its rational/technical agenda [. . .] with prevailing social values and sentiments' (Eccleston, 2011, p. 248). This agenda, creating a politicized social good (Barnett & Finnemore, 2005), is conveyed through techniques of quantification and visualization, in the form of ratings and rankings (R&R). The R&R has helped to increase the total dissemination of OECD content by more than 38 percent across all publishing platforms including Twitter, YouTube and Facebook as well as Sina Weibo, the largest social media platform in China (OECD, 2014, p. 31).

Our world is largely perceived and understood as a giant collage of striking pictures, sound bites, events and personalities in the news. Our chapter explores a particular aspect of the '*PISA effect*' as a media phenomenon. We view media as practices in the production of languages that enter into and order what becomes the content of culture (see, e.g., Postman, 1985). The digital and social media platforms illustrate the way in which PISA appears as events of today connecting the everyday lives of their audiences to the many channels of participation and discussion (Ytreberg, 2017).

This chapter focuses on PISA's social visibility and the resonance in social networks, and, more specifically, its '*mediatization*' via its dissemination on Twitter. Twitter today has become 'one of the most powerful communication mechanisms in history' (Piscitelli, 2011, p. 15), playing an influential role in social life (cf. Hurst, 2017). Twitter is the fastest growing social network in recent years, with 316 million active users sending 500 million tweets a day (Twitter, 2015). As a micro-blogging site, Twitter presents itself as a kind of agora of the digital age and as a practice of acclamation in three ways (van Dijck, 2013, as quoted in Dean, 2017, p. 427): (1) it claims to be a public space, albeit virtual; (2) it is a kind of 'barometer of emotions and opinions'; and (3) it often deals with relatively evanescent emotional responses. The acclamation through social media involves the formation not only of different opinions of atomized and privatized subjects but also of a public mood and social sentiment from the forms of orality and gestures they make available. As Dean (2017, p. 420) states:

> The formation of this new public mood places us on the threshold of the emergence of a new domain of politico-technical calculability and manipulation based on the aggregates of digital data produced and recorded on social media. Moreover, the religious, ritual and liturgical elements of acclamation remain eminent on social media.

PISA as a Media Event

In the first independent publication critical of PISA, the authors Hopmann and Brinek (2007) discuss the methodological merits and shortcomings of PISA in relation to its validity and reliability of its claims. One of their major criticisms is that PISA designers do not attend to PISA restraints but instead reference opaque technical reports that only insiders can understand. Recently, Xavier Pons (2017) produced a review of the mainly qualitative literature on the effects of PISA related to governance of education and the political processes underlining the main theoretical, epistemological and methodological challenges that PISA provokes. While Pons addresses the notion of the PISA effect, he does not measure the marginal effect of PISA on governance.

Despite the fact that there is not a broader view of the PISA effect and its effects on political actors or policy texts, PISA is one of the most important media events in recent decades. The number of students and countries that have taken part in each of the assessments has increased sharply, growing from 250,000 students from 32 countries in 2000 to 565,000 students from 75 countries in 2016. In addition to the sharp increase in the number of students and countries taking part in PISA, the media importance of PISA has also surged, affecting existing practices, policies and structures by introducing new models of educational governance (Steiner-Khamsi, 2014). Meyer and Benavot (2013) claim that one of the effects of PISA has been the contribution of a 'new mode of global education governance in which state sovereignty over educational matters is replaced by the influence of large-scale international organizations' (Meyer & Benavot, 2013, p. 10).

Governance by coordination is exemplified by the OECD's capacity to guide the work of important stakeholders through the organizing of conferences and meetings that offer a space in which experts can discuss these issues. The data, reports and actions of PISA lead to discourses on the transnational regulation of education which generate a specific form of knowledge for educational policy (Carvalho, 2009). Governance by opinion-forming denotes the creation and influencing of education-related discourses (Henry et al., 2001; Sellar & Lingard, 2014).[1] This influence leads member states to have a common language that guides them toward similar goals. Governance by instruments signifies the regulations that the OECD member states agree to abide by as members of the organization. This refers to their capacity to transform common objectives into specific political proposals by means of international agreements. This gives the OECD a very powerful influence, as it issues regulations that can be applied directly to its members and with which they are obliged to comply (Martens, Knodel, & Windzio, 2014).

In addition to these three dimensions, PISA has also enabled the creation of a global space to standardize and measure education indicators and make comparisons between countries that often have diametrically opposed educational systems, socio-economic levels and cultural standards. PISA has led to a new form of governance in education, which promotes and spreads a type of '*instrumental reason*' based on a conception of science that prioritizes the prediction and control of the reality of our society over the adaptation of ways of proceeding to goals, ways that are generally accepted and, therefore, not debated (as explained by Max Horkheimer in his 1947 well-known *Eclipse of Reason*). PISA consolidates what is known as the '*comparative turn*' (Grek, 2009) or '*governance by comparison*' (Nóvoa & Yariv-Mashal, 2003) in which data has become a powerful instrument as techniques of governance are embedded in the metrics, statistics, databases, rankings and comparisons of policymaking:

> Democratic mentalities of government prioritize and seek to produce a relationship between numerate citizens, numericized civic discourse and numerate evaluations of government. Democracy can operate as a technology of government to the extent that such a network of numbers can be composed and stabilized. In analysis of democracy, a focus on numbers is instructive for it helps us turn our eyes from grand texts of philosophy to the mundane practices of pedagogy, of accounting, of information and polling, and to the mundane knowledge and 'grey sciences' that support them.
> *(Rose, 1999, p. 232)*

PISA is a media event because it triggers, justifies and/or legitimizes educational reforms. For example, in Germany, poor ranking results published in PISA 2000 inaugural document created social '*shock*' thereby convincing politicians fearful of future economic failure to introduce a wide range of educational reforms in the following year (Fend, 2011; Bank, 2012).[2]

In other countries, such as Spain, PISA has helped form hegemonic discourses about education and educational policies and practices through the establishment of frames for what is thinkable and reasonable (Bonal & Tarabini, 2013). In order to resolve their poor performance in PISA, some countries even resort to solutions which are offered and sold to them within what is known as the global education industry (Kamens, 2013).

But the decisive factor that converts PISA into a media event is the enormous interest it generates within the media, on social networks and in society in general. Figazzolo (2009) argues that the publication of the PISA results has created an enormous level of anticipation not only within the different tiers of government, but also in the mass media. The media reception of PISA has fashioned a complex process of '*mediatization*' (Rawolle & Lingard, 2014). The dynamics of the mass media and its products operate in the production of meaning. According to Rawolle and Lingard (2014), the relation produced in PISA between educational policy and the effects of journalism on education and its practices is a genuine, specific form of mediatization, in which different forms of discourse seeking to maintain their influence create multiple interests. The process of mediatization involves a transformation at a symbolic level in which media are sources not only of information but also of construction of collective imaginaries (Mata, 2005).

The media's increased interest toward global educational ideas and narratives about education has affected the debates about educational policies in spite of the national and local impacts they may have (Wiseman, 2013; Steiner-Khamsi, 2014). Over the last decade, various research studies have analyzed the media's reception of PISA. The OECD's most significant media event follows very carefully defined media strategies for the dissemination of the results using wide media coverage at the international level through the website https://webcast.ec.europa.eu/pisa-launch-event# and different media platforms. The results are always published in a media event taking place in global cities the first week of December after the tests are held. The OECD shares the results with journalists before the event, but they cannot publish the results until they are officially released by the OECD. So, a few weeks before the PISA results are released, a notification is sent to a list of 4,500 journalists alerting them to the imminent publication of PISA results (Lingard, 2016).

The organizations responsible for the administration of PISA in each country also contribute to the research by making their own specific reports and specific press-friendly documents (Rawolle & Lingard, 2014). These reports are normally focused on the most general aspects of the test and on the competition in terms of results between the countries taking part. This is expressed in the form of league tables as well as data referring to quality and equity aspects (Wiseman, 2013). Although the PISA effect and the way its results have been represented in the media have been analyzed from different academic perspectives, the mediatization of the dissemination of the data is a field that is relatively unexplored.[3]

Social media plays a central role in the media strategy orchestrated by the OECD. As stated in its OECD (2014): 'The OECD continued to expand its traditional and social media presence during 2013, with the timing and nature of press events and publication launches frequently timed to complement major international events, capitalizing on the worldwide media attention' (Annual Report, 2013, p. 34). The OECD's Media Unit and its Directorate of Education and Skills have used Twitter to actively promote the PISA results presentation. As stated in the Secretary-General's *Report to Ministers* (2014), on the day on which the results of PISA 2013 were released, there was an important peak of activity with 612,000 visits to their website (10 times more than average) and a 150 percent increase in the number of Twitter followers; by the end of 2013, the OECD had a total of 355,000 followers on Twitter.

Scope and Method

We analyzed the social perspective of the 'PISA phenomenon' from its presence on social networks, particularly Twitter, which is increasingly used in the dissemination of activities of this kind (Álvarez-Bornstein & Montesi, 2016; Hurst, 2017). We opted for Twitter because of its increasing importance in society, the way it disseminates information, its ease of access and the particular characteristics of this form of micro-blogging in the transmission of messages in a direct, personal way that also encourages interaction.

Twitter offers users and organizations the chance to post a tweet, that is, a short message of up to 280 characters. Once the tweet has been posted, other users and/or organizations can share it using the hashtag. A hashtag (#) is a keyword assigned to a piece of information that describes a tweet and organizes the discussion about a specific event or topic. In this way, it is easier for individuals to get involved in more specific discussions, by following or tweeting certain hashtags. Second, Twitter enables interesting and complex discursive interactions that allow people to develop new forms of relating to each other. This in turn changes the way people relate to technology, creating what has been dubbed '*digital citizenship*' in the era of social networks (Vromen, 2017). As a result, Twitter has become a question of great interest for scholars from many disciplines including computer science, psychology, sociology and education.

We studied Twitter's responses of the 2015 PISA results by analyzing 11,386 tweets gathered between December 6 and 14, 2016, the week after results were published. To extract this data, we used the Chrome extension 'Twitter Archive' with the following search content #pisa2015 or #pisaoecd or #pisaOECD. We selected the day on which the results were launched because as a deliberate part of the OECD's communication strategy, this has become a genuine '*media circus*', in that it contains rituals of conquest or coronation which are broadcasted live, preplanned and presented with reverence and ceremony (Gilboa, 2005).

In addition to the spatial and temporal dimension described earlier, the aim of our analysis was to discover the authorship and content of the tweets in order to understand how a specific narrative is assembled through the message. We decided to conduct a critical discourse analysis by focusing on the process, context and situation in which the narratives appear in order to identify and understand the '*semantic macrostructures*' derived from the (micro) structures of meaning, the themes of the discourse and their orientation (Van Dijk, 1980). The large number of tweets in our research made an in-depth analysis very difficult, so we decided to analyze one of the most important communicative devices, the retweet. The retweet (hereinafter, RT) saves time and space in an established conversation, making it more effective. According to Mancera Rueda and Pano Alamán (2013), the RT performs a communicative function of recognition. When a message is forwarded to others, we are recognizing its authority on the information that is being shared; it also has a dialogue function when we seek to converse with somebody by inserting "@usuario" in the message. In this way, it allows a choir of voices who support or reject what we are saying to be included in the discourse and it, therefore, becomes a fundamental strategy in communication policy and in the formation of public opinion on Twitter, as it offers users the chance to take up another person's discourse for argument and persuasion purposes.

The Reception of PISA on Twitter: The Results

We used the Google Trends tool to ascertain the number of visits to the OECD website in a 4-hour period during the immediate release of the 2015 PISA report. During this time, the highest frequencies were recorded in Sweden, Finland and Belgium followed by Hungary, Denmark, Canada and Norway (See Figure 10.1):

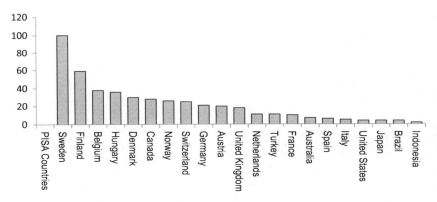

FIGURE 10.1 The Launch of PISA 2015 (Between 10:28 Hours and 14:28 Hours) The countries with the highest impacts in terms of the number of visits to the OECD website during the launch at the OECD headquarters on December 6, 2016.

By contrast, there were considerably fewer visits from countries such as Spain, Italy, the United States and Brazil (see Figure 10.1). The reaction to the Report on Twitter showed 7,629 users posted a total of 11,386 tweets, which were then retweeted 407,306 times.[4] Table 10.1 shows the breakdown of tweets per country. With regard to the busiest period of posting and exchanging information, 50 percent of the tweets were published during the event broadcast over the first 11 hours (Figure 10.2). As days went, by the activity on Twitter diminished considerably. This information reaffirms Twitter's capacity to inform in real time and the possibility of immediate feedback as a microblogging tool.

TABLE 10.1 Number of Tweets per Location, Top 10 Countries

Country	Number of Tweets
Spain	535
United Kingdom	350
France	329
Uruguay	279
Mexico	244
Argentina	185
United States	177
Chile	162
Sweden	165
Finland	156

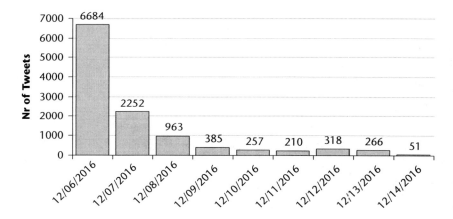

FIGURE 10.2 Number of Tweets by Day

The Making of What Is Normal and What Is Pathological: The Voice of the Winners and Losers on Twitter

Similar to other media studies of PISA, we found that the discourses of PISA in tweets tended to emphasize the aspects related with rankings or league tables (Takayama, 2008; Figazzolo, 2009; Pons, 2011; Martens & Niemann, 2013). PISA functions in a manner analogous to a system of global positioning or geolocation. As Popkewitz states: 'PISA globally positions the child and the nation through a style of thought that differentiates and divides through the creation *categories of equivalence among countries*' (Popkewitz, 2011, p. 36, emphasis added). By exclusively valuing tweets, we are faced with an important dichotomy between those countries who consider themselves '*winners*' and '*losers*' and between countries who offer a good education and others with more mediocre results (Bolívar, 2011). Here are some examples of tweets which were retweeted from countries or regions considered as successful:

[RT @KemPendidikan: CONGRATULATIONS !!.. Results # PISA2015 #OECDPISA Malaysia increased (Translation courtesy of Google Translator).

This tweet was sent from the Malaysian Government's official account and was retweeted 18,522 times.

[RT @ccifuentes: Success of education in Madrid: #PISA2015 puts our students in the worldwide elite in Reading and Sciences]

This tweet was sent from the official account of the President of the Regional Government of Madrid to praise the results of 15-year-old students in Madrid and retweeted on 15,344 occasions by some members of the governing political party and university professors (@ManueldeBuenaga).

Messages such as these seek to glorify and celebrate the results, linking them to the world's elite and associating them with the countries that have become models for others to follow, such as Finland:

[RT @educacyl: #PISA2015: Castilla y León achieves the best academic results of all of Spain's regions]

This tweet was retweeted 11,088 times and was sent from the official account of the Ministry of Education of the Regional Government of Castilla y León. Unlike the message from the President of the Madrid Region, this message was not retweeted by any official Twitter account of the Partido Popular. Instead, the tweet created a conversation between different educational stakeholders.

[@josemherrera80 good results cannot be achieved without good preparatory work". We have to measure what has been achieved in some way.]
[@laclasedejavier The only things that matters is results? We have to tell our students that results are the only thing that matters? I'm sorry but no.]

Far from glorifying the results, these two tweets offer a critical discourse by educational stakeholders in which they champion the work done by teachers and the usefulness of the tests for improving schools.

[RT @junqueras: The work to promote equity, inclusion and the continuous effort made by the schools produce results and educational successes #PISA2015 https://...]

This tweet was retweeted on 7,872 occasions. It was sent from the account of the Vice-President of the Regional Government of Catalonia. It has a triumphalist tone celebrating the results obtained in PISA while also recognizing the work done by the schools. The message produced an extensive conversation in which participants questioned for example the fact that the author made no mention of social inequality data.

5. RT @pasi_sahlberg: Canada now hosts the top school systems in the @ OECD by #PISA2015: Quebec, British Columbia, Alberta & Ontario https://t . . .

This tweet was retweeted 8,633 times. Unlike the previous tweets, this one was sent from the personal account of Pasi Sahlberg, who describes himself in his profile as an 'author, educator and change-maker'. In this case, the tweet generated a debate that went beyond the statistics and analyzed various moments in the live broadcasting of the event and presentation of the results.

In addition to those from the countries at the top of the world ranking, some of the most retweeted tweets were from the '*losers*'. Here are three significant messages from countries that are geographically and culturally different: the Dominican Republic, the Netherlands and Brazil.

[RT @educaindicador: Dreadful results from #RepúblicaDominicana #PISA2015 https://t.co/V8LlSho36X]

This tweet was retweeted 14,490 times and was widely followed in Spain and in different associations with links to Latin America. It is interesting to note that in the hyperlink included in the message (https://t.co/V8LlSho36X), they do not refer to the results obtained by the Dominican Republic, but to those obtained by one of the countries that has recently become a model for others to follow, Singapore ([@cooperaciónIB. Singapore heads the latest PISA survey on education carried out by the OECD worldwide]).

[RT @Lezenschrijven: Nearly 18% of Dutch 15-year-olds has a language delay. An increase of 6.4% relative to 2003. #Pisa2015 https://t. . . .] (Translation courtesy of Google Translator)

This tweet was retweeted 7,740 times and was sent from an official account of the foundation responsible for encouraging literacy in the Netherlands. The information they highlight from the PISA results (the fact that many Dutch students are behind in language skills) is directly related to the purpose of the foundation.

[RT @novaescola: Saiu o #Pisa2015! Brazil is stagnant in science and reading and fell in mathematics. Check it: https://t.co/RvKWLobtnr http. . .]. (Translation courtesy of Google Translator)

This tweet was retweeted 6,816 times and was sent from an official account of the Nova Escola Foundation, a non-profit-making institution that, according to its website, aims to transform Brazilian education by providing high-quality content and services for teachers and managers in the Brazilian education system.

As we can see, these messages, from either political or educational stakeholders, make very general assertions or come to conclusions of little statistical value, beyond those evident in the league tables themselves. In some way, they contribute to creating global discourses about '*good*' or '*bad*' educational systems, or in the making of '*normalcy*' or '*pathology*' frequently excluding criticisms leveled by teachers and researchers. The OECD's communication strategy is geared toward providing information in a clear and simplistic way about the quality of the educational systems and in particular about their performance. As a result, most people whose only knowledge of PISA comes through the media or social media tend to compress various pages of complex analyses by the OECD into overly simplistic ideas such as 'our schools are failing', 'we have the best system in the world' or 'we have an educational crisis'.

Looking Beyond the Ranking: Excellence and Equity or How 'Truth Is Said' About Society and Schooling

In addition to the previous comments on their country's position in the ranking, the tweets also discussed a more critical perspective of the results. These included discussions about equity and quality, public spending and teaching practices at schools. Here are some of the most significant:

> RT @pasi_sahlberg: Lesson from Finland's #PISA2015: Equity & excellence come and go together. When you're in austerity, the smallest & weakest suffer the most.

This tweet, by Pasi Sahlberg, was retweeted 22,046 times. This tweet presents a substantially different discourse from those analyzed previously in that it introduces the concepts of equity and excellence and the need for the two to be linked. It refers to a period of economic crisis of global consequences with clear effects on education.

> [RT @Uhandrea: Relation between the results #PISA2015 (average scores for the three skills) and ESEC (Socio-economic and Cultural Status) for the CC...]

This tweet was retweeted 20,286 times. It was sent from the official account of a Physiology Professor and Chair in Scientific Culture at the University of the Basque Country. In addition to the text, this user illustrates his message with a graph from the PISA results report, which compares the average overall score for the three skills measured in PISA (sciences, reading and mathematics) and

Socioeconomic and Cultural Status (ESEC). Of all the tweets we analyzed, this was the one that generated the largest conversation about the data:

> [RT @CooperacionIB: The #PISA2015 Report and education spending | The Teacher's Tales | @elprofedefisica https://t.co/Il9X52rwAe]

This tweet was retweeted 13,804 times. It was sent from the official account of Cooperación Iberoamericana, a foundation that works in cooperation in Education and Science. In their Twitter profile, they define themselves as specialists in designing, implementing and advising on online education. This message is very similar to the previous one because they analyze the relationship between public spending and scores in science. As well as showing the data, it also has a link to a blog on education (Arturo Quirantes, blog) entitled The PISA Report 2015 and education spending.

In all these messages, certain statistical indicators provided by PISA are causally related with certain political discourses of equity and excellence. This causal relationship occurs between the results offered by PISA and certain public inputs such as public expenditure on education. In these messages, the numbers generated by PISA can be seen as '*facts*' and a way of '*telling the truth*' about society, schooling and children, and because PISA narratives are built on this '*truth*' about national schooling systems, it enables a comparison between them through a supposed equivalence and objectivity (Popkewitz, 2011).

PISA as an Instrument of Legalization/Externalization for the Implementation of Educational Reforms

Some messages refer to the need to design and develop educational reforms on the basis of PISA results. This representation has also been noted in studies about PISA in the media. Generally, these crisis discourses prior to the legitimization of educational reforms arise as a result of the mismatch between public perception of the educational system and the PISA results. For our analysis of this aspect of the PISA effect, we chose this tweet about Mexico:

> RT @aurelionuno: The results of #PISA2015 confirm the urgent need to advance in the implementation of the #ReformaEducativa—Educational Reform].

This tweet was retweeted 17,415 times. It was sent from the official account of the Secretary for Public Education in Mexico, a leading political player. In this case, the PISA results did not trigger a reform movement but instead provided a justification for advancing the implementation of an educational reform process that was already underway.

In this case, as asserted by Zorrilla, PISA, acts as an outside independent voice with the legitimacy and the recognition provided by its status as an international test which demonstrates to public opinion that 'there are very serious problems that must be attended to and if not the country will have to face the consequences in terms of backwardness, inequality and lack of competitiveness' (Zorrilla, 2009, p. 80). This is also an example of what Steiner-Khamsi (2003) described as political reactions in which those concerned claim to be '*shocked*' by the weakness of the educational systems in their respective countries.

In these messages, we can identify what Addey et al. (2017) called '*evidence for policy*', that is, PISA provides evident data for policymaking and the rise of audit cultures. PISA

> has been accompanied by the rise of policy as numbers, and the use of comparative data as a mode of governance in education linked to top-down, test-based modes of accountability [. . .] [However] the PISA data provides another set of evidences for policy-making [although] this evidence does not always result in policy learning or borrowing but more often results in externalization.
>
> *(Lingard, 2016, p. 617)*

Externalization

> refers to the nations using the PISA results to drive reforms that are already underway, using the PISA performance as an argument as a legitimate narrative. PISA has also provoked the construction of new reference societies or reference systems for national schooling systems.
>
> *(Lingard, 2016, p. 611; also see Sellar & Lingard, 2014)*

This was the case of Finland from 2000 to 2009 because of its outstanding PISA performance, which enhanced an educational tourism to this Nordic country by policymakers from around the world.

Concluding Remarks

PISA has become a media event at a global level in spite of the fact that its reception varies greatly between one country/region and the next. This study focuses on how the launch of the results of PISA 2015 was received on social media and in particular on the micro-blogging network Twitter, as a practice of acclamation that has contrived not only the formation of a '*public opinion*' from different individual expressions and/or international organizations like the OECD, but also a public mood related to an inevitable state of crisis and competition, as already stated in this contribution. The presentation of the results on December 6, 2016, produced a sharp peak in online activity, increasing the number of followers of the OECD on Twitter by 150 percent. This strategy of communication and dissemination of PISA results decidedly promoted by the OECD is part of its ability to promote PISA as a social good. In this sense, tweets imply evaluative quantification and visualization that convey comparative distinctions that favor the creation of a logic of the competition in the sense that we have expressed.

Our results show that although there was interest from countries all over the world, there were considerable geographic variations. Most of the countries taking part were from the Americas and Europe, especially Spain, whereas the representation of Asian and African countries was considerably lower. The most active stakeholders in this process were from the political and educational spheres. Among the retweets, we noted three distinguishable discourses: the first was related to the perception of PISA as *'league tables'*. The messages were linked not only with a particular country's position in the table but also with the interpretation of this position as an educational and/or political success or failure. The second discourse was related to a more critical reading of the results and looked beyond a simple observation regarding the position occupied by a particular country in the ranking. In this case, the messages included references to other indicators analyzed by the OECD, producing a discourse on equity and excellence and their relation with other educational indicators such as public spending or performance in each of the different skills analyzed. Finally, the third discourse refers to the use of PISA as a tool for initiating *'necessary'* educational reforms to improve the results or to legitimize educational reforms that are already underway. As we argue, PISA establishes frameworks to help us understand what is thinkable and doable. The communication strategy of the PISA results through Twitter is an effective way of transmitting the OECD rationale that generates a wide diffusion of 'its' own way of thinking and *'truth telling'* of education systems.

Notes

1. Some authors view the OECD as a *think tank* or factory of ideas which generates knowledge or even as an important *'epistemic community'* (an important network of professionals from different fields with recognized experience and skills in different areas) who aspire to reach a hegemonic position in our times (Kallo, 2009; Addey, 2016; Normand, 2016).
2. This movement of educational reforms has been implemented in comparison with previous reforms that occurred during the 20th century, which were in general not fully achieved. Moreover, PISA has also produced in Germany—a European country with the largest academic body in its higher education institutions related to the field of education—a rather notorious consolidation in its educational sciences of a so-called *Empirische Wendung* in educational research, which is also concerning to the field of educational theory.
3. See, for example, the paper by Waldow, Takayama, and Sung (2014), in which they analyze how the media in Australia, Germany and South Korea reported the successful results of the *'Asian Tiger'* countries in PISA 2009 and how these reports exerted media pressure on the governments of these countries.

4. The location of the tweets was made on the basis of the location of the Twitter accounts. Not all users had geolocated their accounts, so the table shows those who were not known as location unknown. This counted for 3,800 tweets.

References

Addey, C. (2016). PISA for development and the sacrifice of policy relevant data. *Educação & Sociedade* (Campinas), *37*(136), 685–706.

Addey, C., Sellar, S., Steiner-Khamsi, G., Lingard, B., & Verger, A. (2017). The rise of international large-scale assessments and rationales for participation. *Compare: A Journal of Comparative and International Education*, *47*(3), 434–452.

Álvarez-Bornstein, B., & Montesi, M. (2016). La comunicación entre investigadores en Twitter. Una etnografía virtual en el ámbito de las ciencias de la documentación. *Revista Española de Documentación Científica*, *39*(4), 1–15.

Bank, V. (2012). On OECD policies and the pitfalls in economy-driven education: The case of Germany. *Journal of Curriculum Studies*, *44*(2), 193–210.

Barnett, M., & Finnemore, M. (2005). The power of liberal international organization. In M. Barnett, & R. Duvall (Eds.), *Power in global governance* (pp. 161–184). Cambridge: Cambridge University Press.

Bolívar, A. (2011). The dissatisfaction of the losers: PISA public discourse in Ibero-American countries. In M. A. Pereyra, H.-G. Kothoff, & R. Cowen (Eds.), *PISA under examination. changing knowledge, changing test, and changing schools* (pp. 61–73). Rotterdam: Sense Publisher.

Bonal, X., & Tarabini, A. (2013). The role of PISA in shaping hegemonic educational discourses, policies, and practices: The case of Spain. *Research in Comparative and International Education*, *8*(3), 335–341.

Breakspear, S. (2012). *The policy impact of PISA: An exploration of the normative effects of international benchmarking in school system performance.* OECD Working Papers, N° 71, OECD Publishing, Paris.

Carvalho, L. M. (2009). Production of OCDE's. Programme for International Student Assessment (PISA). *Knowledge and Policy Project.* Retrieved from www.knowandpol.eu

Carvalho, L. M., & Costa, E. (2014). Seeing education with one's own eyes and through PISA lenses: Considerations of the reception of PISA in European countries. *Discourse: Studies in the Cultural Politics of Education*, *36*(1), 1–9.

Dean, M. (2017). Political acclamation, social media, and the public mood. *European Journal of Social Theory*, *20*(3), 417–434.

Eccleston, R. (2011). The OECD and global economic governance. *Australian Journal of International Affairs*, *65*(2), 243–255.

Fend, H. (2011). New governance of education. Potentials of reform and risks of failure. In D. Tröhler & R. Barbu (Eds.), *Education systems in historical, cultural, and sociological perspectives* (pp. 39–53). Rotterdam: Sense.

Figazzolo, L. (2009). *Testing, ranking, reforming: Impact of Pisa 2006 on the Education Policy Debate.* Brussels: Education International.

Gilboa, E. (2005). The CNN effect: The search for a communication theory of international relations. *Political Communication*, *22*(1), 27–44.

Grek, S. (2009). Governing by numbers: The PISA 'effect' in Europe. *Journal of Education Policy*, *24*(1), 23–37.

Henry, M., Lingard, B., Rizvi, F., & Taylor, S. (2001). *The OECD, globalization, and education policy*. Oxford: Elsevier Science Ltd.

Hopmann, S. T., & Brinek, G. (2007). Introduction: PISA according to PISA—Does PISA keep what it promises? In S. T. Hopmann, G. Brinek, & M. Retzl (Eds.), *PISA zufolge PISA—PISA according to PISA: Hält PISA, was es verspricht?—Does PISA keep what it promises?* (pp. 9–19). Vienna: LIT VERLAG.

Horkheimer, M. (1947). *Eclipse of reason* (Reprint, Continuum International Publishing Group, 2004). Oxford: Oxford University Press.

Hurst, T. M. (2017). The discursive construction of superintendent statesmanship on Twitter. *Education Policy Analysis Archives, 25*(29). Retrieved from http://epaa.asu.edu/ojs/article/view/2300

Kallo, J. (2009). *OECD educational policy*. Jyväskylä: Jyväskylä University Press.

Kamens, D. H. (2013). Globalization and the emergence of an audit culture: PISA and the search for 'best practices' and magic bullets. In H. D. Meyer & A. Benavot, (Eds.), *PISA, power, and policy the emergence of global educational governance*. Oxford: Symposium.

Kotthoff, H. G., & Pereyra, M. A. (2009). La experiencia del PISA en Alemania. *Profesorado. Revista de Curriculum y Formación del Profesorado, 13*(2). Monograph issue. Retrieved from www.ugr.es/~recfpro/?p=435

Lindblad, S., Pettersson, D., & Popkewitz, T. S. (2015). *International comparisons of school results: A systematic review of research on large-scale assessments in education*. Stockholm: Swedish Research Council.

Lingard, B. (2016). Rationales for and reception of the OECD's PISA. *Educação & Sociedade* (Campinas), *37*(136), 609–627.

Lingard, B., Martino, W., & Rezai-Rashti, G. (2013). Testing regimes, accountabilities and education policy: Commensurate global and national developments. *Journal of Education Policy, 28*(5), 539–556.

Mancera, A., & Pano Alemán, A. (2013). *El español coloquial en las redes sociales*. Madrid: Arco Libros.

Martens, K., & Jakobi, A. J. (2010). Expanding and intensifying governance: The OECD in education policy. In K. Martens & A. P. Jakobi (Eds.), *Mechanisms of OECD governance: International incentives for national policy-making?* (pp. 163–179). Oxford: Oxford University Press.

Martens, K., Knodel, P., & Windzio, M. (2014). *Internationalization of education policy: A new constellation of statehood in education?* Basingstoke: Palgrave Macmillan.

Martens, K., Nagel, A. K., Windzio, M., & Weymann, A. (2010). *Transformation of educational policy*. London & New York: Palgrave-Macmillan.

Martens, K., & Niemann, D. (2013). When do numbers count? The differential impact of the PISA rating and ranking on education policy in Germany and the US. *German Politics, 22*(3), 314–332.

Mata, M. C. (2005). Los medios masivos en el estudio de la comunicación/cultura. *Conexão—Comunicação e Cultura, 4*(8), 13–21.

Meyer, H-D., & Benavot, A. (2013). *PISA, power, and policy the emergence of global educational governance*. Oxford: Symposium Books.

Normand, R. (2016). *The changing epistemic governance of European education: The fabrication of the Homo Academicus Europeanus?* Dordrecht: Springer.

Nóvoa, A., & Yariv-Mashal, T. (2003). Comparative research in education: A mode of governance or a historical journey? *Comparative Education, 39*(4), 423–438.

OECD. (2014). *Secretary-General's report to ministers, 2014*. Paris: OECD Publishing.

Pereyra, M. A., Kothoff, H.-G., & Cowen, R. (Eds.). (2011). *PISA under examination: Changing knowledge, changing tests and changing schools*. Rotterdam: Sense Publisher.
Piscitelli, A. (2011). Twitter, la revolución y los enfoques ni-ni. In J. L. Orihuela, *Mundo Twitter*. Barcelona: Alienta.
Pons, X. (2011). *L'évaluation des politiques éducatives*. Paris: Presses Universitaires de France.
Pons, X. (2017). Fifteen years of research on PISA effects on education governance: Critical review. *European Journal Education*, *52*(2), 131–144.
Popkewitz, T. S. (2009). The double gestures of cosmopolitanism, globalization, and comparative studies of education. In R. Cowen & A. M. Kazamias (Eds.), *International handbook of comparative education* (pp. 379–395). Dordrecht, The Netherlands: Springer Science.
Popkewitz, T. S. (2011). Numbers, standardizing conduct, and the alchemy of school subjects. In M. A. Pereyra; R. Cowen, & H.-G. Kothoff (Eds.), *PISA under examination: Changing knowledge, changing tests, and changing schools* (pp. 31–46). Rotterdam: Sense Publishers.
Postman, N. (1985). *Amusing ourselves to death: Public discourse in the agency of spectacle*. Athens: Dromeas.
Rawolle, S., & Lingard, B. (2014). Mediatization and education: A sociological account. In L. Knut (Ed.), *Mediatization of communication* (pp. 595–614). Berlin: De Gruyter Mouton.
Rose, N. (1999). *Powers of freedom*. Cambridge: Cambridge University Press.
Sellar, S., & Lingard, R. (2014). The OECD and the expansion of PISA: New global modes of governance in education. *British Educational Research Journal*, *40*(6), 917–936.
Steiner-Khamsi, G. (2014). Cross-national policy borrowing: Understanding reception and translation. *Asia Pacific Journal of Education*, *34*(2), 153–167.
Steiner-Khamsi, G. (2003). The politics of league tables. *Journal of Social Science Education*, 1. doi:10.4119/UNIBI/jsse-v2-i1-470
Takayama, K. (2008). The politics of international league tables: PISA in Japan's achievement crisis debate. *Comparative Education*, *44*(4), 387–407.
Twitter. (2015). *About company*. Retrieved from https//about.twitter.com/company
Van Dijk, T. (1980). *Texto y contexto Semántica y pragmática del discurso*. Madrid: Cátedra.
Vromen, A. (2017). Social media use for political engagement. In A. Vromen (Ed.), *Digital citizenship and political engagement: The challenge from online campaigning and advocacy organisations* (pp. 51–75). Basingstoke: Palgrave Macmillan.
Waldow, F., Takayama, K., & Sung, Y. (2014). Rethinking the pattern of external policy referencing: Media discourses over the 'Asian Tigers' PISA success in Australia, Germany, and South Korea. *Comparative Education*, *50*(3), 302–321.
Wiseman, A. W. (2013). Policy responses to PISA in comparative perspective. In H. Meyer & A. Benavot (Eds.), *PISA, power, and policy: The emergence of global educational governance* (pp. 303–322). Oxford: Symposium Books.
Ytreberg, E. (2017). Towards a historical understanding of the media event. *Media, Culture & Society*, *39*(1), 309–324.
Zorrilla Alcalá, J. F. (2009). El efecto de los resultados de PISA sobre la política educativa de México. In A. Teodoro & A. Montané (Eds.), *Espejo y reflejo: Políticas curriculares y evaluaciones internacionales* (pp. 113–129). Alzira: Germania

11

WHO GOVERNS THE NUMBERS?

The Framing of Educational Knowledge by TIMSS Research

Christina Elde Mølstad and Daniel Pettersson

Introduction

In contemporary society, different tests of educational performance have been given importance in educational research, policy initiatives and curriculum change as well as in media. Consequently, performance in schools has been increasingly judged on the basis of effective student learning outcomes. One of the most active agencies in performing international comparative tests is the IEA—International Association for the Evaluation of Educational Achievement. The IEA has a history dating back to the 1950s (for a discussion on the history of the IEA see, e.g., Pettersson, 2014), and since 1995 an international large-scale assessment with the acronym TIMSS repetitively has been launched. TIMSS, together with other tests staged by either the IEA or other international organizations, has gradually transformed into reference points for general economic and social policies (Pettersson, 2014). In this context, the phenomenon of international large-scale assessments (ILSA) are serving a global governance constituted by a specific reasoning (cf. Hacking, 1992) connected to the use of numbers. ILSA research, for example, studies using data or results from TIMSS, is based on numbers constructed for partly governance reasons and is a growing interdisciplinary and increasingly international field of study (Lindblad, Pettersson, & Popkewitz, 2015). Hence, the scientific development of the field is highly relevant to analyze. However, it is surprisingly few educational studies that have made use of the data rapidly accumulating with the development of various databases and software. Given the importance of this numbered educational discourse as a social and scientific practice, we propose that it is crucial to take into account how this discourse is framed through different written formats.

We highlight that one important way to investigate both societal and scientific reasoning is to analyze the role played by scientific literature. The research methodology of bibliometrics has demonstrated a potential in using research databases for studying patterns of research activity. Various studies (e.g., Domínguez, Vieira, & Vidal, 2012) have shown how investigating research literature can be both a viable and important aspect of scientific endeavor. What is discussed less is how educational research is transported and transformed at the interface of different scientific fields where varying outcomes and academic capital are interchanged. Also, citation information of scientific papers has long been recognized by bibliometric scholars as indicative of the theoretical and empirical foundations of a study (e.g., Small, 1973; Glänzel & Schoepflin, 1994; Leydesdorff, 1995; Glänzel & Schoepflin, 1999;). Yet, references cited in articles, or citing articles, have become a widely used measure in bibliometric studies that identify trends that develops within research fields and network of authors (e.g., Borgman, 1990; McCain, 1990; White, 1990; White & McCain, 1997).

The main objective of the current study is to visualize and discuss scientific patterns in a specific corpus of research constituted by articles reporting and discussing TIMSS data. From these visualizations, we highlight some conclusions for further discussions. Our interest is primarily focused on the process of legitimating scientific activity and how this is organized. Methodologically, we use research results, as recounted in articles published in international peer-reviewed journals. We use what we call a corpus of articles limited to the most cited articles using or discussing TIMSS data. Focus is on journals, nationalities, authors' affiliations and authors, making it possible to highlight some organizational characteristics of TIMSS research as a scholarly activity. In this handling, we investigate how researchers cross-reference each other and how, in doing so, they establish legitimacy for certain arguments and bits of knowledge (Kandlbinder, 2015). This is conducted by visualizing bibliometric networks and as such we conduct what has been called '*science mapping*' (Van Eck & Waltman, 2014). As such, we are able to explore who inhabits and cultivate a body of academic knowledge (Becher & Trowler, 2001). Our intention is also that the results may serve as a reference useful to guide further study of TIMSS research.

The IEA and TIMSS: Comparative Knowledge Construction

The IEA, was created on a reasoning to conduct comparative studies of educational performance in the late 1950s—staging their first ILSA in the early 1960s—in order to understand more about the effects of educational policies and practices, and hence creating a new typology of educational '*facts*' and '*truths*', based on numbered data. Yet, as a research venture, the IEA was able to foster the exchange of information and numbered data to a technology for educational comparisons, the proliferation of numbered data in education and establish itself as a space for educational comparisons. Further, the IEA laid a foundation for international large-scale assessments and conceptualized a content and methodology used within the ILSA sphere (Pettersson, 2014). However, the organization and its activities also constructed a specific educational language that affected how education, and especially educational performances, was expressed and communicated.

The IEA's purpose was initially said to perform different assessments to make inferences about intellectual functioning from multiple-choice items, to test the feasibility of large-scale assessments and to be exploratory (Foshay, Thorndike, & Hotyat, 1962). Hence, in the beginning, the studies were something new that differed from other, at that time present, comparative studies, mainly because the organization and its activities introduced an empirical approach (by Rouvroy, 2012: this development is discussed in terms of leading to a computational turn in governmentality) to the methodology of comparative education, a scientific field previously said to rely more on cultural analysis (Foshay, Thorndike, & Hotyat, 1962). With the data collected, a new scientific opportunity for researchers for working with international numbered data on education and educational performances was created. Researchers have used this opportunity and published analysis and reanalysis discussing different aspects of education, hence, it can be stated that the IEA was the provider for a new branch within educational research—the ILSA research (Lindblad, Pettersson, & Popkewitz, 2015).

TIMSS, which is the acronym for several studies on mathematics and science achievements, primarily in grade 4 and grade 8, has been conducted several times starting in the year 1995. From the beginning, TIMSS stood for Third International Mathematics and Science Study but it later changed, and today it stands for Trends in International Mathematics and Science Study, and under that name, the study has been performed several times with a contingency of every fourth year.

It became apparent that TIMSS as a test came to promote hierarchies for explaining variance in students' performance. The hierarchies are in the test promoted as '*real*' but, in fact, they are constructed within the technical reports of the different TIMSS tests guiding how the cognitive test is constructed, what type of questions asked in the questionnaires and how the study is framed within a societal context. For making it simple—you get the answers you ask for. As such, the tests construct a specific way to understand society and education based on reasoning that knowledge can be measured and variances can be explained based on various hierarchies. Basically, this is not problematic in the way that performance is explained in relation to differences among students—what is more problematic is that the hierarchies are constructed upfront within the premises of the study based on a specific reasoning looking for '*achievement gaps*' (Lindblad, Pettersson, & Popkewitz, 2015) creating specific epistemological and ontological standpoints. The construction of educational '*facts*' and '*truths*' based on a search for '*achievement gaps*' are then transported to research using the data and results of the TIMSS studies, and these epistemological and ontological standpoints are then framing what most of the TIMSS research is studying and trying to make scientific claims about. This is also a reason for investigating TIMSS research and how this scientific activity is organized and legitimized. In other words, how, by whom and where is educational '*facts*' and '*truths*' epistemologically and ontologically framed within research, using numbered data with the explicit aim of investigating various '*achievement gaps*' based on hierarchies?

Methodology of the Study

The methodological approach, influenced by considerations within bibliometrics, extends to also incorporate a qualitative analysis of research communities, making it possible to describe patterns within a given corpus of research (Mølstad, Pettersson, & Forsberg, 2017). The tension between qualitative theorizing and quantitative methods is pervasive in social sciences and poses a constant challenge to empirical research (e.g., Leydesdorff, 2001). A context of justification is analytically distinguished from a context of discovery, that is, how knowledge is produced. This latter realm was regarded as belonging to a different domain of social sciences. A link between philosophical issues surrounding the growth of scientific knowledge and a sociological quest for explanations of variances in observable distributions was established by historians who investigated the institutional growth of the scientific enterprise. This elaboration provided a bridge between bibliometric approaches and sociological theorizing in science studies (e.g., Cole & Cole, 1973) where the approach was widened from single quantitative bibliometric studies to also include qualitative analysis.

The main objective of the study is to analyze scientific patterns and how a specific corpus of well-cited TIMSS research is inspired, constituted and disseminated. We perform the study by investigating the corpus with an extension to the sources referenced by and referring to the corpus (this larger set of data we call our extended corpus) with the questions addressing the entire set of data: in what journals are the research published, in what countries and institutions are the authors affiliated and who are the dominant authors? Hence, we are able to locate some clusters in which research is organized, and by doing so we are also able to discuss and highlight the process of legitimating research.

In these kinds of studies, losses are always of importance. The databases we use are designed as a self-promoting environment, meaning that they regularly boost scientific materials embedded within their own databases. In our investigation using EBSCO Discovery, Scopus and Web of Science (WoS), this becomes evident. There is a bias in favor of keeping record on articles and journals embedded in the used database. The research on limitations and possibilities with various databases is large but this is not the time and place for discussing these issues, but we claim that the loss of data is considerable especially when it comes to referred publications. As a way of establishing a self-review of our research process, we went through all the articles referred to us by our corpus listed by WoS, and we could conclude that a considerable part of all the referred literature was excluded within the database. As already mentioned, this has to do with the fact that the literature missed is not categorized in WoS as peer-reviewed scientific articles presented in journals, which is the standard form for tabulations. We believe that this observation is not unique for our selection—it might be true for a lot of scientific fields (maybe especially within the fields of Social Science and Humanities) in the contemporary where a shift can be observed from one way of publishing research results into another. Nevertheless, even though these limitations we can observe some state of the arts within TIMSS research.

The Corpus

In a previous systematic research review (Lindblad, Pettersson, & Popkewitz, 2015), a database of ILSA articles was developed consisting of more than 11,000 articles by using the search tools of EBSCO Discovery and Scopus. These articles were further categorized on the basis of differences in research focus. After filtering and categorization, the 20 most cited articles were located (Lindblad, Pettersson, & Popkewitz, 2015, pp. 122–125). We use this compilation as a selection criteria for collecting our data in WoS, namely the most cited scientific articles using or discussing TIMSS data. Because of the software we chose for our analysis—VOSviewer (van Eck & Waltman, 2010)—we later had to change our strategy of perceiving our bibliometric data from EBSCO Discovery and Scopus to WoS because we found that WoS data were better adopted for the environment of VOSviewer. As a result of this transfer, three articles were excluded because they were not embedded in WoS. Consequently, we use 17 of the most cited articles as a corpus of research for further investigations, also the total number of citations changed when moving our search strategy to WoS. In Table 11.1 we present the 17 most cited articles, which constitute our corpus of research.

Analyzing a TIMSS Corpus of Research

With bibliometric methods, we are able to visualize and discuss scientific patterns in a specific corpus of research. By doing so, we are able to map and present a section of TIMSS research. The data and analysis process of this study is presented in the Figure 11.1:

To analyze our data, we have used the software VOSviewer by Van Eck and Waltman (2010). Output files from WoS are transported into VOSviewer for tabulation, which generates interactive maps, that can be zoomed in and out, visualizing bibliometric networks (Zhou & Pan, 2015). Bibliometric networks consist of items such as journals, countries, institutions, authors or publications (Van Eck & Waltman, 2014). Each item is then represented as a dot in a map (Durrant, 2015). We have conducted analysis for portraying relations of bibliometric couplings.

TABLE 11.1 The Most Cited Articles

Articles	Citations in WoS
Else-Quest, N.M.; Hyde, J.S., & Linn, M.C. (2010). Cross-national patterns of gender differences in mathematic: A meta-analysis. *Psychological Bulletin, 136*(1), 103–127.	149
Baker, D.P., Goesling, B., & Letendre, G.K. (2002). Socioeconomic status, school quality, and national economic development: A cross-national analysis of the "Heyneman-Loxley Effect" on mathematics and science achievement. *Comparative Education Review, 46*(3), 291–312.	84
Akiba, M., LeTendre, G.K., Baker, D.P., & Goesling, B. (2002). Student victimization: National and school system effects on school violence in 37 nations. *American Educational Research Journal, 39*(4), 829–853.	63
Spring, J. (2008). Research on globalization and education. *Review of Educational Research, 78*(2), 330–363.	54
Hanushek, E.A., & Luque, J.A. (2003). Efficiency and equity in schools around the world. *Economics of Education Review, 22*(5), 481–502.	53
Hiebert, J., Stigler, J.W., Jacobs, J.K., Givvin, K.B., Garnier, H., Smith, M., ... Gallimore, R. (2005). Mathematics teaching in the United States today (and tomorrow): Results from the TIMSS 1999 video study. *Educational Evaluation and Policy Analysis, 27*(2), 111–132.	42
Van de Werfhorst, H.G., & Mijs, J. (2010). Inequality and the institutional structure of educational systems: A comparative perspective. *Annual Review of Sociology, 36*, 407–428.	38
Tatsuoka, K.K., Corter, J.E., & Tatsuoka, C. (2004). Patterns of diagnosed mathematical content and process skills in TIMSS-R across a sample of 20 countries. *American Educational Research Journal, 41*(4), 901–926.	26
Ammermüller, A., Heijke, H., & Wößmann, L. (2005). Schooling quality in Eastern Europe: Educational production during transition. *Economics of Education Review, 24*(5), 579–599.	24
Takayama, K. (2007) "A Nation at Risk" crosses the Pacific: Transnational borrowing of the U.S. crisis discourse in the debate on education reform in Japan. *Comparative Education Review, 51*(4), 423–446.	23
Papanastasiou, E.C., & Zembylas, M. (2004). Differential effects of science attitudes and science achievement in Australia, Cyprus, and the USA. *International Journal of Science Education, 26*(3), 259–280.	22
Schiller, K.S., Khmelkov, V.T., & Wang, X-Q. (2002). Economic development and the effects of family characteristics on mathematics achievement. *Journal of Marriage & Family, 64*(3), 730–742.	21

(Continued)

TABLE 11.1 (Continued)

Articles	Citations in WoS
Liu, X., & Lesniak, K.M. (2005). Students' progression of understanding the matter concept from elementary to high school. *Science Education*, 89(3), 433–450.	21
Penner, A.M. (2008). Gender differences in extreme mathematical achievement: An international perspective on biological and social factors. *American Journal of Sociology*, 114, 138–170.	21
Schreiber, J.B. (2002). Institutional and student factors and their influence on advanced mathematics achievement. *The Journal of Educational Research*, 95(5), 274–286.	20
Luyten, H. (2006). An empirical assessment of the absolute effect of schooling: regression-discontinuity applied to TIMSS-95. *Oxford Review of Education*, 32(3), 397–429.	20
Chudgar, A., & Luschei, T.F. (2009). National income, income inequality, and the importance of schools: A hierarchical cross-national comparison. *American Educational Research Journal*, 46(3), 626–658.	17

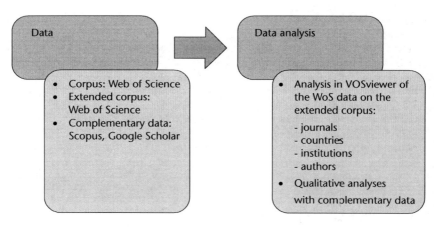

FIGURE 11.1 Overview of the Data and Analysis

Bibliometric couplings are basically the overlaps in the reference lists of publications (Van Eck & Waltman, 2014).

VOSviewer provides distance-based visualizations of bibliometric networks where the distance between items indicates the relatedness between specific items. Hence the items are located in a two-dimensional space so that strongly related items are located close and weakly related items are located far away from each other (Van Eck & Waltman, 2014). As such, the network portrays which items cite the same publications (Van Eck & Waltman, 2015). We have applied fractional counting methodology in VOSviewer so that publications with long reference lists (e.g., review articles) play a less important role in the construction of the networks (Van Eck & Waltman, 2014). Further, VOSviewer assigns items in clusters, which is a set of closely related items. Items are assigned only to one cluster, and the items are ascribed colors to indicate which cluster they are associated with (Van Eck & Waltman, 2014). These clusters illuminate patterns in our data. Our analysis is conducted by highlighting bibliometric couplings on journals, countries, institutions and authors in our data. We focus on clusters with a threshold of 4 for all of our visualizations, meaning that each item has more than at least four couplings to other items in the visualization. The threshold is lower than defaults since we have a relative small sample of bibliometric data.

The strength of using visualizations of bibliometric networks is that it provides a possibility to analyze large amounts of complex bibliographic data by visualizing core aspects of the data. However, the visualizations are, in a way, also simplifications of data, and as such it implies a loss of information. Bibliometric couplings in the visualizations are demanded to position the items in such a way that the distance between the items reflects the relatedness with a high level of precision. However, the distance reflects relatedness only approximately, and as such, some information might be lost, or at least not illuminated in a representative way with perfect accuracy (Van Eck & Waltman, 2014).

Characteristics of a TIMSS Corpus

We use the extended corpus for investigating our specific field of interest. By doing so, we are able to frame the intellectual context of TIMSS research. This we conduct by investigating some selected characteristics of how research is organized and legitimized, and from our example, we are able to discuss some premises on how numbered educational '*facts*' and '*truths*' are transported to and framed within a minor part of educational research—the TIMSS research.

Journals

To explore the intellectual organizing of our extended corpus, we start by investigating which journals that are involved for publishing articles using or discussing TIMSS data. This indicates which research fields that are involved and between which journals intellectual exchange is taking place:

In Figure 11.2, there are three clusters with 42 journals altogether. The three clusters are separately located, indicating that the relevance between the journals is highest within the distinct clusters. Within the bottom-left cluster there are 20 journals, making it the cluster with the highest number of journals. Further within the bottom-left cluster, the journals are mainly covering educational research. The right-most cluster has 14 journals, and most of the journals have a psychological profile. The top-most cluster has seven journals, which mostly focus

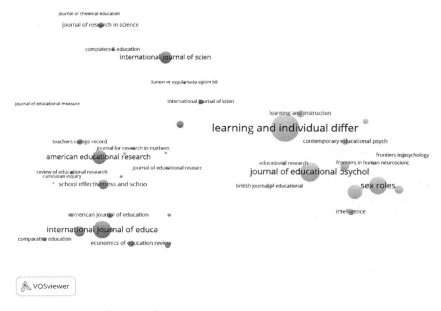

FIGURE 11.2 Visualization of Journals

on specific types of subject topics within education. When it comes to the highest number of bibliometric couplings, it is the journal *Learning and Individual Differences* that has the highest number, meaning that articles in this journal are articles most used and disseminated. Second highest is the journal *International Journal of Educational Development*, followed by *Journal of Educational Psychology* and the journal *Sex Roles*. It is within the right-most cluster that several of the journals with the highest number of bibliometric couplings are located, indicating that the right-most cluster is more evident in the framing of the TIMSS corpus than the other two clusters. Taken together, our findings illuminate that the corpus is mainly intellectually organized within three categories: the field of psychology, educational research and subject specific research.

Countries

One important factor to investigate is in which countries the authors of our extended corpus are active. This provides us with information concerning where the authors are established in terms of cultural frames for their research, also most important for discussing lingua-dependent frames in the construction of epistemological and ontological concepts. Moreover, a reason is also to investigate cultural biases within research, which are important factors in explaining how knowledge is established and disseminated. In Figure 11.3, we present the countries involved in the corpus.

The Framing of Educational Knowledge   175

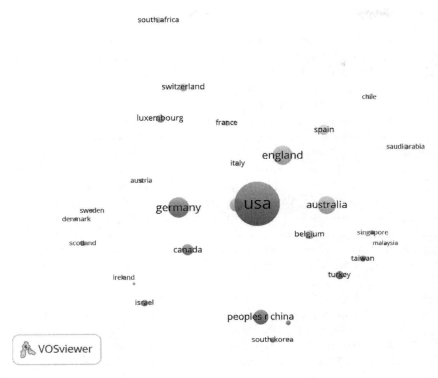

FIGURE 11.3   Visualization of Countries

In Figure 11.3, there are seven clusters of countries with 26 countries altogether. Some of the clusters are separately located; illuminating that the relevance is higher within the clusters then between the other clusters. However, the dark cluster, the cluster with England and the cluster with Spain, Italy and Chile are located across from each other and hence have more in common. Bottom-left is the cluster with most countries, in total nine countries. The smallest cluster is Luxembourg by itself. The United States is the country with the highest number of bibliometric couplings. The number of couplings is 6,450, which is three times the number of couplings of Germany, the country with the second highest number of couplings, which in total has 2,181 couplings. Germany is then followed by England and Australia.

Some of the clusters seem to be geographically and culturally logical, for instance, the cluster represented by Peoples Republic of China, South Korea and Japan (the third item not labeled in the figure). However, other clusters have a greater geographical and cultural spread, for example, the cluster with countries like England, Australia and Saudi Arabia. Another is the cluster with countries like the United States, Turkey, Taiwan, Malaysia and Singapore. These findings illustrate that the United States is the most dominating country within TIMSS research; however, there is a variety of countries active within the corpus.

Institutions

Narrowing further down, we also investigate which institutions that are involved in our extended corpus representing TIMSS research. This analysis indicates which institutions are active, and as such, more precisely indicate at which institutions the extended corpus is intellectually framed.

In Figure 11.4, there are 57 institutions present organized in seven different clusters. The institution with most bibliometric couplings is the University of Southern California, with 1,100 couplings in total. The second most important is Northwestern University, with 949 couplings. The next two institutions on the list are Chinese University Hong Kong, with 656 couplings followed by University of Buffalo (not labeled in the figure, but evident in the tables connected to the visualization provided in VOSviewer). Both of these institutions are located in the bottom-center cluster. Not surprisingly, on the basis of the previous section, many of the institutions in the figure are located in the United States.

Most striking of the clusters is the right-most cluster. It is the smallest cluster with three institutions; however, it contains the two universities with the most bibliometric couplings (University of Southern California and Northwestern University). This indicates the cluster as being of importance in intellectually framing for example, reasoning on 'achievement gaps', separation into different hierarchies and, epistemological and ontological standpoints within the field of TIMSS research in an interlinked process with the data aggregated and presented within various TIMSS studies. Further, the cluster is located in a way that only one

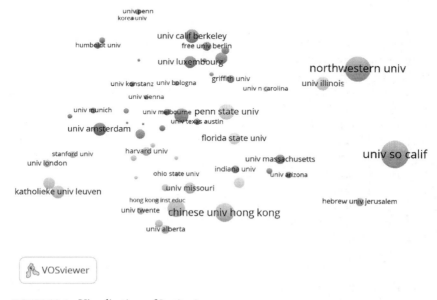

FIGURE 11.4 Visualization of Institutions

The Framing of Educational Knowledge   **177**

other university is close (University of Illinois). This illustrates that the universities within the right-most cluster are mostly related to each other, more than to other clusters. This also goes for the left-most cluster and the mid-bottom cluster. However, the mid-bottom cluster is located more closely to other clusters. Further the clusters in the three mid-top are located across each other, hence, these clusters are more tightly connected to each other, then the left-most and right-most clusters.

Authors

Narrowing even further down, we investigate which authors are involved in the extended corpus. This illuminates the central actors in the construction of TIMSS-research.

In Figure 11.5, there are 20 authors organized in five clusters. The clusters are separately located with the two middle clusters as the main interchange between the three other clusters. The author with most bibliometric couplings is Ming Chiu with 446, followed by Catherine McBride-Chang with 387, Ron Avi Astor with 384, Janet Shibley Hyde with 381 and Marcia C Linn with 369 (the item second to the right). This implies that the two authors with the most bibliometric couplings are located in the top-center cluster. Hyde and Linn are both located in the right cluster. The two authors in the top cluster, McBride-Chang and Chiu, have written five articles altogether within our extended corpus. *Journal of Educational Psychology* is the journal in which McBride-Chang has the highest number of articles. Chiu has the highest number of publications in the journal *Computers in Human Behaviour*. This is the cluster with a substantially higher number of bibliometric couplings per author. This indicates that the both authors and the cluster are important for the intellectual organization within our extended corpus.

FIGURE 11.5   Visualization of Authors

The right-most cluster is the most numerous one with five authors: Alice H. Eagly, Nicole M. Else-Quest, Linn, Xinfeng Liu and David Reilly. The authors in this cluster publish mostly on the topics of psychology, but also on subject specific issues as science teaching.

The middle cluster is the next largest cluster with six authors: Hans Luyten, Ebrahim Mohammadpour, Keita Takayama, Herman G. van de Werfhorst, Mieke van Houtte and Ludger Wossman. They publish predominantly on various aspects of sociology and education. This cluster has a substantially lower number of bibliometric coupling for each author then the other clusters. Further, the left-most cluster has three authors and the bottom-center cluster, labeled with the name Akiba, has two authors. In the left-most cluster, Astor has published articles with both of the other two authors, J.K. Chen and Mona Khoury-Kassabri. These authors have all published in the journal *Child Abuse and Neglect* and in various journals covering the topic of social work.

Summing up our analysis, we conclude that some aspects become more important than others in how our extended corpus is intellectually organized.

Our findings indicate an interchange of legitimization where the United States and other Western countries are major actors who set the scene for academic discourse and transformation, but also that non-Westernized countries play an important role, especially in terms of referencing the corpus. TIMSS research, therefore, seems to organize knowledge in favor of the English language, but also that an important transformation into non-Westernized contexts occurs. Moreover, the fields of education, psychology and subject-specific issues seem to be of especially importance in the framing of TIMSS research.

Scholarly Framing of Educational Knowledge

Porter (1995) raises the question, is science s made by communities? In arguing that objectivity is one of the classical ideals of science, he questions how this will be possible parallel to embracing a social conception of rationality. Rationality

TABLE 11.2 Overview of Main Findings

	Findings
Journals	There are three clusters of journals, which mainly focus on psychology, education and subject-specific issues.
Countries and Institutions	The field is dominated by researchers and institutions situated or closely connected to an American context. There is also Westernized dominance within the field.
Authors	There are some main actors within the corpus in terms of relevance and dissemination. A majority of these actors are established within an American context.

in the modern society tends to be individually performed by researchers with a tendency to gather in clusters appearing as scientific communities. Within these communities' specific rationalities are framed in a scientific discourse where 'facts' and 'truths' are presented. These 'facts' and 'truths' are indeed not trivial; instead they are at the very center of how science interprets and explains the world, but also central in policy implementation. When Kuhn (1970) wrote his influential discussion on scientific communities, he stated that these disciplinary communities defined the standards, the tools, the concepts and the problems that would be regarded as valid in that particular field. This highlights why it is important to map such clusters.

Today, in what has been called the new sociology of science, the concept of negotiation has turned up to be a most influential discussion (Porter, 1995). Negotiation conveys an idea that general principles, so-called universal scientific laws, are never sufficiently definite or concrete. Hence, important scientific claims can never be settled by general principles. Instead, they have to be worked out by rather small groups of specialists. Because of this, large problems and broad scientific questions are brought down to issues of detailed and abstract matters, and 'facts' or 'truths' are settled through close personal or institutional interactions; one of these interaction activities is referencing each other's articles published in peer-reviewed journals.

Consequently, self-referential and self-authorizing becomes an evident issue in these smaller communities where scientists tend to reference each other's work for settling issues of relevance within the smaller community. Self-authorizing and self-referential as principles works as follows: (a) Author A is saying that x is a scientific fact by referring to Author A, or (b) Author A and B are working together and then A is saying that x is a scientific fact by referring to Author B. In both examples, x is presented as a fact on the basis of evidence (consequently a 'truth'). Hence, we are wondering if self-authorizing and self-referential is overemphasizing specific reasoning within the field, and as such, is self-generating just as Hacking (1992) pointed out in his important work. We raise this question on the basis of a tendency for overlapping bibliometric couplings between and inside the different clusters within TIMSS research, as exemplified though the analysis of the extended corpus. Within the corpus we use, there is a tendency that cliques of researchers (organized in clusters) construct and manage the narratives surrounding the construction of scientific 'facts' and 'truths' using or discussing TIMSS-data. We argue that this capacity building of dominant clusters within the studied field contains activities of legitimization of knowledge through self-authorizing and self- referential publishing patters and coauthorship. Accordingly, just as Porter (1995) states, important scientific claims are worked out in rather small groups within demarcated communities.

In analyzing our extended corpus, we have focused our interest toward journals, countries, institutions and authors for investigating the organization and legitimation of knowledge. As described, the expansion of ILSA (e.g., Kamens, 2009), and to a lesser extent ILSA research (e.g., Lindblad, Pettersson, & Popkewitz, 2015) is well documented. In this, we were especially interested in mapping the frames of knowledge concerning TIMSS research within the scientific field. This provides information of the cultural frames and possible bias in the TIMSS research, which are important factors in explaining how knowledge is established and legitimized. Our results show that, first, there are three clusters of journals in which well-cited TIMSS research is published. These journals are mainly focusing on psychology, education and subject-specific issues. Evidently, we are able to state that the corpus is predominantly constructed within the scientific communities of psychology, education and subject-specific recognitions. From other discussions in this book, we know that comparisons and an emphasis on 'achievement gaps' (e.g., Lindblad, Pettersson, & Popkewitz, 2015) are in focus. As such, we can conclude that the various communities are driven in the construction of *'facts'* and *'truths'* on what is causing these *'achievement gaps'* and how can these *'gaps'* be compared in relation to other contexts. Dependent on this construction various hierarchies are elaborated on in explaining community-based findings. Because of this, the different communities made up by clusters of researchers and institutions tend to give different answers between the communities, but the same or similar within one single community. Another aspect of this is that epistemological and ontological statements tend to be the same or similar within the located communities, but if you consider the entire scientific society; conceptualizations might appear with a larger variance. One reason for this is that the various communities tend to be both self-authorizing and self-referential practices.

Second, our study concludes, on the basis of bibliometric analysis, in that even though different communities appeared most of them are situated in either American or other Westernized contexts, even though other national settings appear as important, especially for referencing our corpus. Findings like these are not surprising, but nevertheless important to recognize because the construction of various hierarchies and epistemological and ontological issues tend to be, when constructed, highly dependent on language. This means that even though science is truly international, the languages used are important for how phenomenon is recognized and concepts constructed. In a situation where the most cited TIMSS research, but also the TIMSS studies themselves, are so dependent on the English language, other contextual prerequisites might be underemphasized. Also important is the notion on negotiations. When 'facts' and 'truths' are negotiated, language-dependent conceptualizations not based on English are lost within bibliometric analysis using databases mostly consisting of English-speaking articles. This might, in the long run, lead to that non-English-speaking scientific findings tend to 'disappear' in both scientific communities and on a society level. This is not the same as stating that these communities not exist, it is just saying that these communities are lost in these kinds of studies that we have performed. Another question that can be worth asking: is English slowly transgressing to the language to use for launching 'facts' and 'truths' within science? Because English today more or less is the language in use when to make objective claims on either hierarchies, epistemological or ontological issues. Is English internationally the new Latin, where we can speak a more objective non-contextual language based on 'big data' on an international arena, and other languages might primarily be used to describe national contexts more emphasizing behaviors and national practices? In this text, we do not have the answers on these questions, we are in a position only to discuss these matters in relation to one rather small corpus of TIMSS research, and we can point only to the importance and dominance of English.

Third, we conclude that most of the actors are established in institutions in the United States. This can seem to come naturally from the dominance discussion earlier, but at the same time evident is that a lot of the researchers originally stem from other countries but if you are going into TIMSS research, the United States seems to be the best place. One notion that we highlight is that if most researchers are situated in an American context—American context and issues related to this context might be overemphasized within our corpus. For answering this question, extensive content analysis of the corpus must be performed, but it is not unbelievable that for instance various 'achievement gaps' are interpreted and understood dependent on an American context.

Since TIMSS research is constantly used in arguments for reform initiatives and curriculum development as either rhetoric or symbolic action, it is important to study and analyze this specific discourse in order to understand how knowledge is organized and legitimated within the field. This ought to lead to better understanding of how notions such as for example, knowledge, curriculum, assessment and evaluation are discursively formed inside and outside of a scientific community and how different research fields function as interfaces where intellectual yielding occurs and academic capital is interchanged in the construction of research based on comparative numbered data. It has been stated by Rouvroy (2012) that operations of collection, processing and structuration of data for helping individuals and organizations to cope with circumstances of uncertainty or relieving them from the burden of interpreting events and taking decision in routine, trivial situations have become crucial to public and private sectors activities. In relation to this, an implicit belief developed stating that data are able to anticipate most phenomena of the world. With the help of rather simple algorithms, it is possible to build models of behaviors or patterns, without having to consider either causes or intentions. This creates '*data behaviorism*' (Rouvroy, 2012, p. 1) that is a new recognized way of producing knowledge about future preferences, attitudes, behaviors or events without considering the subject's psychological motivations, speeches or narratives, but instead relying on data. The intellectual organization and legitimization is as such in no way trivial; instead, it is at the very core of how knowledge is constructed and made into '*facts*' and '*truths*' about education.

Further, Porter (1995) makes an argument that the reason that numbers came to be central in the development of society is that numbers are perceived as '*objective*' and as such '*neutral*', but in reality, this is in many respect false, and even contradictory. Instead, numbers should be perceived as a technology of steering and managing society and the state, a technology based on connotations of '*objectivity*', but also as a technology of distance and neutrality. What we are making an argument about is connected to Porter's statements. We state that comparisons and the use of numbered data for describing education came to be perceived as education per se. In this, we have investigated a corpus of well-cited TIMSS research for raising questions on how educational knowledge based on numbered data is organized and legitimized. In this, we conclude in that different research communities preferably in psychology, education and subject specific matters are organized to some extent of self-authorizing and self-referential activities presenting '*facts*' and '*truths*' on educational knowledge. These '*facts*' and '*truths*' are predominantly dominated by researchers situated in the United States or other Westernized countries, and concepts, reasoning on hierarchies and epistemological and ontological claims, are performed in English, leaving a rather extensive corpus of research aside.

In the end, we highlight that in contemporary society, it is widely recognized that power and influence are distributed across all levels of educational systems creating a variety of institutions involved in education. Hence, policy processes consist of a complex configuration of actors and institutions that are connected and interact, sometimes in conflict and sometimes reinforcing each other. The classical question raised is—who governs? The concept of globalization has been used as a description, but also an answer, of these recent developments. The concept has also been fueled in connection to a massive economic and technological development. Other chapters in this book describing the development of how numbers came to be a natural way of discussing education and how specific organizations were created for communicating education through numbers and comparisons. We emphasize on a special branch of this development—the ILSA research narrowed down to a smaller field of a corpus of TIMSS research. By doing so, we have been able to discuss how a specific scientific field created on numbers is organized and legitimated disseminating specific educational '*facts*' and '*truths*' that frames how we think and discuss education in a globalized world. In this chapter, we have mapped and illuminated the actors and settings where '*facts*' and '*truths*' are framed, which in fact is one small observation on a larger question on who '*governs*' the TIMSS numbers.

References

Becher, T., & Trowler, P. R. (2001). *Academic tribes and territories*. Great Britain: Open University Press.

Borgman, C. L. (1990). *Scholarly communication and bibliometrics*. Thousand Oaks, CA: Sage.

Cole, J. R., & Cole, S. (1973). *Social stratification in science*. Chicago: University of Chicago Press.

Domínguez, M., Vieira, M. J., & Vidal, J. (2012). The impact of the Programme for International Student. Assessment on academic journals. *Assessment in Education: Principles, Policy, & Practice, 19*(3), 393–409.

Durrant, P. (2015). Lexical bundles and disciplinary variation in university students' writing: Mapping the territories. *Applied Linguistics, 38*(2), 165–193.

Foshay, A. W., Thorndike, R. L., & Hotyat, F. (1962). *Educational achievements of 13 year olds in twelve countries*. Hamburg: UNESCO Institute of Education.

Glänzel, W., & Schoepflin, U. (1994). Little scientometrics, big scientometrics . . . and beyond? *Scientometrics, 30*(2–3), 31–44.

Glänzel, W., & Schoepflin, U. (1999). A bibliometric study of reference literature in the sciences and social sciences. *Information, Processing and Management, 35*(1), 31–44.

Hacking, I. (1992).'Style' of historians and philosophers. *Studies in the History and Philosophy of Science, 23*(1), 1–20.

Kamens, D. H. (2009). Globalization and the growth of international educational testing and national assessment. *Comparative Education Review, 54*(1), 5–25.

Kandlbinder, P. (2015). Signature concepts of key researchers in North American higher education teaching and learning. *Higher Education, 69*(2), 243–255.

Kuhn, T. (1970). *The structure of scientific revolutions*. Chicago: University of Chicago Press.

Leydesdorff, L. (1995). *The challenge of scientometrics: The development, measurement, and self-organization of scientific communications*. Leiden: Leiden University, DSWO Press.

Leydesdorff, L. (2001). *The challenge of scientometrics: The development, measurement, and self-organization of scientific communications*. Leiden: Universal Publishers.

Lindblad, S., Pettersson, D., & Popkewitz, T. S. (2015). *International comparisons of school results: A systematic review of research on large-scale assessment in education*. Stockholm: Sweden: Swedish Research Council.

McCain, K. W. (1990). Mapping authors in intellectual space: A technical overview. *Journal of the American Society for Information Science, 41*(6), 433–443.

Mølstad, C., Pettersson, D., & Forsberg, E. (2017). A game of thrones: Organising and legitimasing knowledge through PISA-research. *European Educational Research Journal*. Retrieved from http://journals.sagepub.com/doi/pdf/10.1177/1474904117715835

Pettersson, D. (2014). Three narratives: National interpretations of PISA. *Knowledge Cultures, 2*(4), 172–191.

Porter, T. M. (1995). *Trust in numbers: The pursuit of objectivity in science and public life*. Princeton, NJ: Princeton University Press.

Rouvroy, A. (2012). The end(s) of critique: Data-behaviourism vs. due-process. In M. Hildebrandt & E. De Vries (Eds.), *Privacy, due process, and the computational turn. Philosophers of law meet philosophers of technology* (pp. 143–168). Oxford: Routledge.

Small, H. (1973). Co-citation in the scientific literature: A new measure of the relationship between two documents. *Journal of the American Society for Information Science, 24*(4), 265–269.

Van Eck, N. J., & Waltman, L. (2010). Software survey: VOSviewer, a computer program for bibliometric mapping. *Scientometrics, 84*(2), 523–538.

Van Eck, N. J., & Waltman, L. (2014). Visualizing bibliometric networks. In Y. Ding; R. Rousseau, & D. Wolfram (Eds.), M*easuring scholarly impact: Methods and practice* (pp. 285–320). Berlin & Heidelberg: Springer.

Van Eck, N. J., & Waltman, L. (2015). *VOSviewer manual*. Leiden: Universiteit Leiden, CWTS Meaningful metrics.

White, H. D. (1990). Author co-citation analysis: Overview and defense. In C. L. Borgman (Ed.), *Scholarly communication and bibliometrics*. Thousand Oaks, CA: SAGE.

White, H. D., & McCain, K. W. (1997). Visualization of literatures. *Annual Review of Information Science and Technology, 32*, 99–168 (20 p. 1/4).

Zhou, P., & Pan, Y. (2015). A comparative analysis of publication portfolios of selected economies. *Scientometrics, 105*(2), 825–842.

12

OECD AS A SITE OF COPRODUCTION

The European Education Governance and the New Politics of 'Policy Mobilization'[1]

Sotiria Grek

Introduction

The story of education governance in Europe, much like most accounts narrating this old continent, is one of travel and prejudice. On the one hand, travel is integral to Europe, since most of what we identify with a degree of *'Europeanness'* has always connected people and ideas through movement and mobility; education, either in its institutionalized or in its less formal guises, has always been central to the *'traveling'* of cultures, practices and peoples around Europe. Paradoxically however, the national education system has always been relatively closed off; seen as a bounded entity in itself, it became one of the last fortresses of the nation-state against the predicament of *'global'* dictates and shifts. Despite borrowings and *'policy lessons'*—which have largely been silenced by education historians for a long time (Lawn, 2008)—education has been one of the main pillars of building the *'national'*, as national stereotyping would continually separate and therefore define *'us'* from *'them'*.

Yet, this chapter will suggest that it is precisely in the dialectical relationship between travel and prejudice that the governing of European education can more productively be understood. It suggests that this antithetical relationship—which has to a large extent shaped European history—between a desire to move, travel, get to know one another, yet routinely, almost subconsciously finding those *'others'* as different and hence unintelligible, is a particularly productive setting in which to investigate the production of European education policy.

Located in the field of the transnational governance of education, the chapter examines the case of the Organisation for Economic Cooperation and Development (OECD) as a key expert organization in the governing of European education; rather than focusing on higher education, the mobility and travel of which has been well-documented through scholarly work on the Bologna Process (Corbett, 2005; Reichert & Tauch, 2005; Keeling, 2006), it focuses on the area of compulsory education which has been much firmer rooted within national traditions and curricula, and thus considered fairly bounded and fixed. The chapter builds on previous research (Ozga et al., 2011) that suggested that European Commission (EC) and OECD recommendations are often received at the national level as homogeneous. Thus, questions about the relationship between the two organizations in terms of policy direction emerge.

More specifically, we build on empirical research which aimed at moving beyond top-down accounts of the mere and one-directional transfer of policy from the international to the national, toward more attention to the interaction and mediation across '*levels*' and actors. The empirical study which informs this chapter focused mainly on the analysis of discourse through an examination of eight key texts, through a focus on their '*texturing*' effects and their role in establishing a new '*order of discourse*', their chaining, and the extent to which boundary genres were being produced. A firm set of 15 actors from both the Commission and the OECD, as well as other relevant research agencies, was identified and interviewed; the interviews focused on the actors' role in processes of coordination (conferences, meetings, project work), their interactions with other actors within and beyond their organizations and other relational ties that link them and others through channels of flow of data, ideas and/or material resources. This chapter is built using mainly this latter work, namely, the interviews with the key policy actors. The policy actors interviewed and quoted here have had positions of power and significant decision-making leverage, and therefore in all cases first-hand experience and participation in meetings and debate between Directorate General Education and Culture (DGEAC) and the OECD in regard to the financing and conduct of large international assessments.

Hence, although previous work showed how the OECD became a major Europeanizing actor, having not only entered the European education policy arena but in fact monopolizing the attention and policy influence within it (Grek, 2009), this chapter goes one step further; working with the specific case of international comparative testing, it examines how the OECD became a dominant education policy actor as a result of its deliberate and systematic mobilization by the European Commission, which found in the OECD not only a great resource of data to govern (which it did not have before) but also a player who would be pushing the Commission's own policy agenda forward, albeit leaving the old subsidiarity rule intact. As I will show, testing is important because it produces numbers and consequently ratings and rankings; once the OECD has created this unprecedented spectacle of comparison in European education, no system can remain hidden and separate any longer. The field of measurement becomes instantly the field of the game.

In order to contextualize the case under question, we begin by offering a brief sketch of the rise of international comparative testing; we will briefly discuss the main studies which have metamorphosed it into a spectacle of surveillance and control for national education systems and have had significant effects on education policy making not only on participant countries but also on European education policymaking overall. I move on to explain and discuss the role of experts in this emergent European policy field and finish off by an examination of '*policy mobilization*'; applying theory from the field of social studies of science and technology, the concepts of boundary work and '*boundary organization*' (Guston, 2000; Jasanoff, 2004; St Clair, 2006) are used in order to show the ways that the OECD has transformed into a '*site of coproduction*' of both knowledge and social order (St. Clair, 2006).

The Case of International Comparative Assessment: OECD, International Adult Literacy Survey (IALS) and PISA

Comparative testing has become the lifeblood of education governance in Europe and globally. It is more than simply a statistical project; rather, it has become part of consistent efforts to restore legitimacy and trust between populations and their governments. As Hall contends—building legitimacy requires potential users in the process, as well as technical experts. The most important role of indicator sets may be in framing the issues and defining the problems, rather than suggesting the solutions (Hall, 2009).

The governance of international comparative testing reflects these values. Project boards usually work in conjunction with a large range of consortia of international partners and technical advisors (statisticians, media specialists and, interestingly, philanthropists); they also consult with a vast array of different actor groupings, such as academics, private companies, policy makers, associates, country correspondents, regional working groups and others. Regular training courses are delivered as well as seminars, and regional, thematic and global conferences. Although all these initiatives suggest sustained efforts to include and create consensus with the greatest number of stakeholders possible, the role of experts remains central; before they acquire a more '*public*' and visible face, tests are being discussed, negotiated and indeed fought over among field experts for a long period of time.

The case of the OECD is particularly interesting because, unlike the EU, it has neither the legal instruments nor the financial levers to actively promote policymaking at the national level within member nations. Nonetheless, through ranking exercises such as the Education at a Glance annual reports, the IALS, its Indicators in Education project, the more recent Teaching and Learning International Survey (TALIS), which focuses on teachers, through PISA and national and thematic policy reviews, its educational agenda has become significant in framing policy options not only at the national but also, as it has been argued, in the constitution of a global policy space in education (Lingard, Rawolle, & Taylor, 2005;

Grek & Lingard, 2007; Ozga & Lingard, 2007). This raises the question—what has transformed the OECD to one of the most powerful agents of transnational education governance? Martens (2007) has contributed substantially to this discussion suggesting that the *'comparative turn'*—'a scientific approach to political decision making' (Martens, 2007, p. 42)—has been the main driver of OECD success. Through its statistics, reports and studies, it has achieved a brand which most regard indisputable; OECD's policy recommendations are accepted as valid by politicians and scholars alike, without the author seeing any need beyond the label 'OECD' to justify the authoritative character of the knowledge contained therein (Porter & Webb, 2004).

There has been a range of such studies that the OECD has been organizing since the early 1990s, the majority of which were adult literacy studies initially, followed by the delivery of the most successful one, PISA, and more recently, from 2011, PIAAC, the Programme for the International Assessment of Adult Competencies. The first literacy study, for example, the IALS was the first and largest international comparative testing regime of its kind. Conducted from the early 1990s, it was an innovative study, as it was the first time ever that an international comparative dimension was added to the construction of a literacy survey instrument. Thus, it heralded a new era in the construction and evolution of international comparative studies, as for the first time ever it gave international testing a comparative dimension, where measurement against other countries' performance offered unprecedented visibility and thus exposure. As it was an original and new endeavor, slowly at the start but increasingly later on, IALS boosted confidence in the construction of measurement tools of this kind, increased their persuasive power in regard to their validity and transparency and created substantial revenues to the research agencies administering them. Finally, and perhaps above all, it created a circle of like-minded expert communities, who found in these studies a platform for promoting the problematization of specific issues, their institutionalization through their exchanges and the setting up of the study, as well as their legitimation, in the form of advice to failing countries, once the results were published.

Following the successful IALS endeavor, PISA became a major instrument in providing data for the European education systems almost from the start. The international dimension of the survey, which overrides the boundaries of Europe to compare student performance in countries as diverse as the United States, Greece and Indonesia, gave PISA a particularly significant weight as an indicator of the success or failure of education policy. While always testing reading, mathematical and scientific literacy, its innovative dimension—and part of its interest as a governing device—lies in the fact that it does not examine students' mastery of school curricula, rather the focus is on an assessment of young people's ability to practically apply their skills in everyday life situations. The focus on 'real-life' circumstances and on students' capacity to enter the labor market with core skills, such as literacy and numeracy, has taken PISA's focus of interest away from less explicit educational aims that resist measurement (e.g. democratic participation, artistic talents, understanding of politics, history, etc.), towards a more pragmatic view of education's worth: 'its relevance to lifelong learning' (OECD, 2003). Finally, and perhaps most significantly, a key feature of PISA is:

> its policy orientation, with design and reporting methods determined by the need of governments to draw policy lessons.
> *(OECD, 2003, no page numbers)*

Hence, this is not simply a testing regime—it is constructed and operates under a clear and specific frame of policy recommendations, which are to be adopted by the participant countries if the latter are to improve their future PISA assessments and thus improve their standing in attracting economic and human capital investment. In other words, the involvement of the OECD with the steering of education policy in participant countries does not stop with the publication of the PISA results; on the contrary, this is perhaps where it begins. Expert groups write expert reports, analyzed and taken forward by other national and local experts, while the Commission expert committees are also on board in order to keep the game in sight and keep it running. It is to the role of the experts therefore that we now have to turn to.

Steering the Soup? Experts, Conflicts, and Management of Knowledge

The brief discussion of IALS and PISA above shows some of the reasons why international comparative testing has become one of the prime instruments in the steering and exchange of governing knowledge in education in Europe today. Their development has created the necessary preconditions for achieving policy understanding, travel, translation and thus, despite local idiosyncrasies and histories, policy consensus.

Nonetheless, the story of the development of international assessment should not misguide us toward the sketching of an ideal type of policy generation process where genuine debate and the building of relationships and collaborations produce new knowledge. Hugh Heclo, as cited by Freeman (2012), described policy as a *'reverberating'* cobweb of conditions, people and practices. Freeman uses this eloquent image to discuss the collective production of meaning through meetings and documents; using Heclo's idea of *'collective puzzling'* for the making of policy, he argues that:

> this puzzling entails multiple acts of translation, but only to the extent that we can think of translation as generative, an active process of the production

of meaning. It seems impossible to ask, at any given moment, 'where is policy?' for it seems to be always incipient, mobile, somewhere between.

(Freeman, 2012, p. 17)

International comparative testing is an excellent example of the kind of mobility of the policymaking process that Freeman describes; the discussion of the organization, preparation and delivery of international tests makes a case precisely for a close examination not only of the movement of policy in itself, but crucially of those who move it. The role of experts is central as their own in-depth and trusted knowledge allows them to be highly mobile; in the name of their specialized expertise, experts have to be numerous; they are employed by different policymaking and research organizations and are accountable to them alone; their expert knowledge suggests the need for them to be present and offer advice at different stages of the policymaking process, yet it is precisely this same trusted and objective knowledge that renders them invisible. They offer evidence for policy, yet their most important role is symbolic, that of the legitimization of knowledge (Boswell, 2009).

This is the kind of status that the OECD acquired with the conduct of the big international tests; the seal of unequivocal, trusted truth which, as we will see further on, it took one step further into an almost amalgamation of knowledge into policy. Quantification, simplicity and measurability were the trio of the key ingredients of its success, as slowly yet surely the OECD managed to persuade that its statistical reasoning was not simply the conventional, partially constructed representation of very complex and different contexts but rather the objective reality. Econometrics became the single methodology for its measurements, whereas questions in regard to the epistemology or ethics of its analyses were never asked. Following Kingdon's (1984) policy soup model, OECD slowly gathered all the ingredients and the know-how in order to produce best-selling 'knowledge soup'; through its management and steering of knowledge production, it manages and steers new policy agendas and directions. Similar to Kingdon's (1984) idea of the primeval soup, ideas for research float around for some time; new avenues of researching education performance are always open. Given the expert marketing of the studies' results globally, failures in performance are broadcast widely; thus, the need for immediate action is necessary. Indeed, the persuasive power of the OECD lays in its construction and measurement of education indicators; the quantitative knowledge it produces is knowledge and action simultaneously, as no indicator has any purposeful existence unless it signals action (Lawn & Grek, 2012).

In other words, OECD not only produces evidence quickly and effectively but also digests it and offers it to policymakers in the format of policy solutions. In a sense, if we are used to accounts of European policymaking as slow, cumbersome and "coming from nowhere" (Richardson, 2001, p. 21), the OECD bypasses these obstacles in four key ways; first, it defines the limits of the possible by suggesting what can be measured, hence what can be 'done'; second, it carries no political jurisdiction therefore it carries no external threats to national policymaking, as perhaps the Commission or other EU institutions might have done; it now has the experience, networks and the technical and material resources to speed up the policy process so that it can show '*results*' within the usually short timeframe that policymakers are in power; and last but not the least, it carries all the '*right*' ideological messages for education systems in the twenty-first century—that is, it connects learning directly to labor market outcomes and human capital.

Nonetheless, how has the OECD become such a powerful player in education governance in Europe? As some of the people who work there might have argued, the Education Directorate staffs who are based in Paris take a few decisions, if any; the OECD, as they argue, is no other than the participant countries and the national actors and experts sent to the OECD committees and meetings. Thus, how accurate is to examine the emergence of this new policy arena by simply focusing on this single international actor? This is where the initial juxtaposition between travel and prejudice is helpful again, as the story of the emergence of the OECD as an influential actor (mostly on the basis of its large international tests) is yet again a story of tension—the expert loves and expert wars that have been forming the history of international comparisons of performance measurement for over a decade:

> So around 2003–04, we [OECD and Commission] started becoming far more involved. Meetings all over the world [. . .] The European member states should see that the Commission is there because one of the criticisms of the Commission since all this started was that we didn't take into account all the good work of the OECD. Which was wrong but they said it. The way of showing them was to actually be there—not an empty chair.
>
> *(EC4)*

Indeed, although the Commission and the OECD had been leading quite separate ideological paths, a new love affair began emerging—this relationship would gradually strengthen and eventually become the *sine qua non* for the governing of European education systems. Another interviewee was even more eloquent in his discussion of this flourishing relationship:

> We used to have great competition between the two institutions [OECD and the EC] which was that they were research-based, we were policy-based. And we needed that. They needed the policy aspect to mobilize the European consciousness [. . .] it was in their interest working with us . . . We had some differences but we are working closer and closer together, we are very, very, good friends now, there is no conflict.
>
> *(EU3)*

And of course, love is power:

> When the OECD started speaking about TALIS [survey on teachers] it attracted the attention of the member states that all this is very good but it is expensive. [. . .] So, I managed to convince my Director General of supporting (the OECD) with an awful lot of millions of euros. And I went back to the OECD with that message and said that of course if we pay we want influence.
>
> *(EC7)*

On the other hand, OECD actors appear also as quite open to the Commission, stressing from their own point of view, the reasons that the DG Education would work closely with them:

> First of all, I think we've been very lucky that on the Commission side, that they've given a lot of emphasis to skills recently [. . .] so I think we were fortunate that the work that we decided to do on PIAAC corresponded extremely well with their areas of interest and research priorities [. . .] I think they have been attending these international expert meetings that have taken place developing the proposal for PIAAC and so they were already onboard at that stage and then when it looked like the project was going to go ahead [. . .] we went out to speak to them and get them to agree to also provide some funding. So, they made a direct contribution, an actual contribution to the international costs and also eventually agreed to subsidize EU countries, the cost that they had to pay as well to the OECD. So, we got just a block of direct funding and indirect funding to countries that they then had to pay us for the international costs. That made a big contribution in financial terms and therefore of course enhanced interest in the project.
>
> *(OECD3)*

Another OECD actor also suggested the way that the relationship, rather than hostile, has been much closer recently, in fact '*hand in hand*':

> We have the same perceptions like other international organizations that it is important that we work together and that we avoid duplication of effort and that we know what the other organizations are doing and that there are often occasions that jointly we can do more than what we can do individually. I think we were always aware of that but I think that has become increasingly important that we work hand in hand. And inevitably because we have some common goals. The OECD has had for some time its own job strategy, the Commission has its own employment strategy and

its Lisbon goals and there is a lot of overlap. So, I think it is quite normal that we can cooperate on a lot of areas.

(OECD5)

However, there is also a reverse side to the coin. If this is a world of travel, exchange and collaboration, more often than not these exchanges take place in a competitive field, where most large international research organizations strive to secure the limited and diminishing funding available from national governments for the conduct of these studies. As a result, collaboration among them for the delivery of studies and the collection of education statistics is not a choice anymore, but a necessity. Conflict and tensions can run deep:

> The main reason is that they are competitors and both in scientific and in financial terms it is getting more and more difficult to conduct these surveys. There was a message from member states to the OECD and the IEA3—get together, sit down and discuss it and do it. Now, 6 months later, we all come together and we ask what was the result of that meeting and the answer was that we didn't find a date. They don't work together because they don't like each other.
>
> (EC9)

Interviewees also describe internal conflict within international organizations and their departments, for example, within the OECD itself. The following quotation describes the conflict between the Centre for Educational Research and Innovation (CERI) and the Directorate of Education, similar to the kinds of processes Jullien and Smith (2011) describe when they discuss IOs as internally unstable institutions, rather than the opposite:

> They live in different worlds—the same floor at the OECD but in different worlds. They don't like each other—one is more research-based, the other one more indicators and data, surveys. One is more reflection, the other one is more publicity, the charts—different traditions, the same director.
>
> (EC12)

Finally, another account that describes the conflict and competition for securing contracts for education research in Europe comes from another interviewee, a key member of staff of one of the Commission's research agencies:

> I think because the OECD is very much looking for member states' subsidies and grants and financial support for each separate research activity, they are also keen in showing that they do something unique and innovative in order to get such funding. And so then in a way they are in competition

> with us. An example is they did a recent policy review which is called 'Learning for Jobs' which basically deals with VET. And they didn't invite us to some national expert groups and so on that are in development—and they did very little use of our work because they wanted to do something that was different and specific so that they could sell it to the member states—this is my interpretation, of course. But I think that there is this kind of competition, differentiation between European institutions because we are in competition for funding.
>
> *(EC3)*

The quotations presented above suggest that descriptions of a field of actors who come together regularly and on equal terms to achieve consensus for the pushing of certain agendas might be false. On the contrary, they highlight the need to also focus our attention and study on those meetings that never happen, as well as those actors who are consistently not invited to expert meetings. They direct us to an understanding of a field, which is riddled with internal and external competition for funding, especially in times of reducing national budgets in an era of austerity. Nonetheless, the emerging data make the whole picture even more interesting, especially given the emphasis on the role of the meeting for the development of shared understandings (Freeman, 2012). Here is another EC actor:

> We create an expert group, we do the same as the OECD, we ask member states to designate experts. [. . .] Actually, member states are represented by different people who have different views around the same questions. Very often I would almost kill myself at the meetings because I would say, well that is what we've just decided with the member states yesterday. And the member states were sitting there, saying we've never heard of it [. . .] What you discover [. . .] is that people don't know each other—they don't even know the others exist. They have never heard of them. They come from different institutions, different backgrounds, different interests, policies, objectives. The member states are not even aware of these contradictions. The result of it is that they don't have any influence.
>
> *(EC10)*

And he continues:

> I am not sure if it is in the interest of the OECD or the Commission to solve that problem—because these institutions will benefit from that—the more they contradict each other, the more the institutions decide. [. . .] And with OECD, surely it is the same. This is so obvious—that's what they do—OECD is (NAME). We always have a joke with (NAME)—where he is brilliant, is to conclude. He is fantastic in this—conclusions! He is the

> conclusions expert—they are in before the meeting (laughs). [...] It is very convenient.
>
> *(EC10)*

In order to close this section, I will briefly return to the beginning: there we argued that Europe is constructed through travel and prejudice; this is also reflected in the study of the governing of Europe, given both the exchange of ideas that attempt to understand and explain it, as well as the disciplinary limitations and hierarchies which have so far seen the field of education as of lesser relevance and explanatory significance. On the contrary, the article suggested that the education policy arena is a key perspective in understanding Europe not only because it has become central in the discourses and policy direction followed by the Commission but also, and perhaps more importantly, because the process of learning from, with and at times despite others, is at the heart of the everyday realities of what policymakers do. Having examined the case of international comparative assessment, the article showed how the education policy agenda in Europe was not simply assembled at the Madou corridors and meeting rooms of the DG Education and Culture; on the contrary, an unlikely actor, given its global and (mostly US resourced) research agenda, became influential and soon arose to dominate the field. But how did this come about?

> The OECD didn't have an agenda on education policy [...] [So] the Commission thought, and I fought this for years, that the OECD had to adopt the same agenda as we had developed in Brussels. So, van der Pas, the Director General, went to meetings with the OECD and argued for their work, the annual work of the OECD should be the same as the one we have. He argued for and pushed that what we have as a policy agenda should also be relevant for the OECD.
>
> *(EC10)*

And he continues:

> We ended up inspiring OECD to adopt a policy agenda—and that they did with member states. They see the member states and have meetings with the ministers [...] So, they [member states] go to the institution which they are most influenced by or more easy to work with, or it is more convenient in terms of the political context in the country—which puts the European Commission in a weak situation because in fact we are the threat to the member states despite of the fact that we follow the Treaty etc. and we are a policy organization. The OECD isn't. So, if you want to weaken the European Commission then you go to the OECD and discuss the same subject matters there. That shift has weakened the Commission and signals the need

strongly for the Commission and the OECD to work together. The more you do that the more you have the need to have close cooperation between us, a competitive cooperation, a cooperation of influence, who decides, who draws conclusions.

(EC10)

The case of the OECD adopting a policy agenda is a case of an international knowledge actor being mobilized, influenced, perhaps even pushed, to become a policy actor in itself. This is not simply a case of knowledge informing policy, as is most commonly the case; it is in fact a fusion of the two realms in such a conscious and strategic manner that raises interesting questions regarding the extent of the '*technicization*' and '*de-politicization*' of education problems in particular and perhaps governing problems more broadly. In a way, it signals a shift from knowledge and policy to knowledge becoming policy—where expertise and the selling of policy solutions drift into one single entity and function. The next and final section will attempt a preliminary theorization of these ideas in order to broaden understanding in regard to the role of transnational expert organizations in education governance and governance in more general terms.

Discussion: Policy Mobilization and the Rise of 'Competitive Cooperation'?

A central issue arising from this analysis is the relationship between the production of knowledge and policy. There is a vast literature on the knowledge and policy continuum as well as on their coproduction, especially in the field of 'hard' science. Analyses from the field of studies of science and technology have explored the new regulatory role of transnational expert institutions, like the OECD, that are meant to possess both the knowledge base and the expert networks to produce scientific evidence for policymaking. In an interesting analysis of the World Bank in producing policy to combat global poverty, St Clair has masterfully shown the negotiated nature of the 'objective' data offered by such institutions: "definitions and assessments are not account of facts, but rather 'fact- surrogates', well-structured parts of an ill-structured and complex whole" (St Clair, 2006, p. 59). St Clair draws on Desrosières to discuss the relativity of statistics in the pursuit of knowledge for policymaking; she shows how the choice of what and who counts as expert in producing evidence for policy is not only a methodological question but also an epistemological and a moral one. Applying insights from science and technology studies, St Clair suggests that the transnational expert organizations have to be analyzed on the basis of their '*boundary work*', that is in relation to their ability not only to produce knowledge but also new social orders. She discusses the problematic and self-fulfilling nature of what she calls the 'circular dynamics' of expert knowledge, since—she suggests—the audiences that are meant to legitimate the knowledge produced are in fact audiences that have, to a large extent, been generated by the expert organization itself. Finally, she uses the work of Jasanoff (2004) and Guston (2000) to make a case for the role of international organizations as *'boundary organizations'*:

> The crucial role of these institutions is, then, to assure the stability between the domains of science and politics, to speak to principals in both domains and to do so in a way that integrity and productivity can be assured. Speaking differently to different audiences, boundary organizations can bring stability to usually controversial issues. [. . .] [they] may be a way to avoid the politicisation of science as well as the scientification of politics.
>
> *(St. Clair, 2006, p. 68)*

The OECD has become the boundary organization par excellence in the field of transnational education governance. With its work on the construction of performance indicators and more recently with its success in international comparative testing, it has emerged as central producer of policy-oriented knowledge in the developed world; and it offers not only measurable and comparable data but also—what is considered—reliable guidance for policymaking. Because of the OECD, assessing education is often presented simplistically as an empirical problem open to quantification, and hence improvement, rather than also as an epistemic and political endeavor. Through the networks, it has developed both in the scientific and the policy world, the OECD has become a central node in the structuring of the global education policy field. However, how has this come about? If boundary work is necessary for policymaking in controversial policy fields, such as genomics, climate change, migration or global poverty, what is it about education that requires this kind of dual agency, the need to be speaking to and persuading both patrons and peers?

There may be two answers to this question: first, the nature and history of education policymaking in Europe and second, the lack of a dynamic by DG Education and Culture in shaping policy in European member states. Starting from the latter, the data has shown how, why and when the OECD was influenced by the Commission to adopt a policy agenda. In other words, the OECD became a policy actor and indeed a key one, not simply out of its own accord and expert moves; it was mobilized to become one. This is where the concept of policy mobilization is helpful, as it may offer an explanation of the rise of transnational expert institutions as sites of coproduction of knowledge and social orders. Policy then is perhaps not everywhere, and it might not be as fluid and as ephemeral as previous analyses might have shown it to be. At least in the field of European education policy, and as the data above has shown, policy travel has had clear points of departure and arrival, as well as carriers and receivers; when the OECD developed the expertise to conduct large international comparative tests and thus had for the first time relevant evidence for policymaking, it also acquired reputation and recognition in the field—characteristics that DGEAC had never managed to have. National policymakers began turning to the OECD for evidence to legitimize policy choices at home and so—surprisingly perhaps—did the Commission. Since the OECD had both the data and the persuasive power to change policy direction at nation-states, DGEAC could use it as a point of mediation between its own policy agendas and national education systems. This is where St Clair's description of the circular dynamics' of the policymaking process appears to have also been the case in education governance, too; both organizations, the OECD and the Commission, have been seeking legitimization for the knowledge and policy they produce from continuously turning to one another.

The mobilization of policy however was soon to become policy competition; the OECD acquired such dominance in the field that the Commission and its agencies have often been sidelined in the policy process. What this might mean for the future of European education governance is still to be seen; nonetheless, what is certain is that the Commission now has another policy actor to always take into account—if this actor will be friend or foe remains to be seen.

Friends or foes, loves or wars, travels or prejudice—contrasts and oppositions keep on writing the history of European education policymaking. As I tried to show earlier, the construction of the European education policy space was one of the continuous battles against a resisting nation-state education system which had embedded traditions and histories that were threatened by its emergence. Indeed, in the face of increasing internationalization and globalization, national education systems have been strengthened as education is seen as an important policy area, still administered nationally and locally. Global and European policy actors are faced with strong local pedagogies and traditions, which for some are still seen as the cornerstone of the idea of the nation-state itself. Thus, in contrast to other policy areas like climate change or genomics, for example, the controversy that a boundary organization like the OECD deals with is not a scientific one; rather, it is deeply political and historical, and therefore perhaps presents even greater risk-taking when it comes to proposing reforms both at home and in 'Europe'. And this is perhaps why international comparative testing is of such interest; given the conflictual rather than consensual nature of the relation between the national and 'Europe', the OECD has become not only a site for the coproduction of knowledge and education policy, but also a powerhouse.

Notes

1. This chapter is a shortened and revised reprint of Sotiria Grek (2014) OECD as a Site of Coproduction: European Education Governance and the New Politics of 'Policy Mobilization', *Critical Policy Studies*, 8(3), 266–281 copyright © Institute of Local Government Studies, University of Birmingham, reprinted by permission of Taylor & Francis Ltd, www.tandfonline.com on behalf of Institute of Local Government Studies, University of Birmingham.
2. By 'European Commission', I refer more specifically to the Commission's Directorate General Education and Culture (DGEAC).
3. The chapter reports on research funded by the Economic and Social Research Council (ESRC) research project entitled 'Transnational Policy Learning: A comparative study

of OECD and EU education policy in constructing the skills and competencies agenda' (2010–2012) (RES-000–22–3429). It is also informed by a current research project that has received funding from the European Research Council (ERC) under the European Union's Horizon 2020 research and innovation programme, under grant agreement No 715125 METRO (ERC-2016- StG) ('International Organisations and the Rise of a Global Metrological Field', 2017–2021, PI: Sotiria Grek)

4. IEA is the acronym for the International Association for the Evaluation of Educational Achievement. IEA became a legal entity in 1967, but its origins date back to 1958 when a group of scholars, educational psychologists, sociologists and psychometricians met at the UNESCO Institute for Education in Hamburg, Germany, to discuss problems of school and student evaluation.

References

Boswell, C. (2009). *The political uses of expert knowledge: Immigration policy and social research.* Cambridge: Cambridge University Press.

Corbett, A. (2005). *Universities and the Europe of knowledge: Ideas, institutions and policy entrepreneurship in European Union higher education, 1955–2005.* Basingstoke: Palgrave.

Freeman, R. (2012). Reverb: Policy making in wave form. *Environment and planning A, 44*(1), 13–20.

Grek, S. (2009). Governing by numbers: The PISA effect in Europe. *Journal of Education Policy, 24*(1), 23–37.

Grek, S., & Lingard, B. (2007). *The OECD, indicators and PISA: An exploration of events and theoretical perspectives.* FabQ Working Paper. Retrieved November 21, 2013, from www.ces.ed.ac.uk/ research/FabQ/publications.htm

Guston, D. (2000). *Between politics and science: Assuring the integrity and productivity of research.* Cambridge: Cambridge University Press.

Hall, J. (2009). *The global project measuring the progress of societies: A toolkit for practitioners.* Presentation from the 3rd OECD World Forum, October 27–30, Busan.

Jasanoff, S. (2004). The idiom of co-production. In S. Jasanoff, (Ed.), *States of knowledge: The co-production of science and social order.* London: Routledge.

Jullien, B., & Smith, A. (2011). Conceptualising the role of politics in the economy: Industries and their institutionalisations. *Review of International Political Economy, 18*(3), 358–383.

Keeling, R. (2006). The Bologna process and the Lisbon research agenda: The European Commission's expanding role in higher education discourse. *European Education Research Journal, 41*(2), 203–223.

Kingdon, J. (1984). *Agendas, alternatives and public policies.* New York: Harper Collins.

Lawn, M. (Ed.). (2008). *An Atlantic crossing? The work of the International Examination Inquiry, its researchers, methods and influence.* Oxford: Symposium Books.

Lawn, M., & Grek, S. (2012). *Europeanising education: Governing a new policy space.* Oxford: Symposium Publishers.

Lingard, B., Rawolle, S., & Taylor, S. (2005). Globalising policy sociology in education: Working with Bourdieu. *Journal of Education Policy, 20*(6), 759–777.

Martens, K. (2007). How to become an influential actor—the 'comparative turn' in OECD education policy. In K. Martens, A. Rusconi, & K. Lutz (Eds.), *Transformations of the state and global governance* (pp. 40–56). London: Routledge.

OECD (2003). *Learners for life: student approaches to learning: results from PISA 2000.* OECD Publications: Paris.

Ozga, J., Dahler-Larsen, P., Segerholm, C., & Simola, H. (Eds.). (2011). *Fabricating quality in education: Data and governance in Europe*. London: Routledge.

Ozga, J., & Lingard, B. (2007). Globalisation, education policy, and politics. In B. Lingard & J. Ozga, (Eds.), *The Routledge Falmer reader in education policy and politics* (pp. 65–82). London: Routledge Falmer.

Porter, T., & Webb, M. (2004). *The role of the OECD in the orchestration of global knowledge networks*. Paper prepared for the International Studies Association annual meeting, Montreal.

Reichert, S., & Tauch, C. (2005). *European universities implementing Bologna, EUA trends IV report*. Brussels: European University Association.

Richardson, J. J. (2001). *European Union: Power and policy-making*. London: Routledge.

St Clair, A. L. (2006). Global poverty: The co-production of knowledge and politics. *Global Social Policy, 6*(1), 57–77.

SECTION IV
The Dissolution of the Science/Society Distinction

The fourth and final section focuses on international assessments as 'merely' descriptive of some reality or to examine their effects on policy and school programs and policies. It moves into a different but complementary terrain to think about how as the numbers of international assessments are 'actors' that generate cultural theses about desired societies and populations that the research is to actualized. The numbers as about the future to be governed by the present! The assessments are an anticipatory reasoning about the future. The ordering of numerical qualities and qualities produce rules and standards about what is to be known, how it is to be known and what counts as the future of reasonable knowledge and reasonable people. The first chapter by Thomas Popkewitz and Sverker Lindblad, *Statistical Reasoning, Governing Education and the Making of Differences as Kinds of People*, explores statistics as a particular style of reasoning and technology in the making of people into populations. The use of populations invents inventories or profiles of people that are not descriptive but anticipatory. Anticipatory as they embody cultural and social principles about desired futures about who children, but also families and communities, should be. The chapter explores the inscription produced by the distinctions and classifications of the successful and failing schools that bring into being epistemological principles that are no longer fictions but principles of reflection and action. The numbers of ILSA are inscription devices about desired kinds of people and societies that are to be actualized through the categories, distinctions and classification through numbers are given intelligibility. Finally, Thomas Popkewitz, in *Anticipating the Future Society: The Cultural Inscription of Numbers and International Large-Scale Assessments*, examines how OECD's PISA and the McKinsey reports of education bring into action technologies that govern what is seen, talked about and done. Its expertise is a particular kind of science that creates the abstraction of the school as '*a system*'

202 The Dissolution of the Science/Society Distinction

whose parts function to order and classify how judgments are made, conclusions are drawn, rectification to social and educational programs are proposed and the fields of existence are made manageable and predictable in school reform. The chapter also explores how the very categories and distinctions embodied in the numbers and magnitudes of ILSA fabricate narratives and images of society, but in practice, also kinds of people.

13
STATISTICS REASONING, GOVERNING EDUCATION AND MAKING DIFFERENCES AS KINDS OF PEOPLE

Thomas S. Popkewitz and Sverker Lindblad

Introduction

Numbers in policy and social research are generally seen as merely data that describe events for social planning. International and national statistical reports, for example, invite comparisons over time and space, between categories, and which can be used in various kinds of quantitative analyses, particularly as research relates to educational policy. *Education at a Glance: OECD Indicators* (2014),[1] OECD's PISA (Programme for International Student Assessment), TIMSS (Trends in International Mathematics and Science Studies) and the US NAEP (United States' National Assessment of Educational Progress). for example, use populational indicators to report national progress, in areas such as, in science and mathematics achievement.

The numbers of statistics in educational phenomena, argued in this chapter, are viewed as embodying cultural and social principles. We explore how numbers work, not simply as descriptions but as embodied desires of futures that are to be actualized through planning. Our argument is that numbers are part of social practices that generate principles about '*the nature*' of society and its kinds of people. Further and significant to the chapter, the making of kinds of people entails double gestures and a paradox: the very practices to include and change populations in the name of progress and equity doubles back on itself as processes of exclusion and abjection or the casting of kinds of people into unlivable spaces (Popkewitz, 2008).

We proceed in the following way. The first section explores statistics historically as cultural practices that entail a paradox: the finding of numerical equivalences to understand differences and inclusion produce differences about the qualities and characteristics of people. The second section explores statistics as generating principles about desired kinds of people. Further, we explore statistics as practices about the relation of individuality and society that research is to actualize. And, as in previous sections, a paradox is encountered. The classifications of people produce divisions to differentiate the normal and the pathological. The concluding section focuses on statistics as a social and cultural '*actor*', an agent that anticipates what the future should be in the ordering of the present.

This chapter draws attention to particular but often understudied qualities of the political in schooling, that is, how the ordering and classifying of educational phenomena embodies desires of the future that normalize, divide and exclude. Our approach is diagnostic: to ask historically about '*the reason*' and '*reasonableness*' of numbers as practices for thinking about policy and research; how numbers '*act*' to generate principles for governing the relation of individuality and the society; and the limits of such thought in questions about social inclusion and exclusion.[2]

Statistics as Cultural Practice: Political Arithmetic and the Taming of Chance

Thinking of people through statistical reasoning is so much a part of contemporary life that we are often unaware of this '*belonging*' as a historical invention. Statistical reasoning about large groups of people is one of the important inventions of the 19th century.[3] Statistics did previously exist, but it was about individual phenomenon. It was not possible to '*think*' about populations or large aggregates of people through numbers until different historical inventions came together from mathematics, statistics, physics and state administration. This section explores two qualities of modern statistics as a mode of thinking. One is statistics as a particular way of reasoning in the governing of modern societies. Second is a particular kind of consciousness associated with modernity, that is, of the '*homeless mind*'. That consciousness embodied abstractions about people from which knowledge is produced for ordering daily life, experience and belonging. Statistical reasoning about populations is one such strategy.

One example of this mode of thinking is the national statistics of educational attainment presented by OECD in *Education at a Glance* (2016). The report compares the percentages of individuals in different nations not finishing upper secondary education. Underlying the percentages is a double quality that differentiates the normal from the pathological: high completion is desired and given as the normal, and lower rates indicate a pathology to be corrected (see Table 13.1).

The making of the Table 13.1, however, entails '*back stage*' cultural and social principles. These principles form as a continuum of value in defining the successful and failing educational systems. 'Educational attainment' is correlated with social, cultural and psychological categories about populations—often in terms of gender, socioeconomic background and immigration, such as comparing individuals with native-born parents and individuals who have one or two immigrant

TABLE 13.1 Trends in Educational Attainment, Age Group 25–34 Years Old (2005 and 2015) over countries.
Percent not completed upper secondary education. Level of education defined by ISCED 2011 and ISCED 1997.

Country	2005	2015
Australia	21	12
Finland	11	10
Sweden	9	18
Spain	35	34
Turkey	63	48
United Kingdom	27	15
United States	13	10
OECD average	21	16

parents. The socioeconomic distinctions are linked with psychological qualities, such as motivation, aspirations and individuals working hard in school.

The comparative values about people in the numbers become foundational data for norms defined as educational 'gaps' as differences between categories. Intervention models are designed from the norms to change educational systems. The model of change is to actualize the anticipated characteristics and qualities of the people who are to inhabit its social networks in the future.

Statistics as a Technology of Governing

If we take this example, statistics is not merely a tool for social intervention. It numbers embody a particular system of reason that is never merely that of the numbers themselves. State planning to change social conditions is to change people. *The statistical data not only describe but order and classify what is desired in social relations and people.*

Historically, this relation of numbers, planning and changing is no surprise. Statistics joins with the idea of the welfare state in the governing of the modern nation.[4] *Statistik* in 18th century Germany was the science of police, for regulating and keeping order. Statistics, for example, ordered the populations to control for epidemics and to regulate tax collections. By the 19th century, the French word of *statistique* and the British *statistics* signified the arithmetic of the state. It was to calculate the administration and coordination of populations to secure the ends of wealth, public order, virtue and happiness. State administrators, for example, spoke of social welfare in terms of biological issues—such as reproduction, disease and education (human '*nature*', individual development, growth and evolution).

The numbers of statistics are categories about human conditions and people. Populational categories embody distinctions that overlap with the politics and culture. The representations in the US census after World War II entailed new classification of people for ethno-racial management. The category of Latino emerged, for example, to classify people from, for example, Brazil, Haiti, Argentina and Mexico, among others, as a single population. Once made into the categories, they enter into those social relations as a way of thinking about the present and the future. Today, this category of statistical reporting works into social movements and policy in education to define heterogeneous populations as homogeneous through the system of reason applied.

The statistical construction of populations, then, is a social technology for changing social conditions and, while not often considered, changing people (Hacking, 1990, 1991; Castel, 1991; in education, Popkewitz, 1991). Populational reasoning provides abstractions about how think about, order and act on particular groups of people as well as how people should think about themselves in relation to others. The War on Poverty in the United States in the 1960s, for example, entailed the creating of criteria to classify populations as a schema for social administration and intervention. Poverty existed prior to that but was not classified and tabulated as a device of state policy and research for intervention for moral and economic purposes. Programs are established for remediation of targeted populations, books are written about groups classified as ethnic populations and research is organized to change people through concepts and theories of cultural and social patterns of family child-rearing practices among those populations.

Populational reasoning is no longer deployed solely as state reasoning. It is a social practice of governing about who people are but also who they should be. The numerical distributions in schools become part of the '*reason*' of instruction. From the various characteristics of child development related to age and school grade to social characteristics of children (urban, at-risk, disadvantaged, gifted, adolescent, achievement), contemporary schooling is ordered through statistically derived categories of populations and is heightened, for example, through current US policy discussions of high-stakes testing and of international comparisons of student academic performance (Popkewitz, 1998b).

Numbers and the Paradox of Planning for the Future as Making Differences

The invention of statistics to order and differentiate large groups of people is embodied in this broader historical and political commitment to human agency. European reformation concepts of the person were revised as categories of the human mind whose soul had moral and rational qualities for intervening and changing one's life (Mauss, 1938/1979). Theories of agency in Anglo-Saxon, French and German-speaking worlds, for example, constituted people as autonomous subjects of motives and perceptions to determine the actions that shape the future (Meyer, 1986). Concepts of agency and human interests inscribed an individual who could know and act in the world that was subject to its own laws (Wittrock, 2000). Using the language of political theory, agency entails the movement of the objective order of institutions into the realm of subjectivity that is administered in the name of freedom (Pocock, 2003). The agency of the individual was made into the primordial category of progress through human interventions that would bring perfection to the future.

Yet with the historical invention of agency coincided with the '*invention*' of society and the social. Varela (2000) argues that the formation of individual personalities, individual subjects and the idea of society emerge at the precise historical moment when the legitimacy of power was being based on the idea of a general '*will*'. While the word '*society*' is present prior to the Enlightenment, it emerges to think about collective human existence instituted as the essential domain of human practices. Prior to the 18th century, society was a notion about associations of people and not about collective '*homes*', belonging and populations. The individual in the 18th-century French *philosophé*, for example, was bound to the '*discovery of society*' in a process of disengagement from the religious representations.

This leads us to consider that numbers enter into the cultural and political spaces of policy, research and programs. Statistics brought together large numbers of discrete attributes of the individual into a social whole, envisioned as objects that could be operated on in order to promote the general good and freedom of the individual. If we turn to the progressive political and educational reforms of the turn of the 20th century, the fundamental operations of the new statistical knowledge were embedded in what were called the moral sciences. It was to bring the greatest happiness to the greatest number.

The agency associated with '*happiness*' embodied its others. Happiness could be counted and measured as not so much of men's and women's happiness, but oddly enough as the moral sciences were concerned with populations classified as outside the realms of happiness: the poor, the immigrant '*races*', working classes as different from those embodying '*the nation*' and so on. The populations identified for planning were those constituted as the '*unhappy*', different and outside of normalcy because of immorality, criminality, prostitution, divorces, poverty and hygiene.

Agency, then, is a category codified and standard in relation to principles of the social in which its actions are authorized. But in that relation are simultaneously distinctions that differentiate the normal and pathological. The creating of populations is a way to think about and plan to rectify '*harmful*' social and economic conditions as well as to enable the individual to become a self-governing citizen capable of acting with freedom and liberty (Hacking, 1990; Rose, 1999). The planning, ironically, to recognize differences for inclusion establishes difference. The achievement gap, and categories of the '*urban*', social disadvantaged and at-risk child in North American and many European contexts inscribe distinctions, differentiations and divisions. Statistical tables, such as Table 13.1 earlier, about learning, achievement and the characteristics of the teaching instantiate social and cultural distinctions to compare and divide the attributes of the child who '*achieves*' from the child who does not '*fit*'.

Maybe this comparativeness is the albatross of modern social science. To represents differences inscribes differences as the qualities and attributes of populational kinds of people. The statistical reporting places people in a continuum of values that classifies and enumerates central tendencies with the extremes as the pathological.

This differentiating and dividing is evident in the OECD (2016) report from 2012 on student performance and equity (Figure 13.1). Student performances on achievement tests are correlated to the individual's socioeconomic status. Sweden, for example, is shown having an increasing connection between socioeconomic status and test results. The statistics embody the hope of the future and fears of dangerous populations. The hope, for example, is in the models of change that OECD provides for improving schooling. The hopes coexist with fear that further decline in schooling but the dangers of decline of society itself that become points of reference in Swedish policy and media.[5]

The visual image of the chart embodies a continuum of values about normalcy and pathology. The OECD comparisons of student performances are images that embody narratives of providing direction against the dangers of the increasing socioeconomic segregation, and future programs for making school compensate for society (see, e.g., SOU, 2017, p. 35).

The concern of teacher professional selection and development intersects with social and psychological categories of the child and family that do not succeed in the assessments. These are then related to curriculum designs so as to maximize performance outcomes. The OECD report on Sweden (OECD, 2015), for example, graphs maps measures of social equity and social economic impact of student performance in mathematics. Populational qualities become descriptors of both the qualities of people but also of what is normal and pathological in the development of the nation. This double quality of collective belonging and characteristics of people appear textually through the reporting of the performances of 15-year-olds who do not reach minimum performance levels in mathematic assessments.

The principles generated about normalcy and pathology act indirectly in organizing programs and for the individual to plot, self-monitor and supervise one's life trajectory. *The creation of the social categories about kinds of people in the statistical measures makes biographies*, linking student achievement with psychological qualities (motivation, self-esteem), loop into every life as ordering principles about the specific characteristics ascribed to the individual act. A script or narrative about biographies as the numbers are augmented with qualitative practices related to programs and assessments and self-assessment in schooling.

The categories and assessments embodied *a priori* assumptions about differences in the moral order to measure and calculate as if they did exist in order to think about how to change people. The measures were deployed as systems to realize a desired world about what was hoped for. Its numerical representation

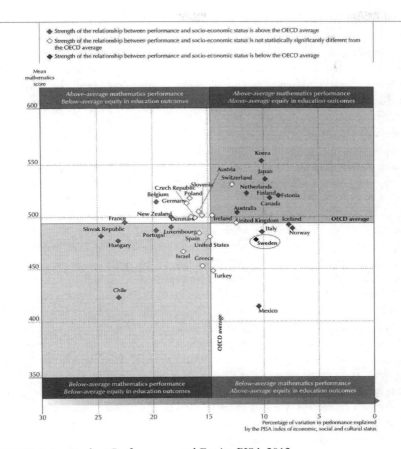

FIGURE 13.1 Student Performance and Equity, PISA 2012

became '*actors*' to describe and change people (actual and theoretically). Numbers as magnitudes were to make visible what counted. The information provided numbers bound a theoretical question to cultural and social practices that make the abstraction significant.

'*The Homeless Mind*'

One of those qualities of the '*reason*' embedded in classifying people as populations is what Berger, Berger, and Kellner (1974). call '*the homeless mind*', that is, being able to reflect about the '*self*' as both an object and subject. Drawing on the sociology of knowledge, Berger et al. view '*the homeless mind*' as a way of acting and '*seeing*' in the modernity.

The consciousness of the homeless mind creates a separate realm for human reason in processes of change that is different, for example, from the reasoning about finding the heavenly rules in God's earthly world. For our purposes, '*the homeless mind*' provides a way to historically understand quantification as embodying broader historical principles about modes of reasoning about the relation of individuality and collective belonging and '*home*'.[6]

'*The homeless mind*' captures, at one layer, the idea of the reason of the '*enlightened*' person as having the capacity to see '*facts*' as external to the self, but it still passed through the consciousness of the subject. This consciousness provides conditions that replace, at least partially, previous reliance on face-to-face relations to assess truth, honesty and honor. Truth is tied to modes of conceptualizing and analyzing, a rational temporary order to daily life and its possibilities of change (see, e.g., Bledstein, 1976; Shapin, 1994). That consciousness of abstractions direct to human qualities embodies possibilities to systemize, conceptualize and administer '*the self*' in social relations. The method for understanding is to create abstract sets of concepts to talk about society, nation, a citizen, family and childhood in ways that were not available previously.

The abstractions perform as a particular '*homelessness*', as human existence can be thought of as having no historical location, cultural specificity or geographical boundaries. The social practices associated with numbers and populations are just the opposite of producing places of belonging. Quantification, for example, is a technology of social distancing from the immediate and the local by providing a common and universal language (Porter, 1995). '*Thinking*' through probability theories about populations provides a way of '*seeing*' oneself in the universal time of humanity. The distancing and abstracting of the self as a reflectivity is a hallmark, if we can use this word, of the modern expertise of the human sciences, and found in Freud, Marx, Durkheim, Weber, Vygotsky and Dewey and carried into contemporary social and educational practices.

Statistics provided new ways to think about changing conditions through the abstractions of society, economy and culture. People were classified within populations to identify or rectify '*harmful*' social and economic conditions as well as for policing and organizing the security of populations. The new probability theories brought into statistical reasoning, for example, enabled the codification and standardization of dispersed phenomena under a singular umbrella of a population's societal attributes and economics.

The distancing is a rapprochement with the immediate and the re-creating of belonging and home. The classifications and measurements that accompany statistical reasoning in the 19th century worked back into everyday life and human experience. Thinking of one's self as a worker, as belonging to an ethnic group, or as an adolescent, is this double quality of abstractions as distancing strategies, which simultaneously serve as a GPS system for everyday life.

This paradox of the rapprochement with abstractions and the immediate are embedded in the categories of the psychologies associated with, for example, the conscious/unconscious, zones of proximal development, and problem solving.

The abstractions for thinking about the child and about how the child should '*think*' and act become the spaces of personal knowledge. The reflective teacher and action researcher, for example, are abstractions about kinds of people. The abstractions embody concepts about what to notice in classroom teaching and as theoretical canopies about the processes for thinking that projects the future as the application of '*reflection*'—not only about what to notice but also to organize action directed to what should be done.

The abstraction of '*the Reflective Practitioner*' loops into the life of the teacher as it is brought into programs, theories and narratives about the expert and professional teacher that the novice is to become. '*The Reflective Practitioner*' entails the '*homeless*' mind, if we can use the phrase, as it finds its home in everyday life. The teacher becomes the problem solver whose reflection flows between universals rules and standards of the abstraction of '*the reflective*' self and the immediate site of acting and experiencing of being '*reflective*'.

The homeless mind, then, is a particular characteristic of numbers and statistics. Statistics is an important '*inscription device*' for governing conducted through processes of distancing and attaching the self to particular sets of rules and standards. It is a technology for placing individuals in a relation to transcendental categories that seem to have no particular historical location or author to establish a home. The comparative distinctions of PISA or the correlations between student achievement and parental and community practices are abstractions that place one's self outside of a particular place, yet give meaning, attachment and affiliation that link individuality to collective spaces of belonging of the nation and the citizen that seem to have no attachments.

Making Up People and Designing Futures

We began the discussion by arguing that statistics embody cultural and social distinctions. We argued further that statistics in educational phenomena embodies a particular form of '*modern*' consciousness related to the homeless mind. In this section, our focus is on how the numbers are cultural practices concerned with making kinds of people. This focus brings us closer to consider the title of the book with this section concerned with how the numbers are not only about the present but also about an anticipated future.

Fabrications

One way to think about the classifications of populations is as making up people. Hacking (1995, 2006) argues that the human sciences produce human kinds in the very processes of discovering '*facts*' about people. This process of producing kinds of people can be thought of as a fabrication. The notion of fabrication helps to explore the particularities of statistics in making inventories or profiles of classes of people that can be managed and self-managed.

Fabrication embodies two nuances that are important in thinking about the distinctions and classifications that order schools. One nuance is fabrication as a fiction about kinds of people. The distinctions about children are fictions in that they are produced historically as ways to think about children in response to particular events and issues of the world. Calling a child '*disadvantaged*', '*at-risk*', '*artistic*' and '*lifelong learner*', for example, are fictions to think about issues, dilemmas and the obligations of schooling. The child study movement's classifications of youth and adolescence, for example, at the turn of the 20th century are fictions about human kinds. G. Stanley Hall's (1904) classification of children's development as an '*adolescence*' is not an object that one can touch but ways of thinking, '*seeing*' and feeling about '*the things*' of the world that were (and are) deemed important. Hall used the notion of adolescence to collect statistical data as a way to respond to perceived events of the world of childhood. It is not that the notion of adolescence was not used earlier. The Romans used the word 'adolescence' to talk about growing up. But they and the medieval world did not make the child as a distinguishable populational group in society whose particular presence required attention.

Adolescence, as a kind of person, was assembled and connected in a grid of different historical practices. The distinctions and differentiations that ordered the child's growth and development in the child study movement, for example, were not created through science alone. Its distinctions and differentiations assembled and connected Enlightenment hopes of '*reason*' and science with political theories of participation, Christian ethics and social biology articulated a psychology of the child as the future cosmopolitan citizen. The fabrication of adolescence, for example, connected discourses of medicine, psychology and pedagogy to calculate what was normal and pathological, treating the problems that arose from calculable deviations.

Fabrication also directs attention to how fictions loop into everyday life to manufacture kinds of persons. This is the second nuance of fabrication. Adolescence was, in part, to order the conduct of children coming into the newly formed mass school and rationalities of science that included '*urban*' youth associated with European immigrant and African American populations that moved from the American South at the turn of 20th-century America. Through the interaction of a range of pedagogical, social, cultural and medical discourses about the child, for example, the fictions loop into and become part of the material existence of schooling to make or manufacture the child and teacher through programs, theories and stories.

The naturalness of adolescence as a category of childhood is unquestioned today. The '*profiles*' or '*personal inventories*' of the adolescent as human kinds are aggregates that are acquired to fill in details for the abstraction about its constituted capabilities and capacities of people (Hacking, 1995).[7] Theories of youth and adolescence are abstractions that create impersonal categories that move across different sectors of schooling that provide benchmarks for teachers to work on the conduct of youth. The fabrication of kinds of people brings us back to the earlier discussion of '*the homeless mind*' in linking individuality with social belonging and '*home*'.

This double nuance of fictions and manufacturing makes it possible to consider new techniques for structuring reality and producing new phenomena to consider. Survey instruments and databases about the worker and non-worker, gifted and delinquent child and immigrant populations order information that can manage programs for rectification of social problems—to provide for diversity and intercultural education and for programs to ease the difficulties of being an immigrant and so on.

Making Difference: The Normal and Pathological

More than we like to think, the human kinds fabricated in schooling targeted for administrative intervention are populations seen as different or deviating from the normal—as in opposition to what is captured in the notions of the normal child, normal speech, normal development (Hacking, 1995). Fabricating people is the mapping of cultural spaces about the qualities and characteristics of kinds of people. Hall's child studies at the turn of 20th century America enunciated a particular cultural thesis of who the child should be. Adolescence was deployed as a particular strategy that not only standardized the normal but also simultaneously recognized kinds of people whose qualities of development and growth were different.

The differences in kinds of people embody double gestures. One gesture is of hope. The hope was that the transitional stage of adolescence could be managed to ensure the proper development in becoming an adult. The other, simultaneous, gesture was fears of youth, which posited youth as a dangerous population that threatened the moral order through, for instance, sexuality, criminality and so on.

That hope and those fears were inscribed as the conditions of urban life and the reforms about how people lived. Hall's study of the adolescent, for example, embodied the Social Question of the turn of the 20th century reform movement; a term used by Protestant Reformers and social scientists in American and Northern European Progressive reform movements. The Social Question was concerned with the moral disorder of the city and differences in the characteristics of urban groups. In the United States, 'urban' was a term to differentiate the kinds of people who embodied the promise of American republicanism and as different from women not in the home, particular immigrant and religious groups (Irish Catholics, Italian, Eastern immigrants) and racialized groups such as Chinese immigrants and African American who were freed from slavery after the American Civil War.

The hopes and fears or double gestures are embedded in contemporary statistics. *The teenage parent*, for example, was constructed as a statistic category in the white American suburbs of the 1960s but connotes the early parenting in the black urban ghettos in the 1980s and 1990s (see Lesko, 2001 Lesko, & Talburt, 2011). The category embodied cultural debates about family deterioration, permissiveness and dependency translated into individual faults related to bad values, hopelessness and lack of a future. The information provided by numbers was a theoretical question bound to cultural and social practices that would make the theoretical abstraction significant (Lesko, 1995). The teenage parent was classified as having succinct chronological, physiological and legal clauses and can be applied to many cultures—*the kind* is teenaged, female, pregnant and—an unwritten premise—unmarried.

The profiles and inventories of the adolescent as a kind of child codified '*youth*' in international assessments follow similar trajectories. The statistical data in *Are Students Ready for the Technology-Rich World? What PISA Studies Tells Us*[8] or *Risks and Outcomes of Social Exclusion: Insights From Longitudinal Data*[9] embody categories of different human kinds. The reports identify students who fail, but in that inscription of failure is inscribed the idea of who is successful that silently travels inside as the notion of difference. Instructional programs were devised for remedial measures of children who fit these categories of '*not passed subject*' and foreign background. Summaries, charts, graphs and tables identify the characteristics of youth to provide profiles of the child who did not fit the picture of the successful student. The distinctions of national and international statistics overlapped with principles generated to interpret experience as different layers of education— among governmental ministry officials, educational system leaders and teacher interviews.[10] Swedish governmental reports describing categories of educational non-performance of students of 'Foreign Background' or 'Newly Arrived', for example, circulated with 'on-the-ground' planning of reforms and organizing instructional programs.[11]

The double gestures point to the effect of populational measures. They generate a comparative system of reason that differentiates, distinguishes and divides. As Dreyfus and Rabinow (1983) argue, all societies have norms. Normalization involves the ordering and individuating of groups in relation to each other for social administration. The distinction imposed through statistical reporting is a special kind of strategic directedness in which norms are always on the move to create standards of the normal in order to isolate and deal with abnormalities given that definition—what earlier we spoke about as double gestures.[12] The categories of '*human kinds*' in statistical reporting distinguish, enumerate, control and order deviations in relation to bureaucratic imperatives.[13] The categories of school dropout or leaver, minority or special education are important administrative categories deployed in the problem of social inclusion.

Abjections

The statistical representations of populational distinctions organize difference. But the differences are not merely about comparing what is '*real*' about people.

They entail comparative installations that differentiate and divide those who are enlightened from those who do not have those qualities—the backward, the savage and the barbarian of the 19th century and the at-risk and delinquent child of the present. School reforms, for example, are to provide an inclusive society where '*all children learn*' and there is '*no child left behind*'. Teaching and learning theories embody the assertion of the homogeneity of values and norms that downplay differences of people by emphasizing what should be common to and '*the nature*' of—all human beings. With this insertion of '*all*' is instantiation of difference. The gesture is to make all child the same and on equal footing. Hope overlaps with fears of the child whose characteristics are not cosmopolitan and a threat to the moral unity of the whole—the disadvantaged, the poor and those populations designated as ethnic and immigrant, signified in the US context as the child '*left behind*'.

The hope to include '*all children*' simultaneously entails a jettisoning of particular groups who stand in a space outside the norms and value that binds '*the all*'. The '*all*' linguistically assumes a unity of the kinds of characteristics and qualities that children are to have in order to be included. The unity presupposes what is outside of that space, children do not belong and thus is not part of the '*unity*'. The differences are jettisoned, cast out or called '*abjected*' in feminist, social and post-Kantian political theory.

The apparatus of abjection is embodied in the manner in which opposites cohere in principles of inclusion to produce others who do not enjoy the status of the subject, but whose lives are circumscribed by the cosmopolitan modes of living. Abjection is embodied in narratives of freedom and democracy in 19th century American literature. Morrison (1992) argues that such literature inscribed a language that 'powerfully evoke[s] and enforce[s] hidden signs of racial superiority, cultural hegemony, and dismissive "Othering" of people and language' (p. x). Today, that '*Other*'—who is not yet inside but recognized to be included yet different—is expressed in notions of the disadvantaged and the '*child left behind*' as signified in recent US legislation.

The process of abjection directs attention to the recognition given to excluded groups marked for inclusion, yet that recognition radically differentiates and circumscribes something else that is both repulsive and fundamentally undifferentiated from the whole (see Shimakawa, 2002). The category of '*immigrant*' is illustrative. The immigrant is a category of a group and individuals whose status is somewhere not quite '*in*'—worthy for inclusion but excluded. The immigrant lives in the spaces between requiring special intervention programs to enable access and equity and at the same time established difference and the Other, outside by virtue of their qualities of life.

We can explore the production of norms that are abject in the '*kind of people*' classified as '*at-risk*'. Classifying children and families as at-risk is a technology of governance through the rules of reason. When national and international statistics are examined, certain indicators of '*at-risk*' children are used to recognize those populations to be included. UK statistics, for example, use the category of '*at-risk*' to differentiate populational groups that are classified as '*ethnic minority*' children, a '*high- risk*' category since 16 percent of permanently excluded children belong to it, with nearly half of the high-risk category being African-Caribbean, even though they make up only 1 percent of the population (Alexiadou, Lawn, & Ozga, 2001). Risk becomes as such foremost a schema of rationality, a way of breaking down, rearranging, ordering certain elements of reality (Ewald, 1991). No one '*properly*' evades it. Its organizing schema of management and rationality can be realized in any and every kind of institution. It can be applied to anyone, depending on how the dangers are analyzed and the events considered (Defert, 1991; Ewald, 1991).

Risk is a category that represents a complex system of ideas that, in a Kantian sense, refers to no specific reality. It is a category that fabricates human kinds: it is a fiction, and it makes kinds of individuals. The recognition of populations at risk addressed is 'factors, statistical correlations of heterogeneous elements' (Castel, 1991, p. 288). As Castel (1991). stated, 'We are situated in a perspective of *autonomized management* of populations conducted on the basis of differential profiles of those populations established by means of medico-psychological diagnoses which function as pure expertises' (p. 291).

Abjection, then, is a way to think about the complex set of relations of inclusion and exclusion—the casting outside and placed in and in-between space and excluded in the same phenomenon as the cosmopolitanism of schooling. *But the processes of abjection are not merely about the present.* Pedagogical practices simultaneously drawing in and yet placing outside certain qualities of life and people recognized for inclusion yet placed in different spaces that can never be '*of the average*'.

Statistics as a Cultural Practice in Making People and Designing the Future

While there is a disciplinary and political reflexivity about the uses and abuses of statistics, such reflexivity does not examine or bring into question the rules and standards that are historically mobilized. Contemporary social and educational research rarely asks about the cultural principles that order the theories, concepts and methods of curriculum research. This is particularly evident where curriculum research takes official categories and distinctions as its framework of investigation—such as the way that state categories of poverty, minority and ethnicity formed the core conceptual assumptions and the origin of studies to correct inequities.

Our focus on the reasoning is to recognize a significant fact of modernity: governing is exercised less through brute force and more through the systems of reason that fabricate kinds of people and biographies. We have explored this governing through the cultural and political principles that are inscribed in statistics and numbers. Statistical reason embodies the hope of social planning that a better life can be produced for individuals. That hope inscribes desired futures that research is to actualize.

But this hope of the future involves tensions and paradoxes. Statistics is never merely its numbers, magnitudes and equivalences. We argued that statistical reasoning connects social, cultural, scientific and political discourses that form a single plan to make kinds of humans—people who are sites for state intervention and as biographies. We focus on populational reasoning in statistics as fabricating particular *'kinds of people'* and biographies that inscribe subjectivities through planning people. The differentiating qualities of the populational data have self-referential qualities that define not only the individualities but also the trajectories that order the problem and solutions for the life that one should live.

The anticipatory qualities of statistical categories and distinctions are the inscription of relations between individuality and the social—inscriptions that are productive and not merely descriptive. The calculations and standardizations through the measurements inscribe a particular temporality about the anticipated future as embodying particular kind of peoples—the participatory person, global competence and the rationalities how to think and act. The images and narratives given as mathematics and science in the curriculum assessed engender principles about what is a child's problem solving. Science and mathematics are given as the '*wisdom*' whose authority in managing the natural work, the majesty of its procedures, styles of argument and expertise to interpret social life as its sacraments of the kind of people to be made. The science, however is not about the rules and standards of reason(s) of these disciplines. What is embedded in the statistics are alchemies that are ordered through psychologies about the social and individual, given expression in the classifications about how children '*solve and interpret problems*', '*motivation to learn*', '*beliefs*' about themselves and attitude.

We argued further that the making of kinds of people inscribes a continuum of values and double gestures that normalizes and differentiates in the efforts toward inclusion. While seeking inclusion, the very principles that are generated for inclusion divide and render certain groups as different, dangerous and in need of intervention. It is possible to examine the territories marked for the freedom of the child and parent as simultaneously internments and enclosures that divide and exclude.

The argument poses a dilemma when focusing on international assessments of student performance as addressing inequities. The very acts of social administration deployed by statistical reporting to address issues of progress require intervention through a practical causality that differentiates, distinguishes and divides individual characteristics in a continuum of values about the normal and the deviant. By not questioning as a system of reason, embodied statistics as numbers circulate in policy and research, as it is never merely that of numbers and mathematics.

The analysis also raises an important set of distinctions that circulate in the folklore of teaching, research and policy.[14] That folklore is the division between research and practice, or theory and the experience of the school, captured in much of the research on '*teacher expertise*' or '*the wisdom of the teacher*'. These divisions make possible the thinking of statistics as a set of tools for policy that is different from what people do with the numbers. The division is seen in the decoupling of policy and practice in organizational theory and the often-found dismissal of research as part of '*the ivory tower*' of the university. The latter is treated as having no connection to '*what happens on the ground*'. We have argued that the system of reason is a material practice that has '*real*' effects in ordering the nature of social problems, creating kinds of humans that are acted on and fabricating biographies. The decoupling and the distinction between theory and practice can, at this point in the analysis, be seen as historically and practically naïve and eliding of issues of power and the political.

The distinction of theory and practice, if we use the previous analysis, serves as an epistemological obstacle, to use loosely Gaston Bachelard's famous term, for understanding the governing functions in modern society and the different circuits through which inclusion and exclusion are produced. Important to the reflexivity of educational and curriculum research is how particular conceptions and rules of reason circulate—how is it that the theoretical notions of probability theories and populational reasoning '*fit*' so well and are '*seen*' as '*practical*' to policymakers as well as to teachers in organizing school improvement plans that we discussed earlier? What is narrated as practice is not something providing a '*real*' and natural knowledge, but something that is produced through a complex set of historically structuring principles that situates one as a historical actor and agent that is not only of the present but also of the possibilities of the future.[15]

Notes

1. www.oecd.org/edu/eag.htm: 'This annual publication is the authoritative source for accurate and relevant information on the state of education around the world. Featuring more than 150 charts, 300 tables, and over 100,000 figures, it provides data on the structure, finances, and performance of education systems in the OECD's 34 member countries, as well as a number of partner countries'.
2. Since we began this project on statistics in 1999 within a European Union 4th Framework study of educational governance and social exclusion, there have been extensive studies of statistics in policy. These studies have generally focused on the social field and networks in which statistics are deployed with Europe (see, e.g., Grek, 2009). Our interest earlier and here complement these studies but is different in its concern with systems of reason (also see, e.g., Lindblad, Pettersson, & Popkewitz, 2015).
3. There are informative histories of the discipline of statistics for the interested reader. See, for example, Stigler (1986) and Alonso and Starr (1987). See also Bowker and Star (1999), Hanson (1993) and Gould (1981).
4. *Staatenkunde*, the systematic study of states, an early form of what was called comparative politics, appeared in municipal censuses in Nuremberg in 1449 (Alonso & Starr, 1987, p. 13). The English tradition of political arithmetic was the application of rational calculation to the understanding, exercise, and enhancement of state power. In the 18th century, it was to reverse the growth of the state. Statistical societies in the 19th century were to gather objective facts, mostly numerical but also data that are today called 'qualitative'.

5. cf. the inquiry of the Swedish School commission. Official Report from the Swedish Government, No 2017: 35.
6. Berger et al. relate '*the homeless mind*' to the emergence of bureaucracy and technology in capitalism. Our use is broader and less institutional bound. See, for example, Popkewitz (2008).
7. Hacking (1995) directs our attention to differences between things of '*nature*', such as quarks and tripeptides, and those of human kinds, such as teenage pregnancies and adolescence. When comparing '*things*' such as camels or microbes, what they do is not dependent on how the categories are used to describe them. But this is not so with human kinds.
8. www.oecd.org/education/school/programmeforinternationalstudentassessmentpisa/35995145.pdf
9. Report by John Bynner: www.oecd.org/edu/school/1855785.pdf
10. Foreign background is an example of the many concepts that form a comparative concept that establishes '*deviancy*' even when created as a moral/political obligation of a society to ensure equity and justice. In one sense, as we will talk about later with the concept of minority, it is only through certain assumptions about the normal '*being*' of the citizen/individual that the classification of foreign born is applied.
11. See, for instance, Table 13.1 and Official Report from the Swedish Government, No 2017: 35
12. While there are multiple modernities, our concern is with the emphasis on reason and science in the European Enlightenment in the 18th century that is transported into the 19th century human sciences, industrialization, urbanization and professionalization that accompanied the newly formed democratic states and its citizens.
13. The categories of school leaver or dropout, minority or special education are important categories deployed in the problem of social inclusion as administrative categories. Hacking (1995) suggests, for example, that the categories of autism or physically or emotionally handicapped are specific administrative kinds. They are not specific disease labels but an umbrella for many.
14. This is not only a problem of educational theory. From Latour's (1999) discussion of science, to Emmanuel Wallerstein's (1991) and Peter Wagner's (2001) discussion of modern social theory, there is a continual questioning of the ways in which modern social theory has divided phenomena—what Latour calls the modernist settlement, which has sealed off into incommensurable problems questions that cannot be solved separately. Latour talks about the relation of human and non-human in science, Wagner about the relation of certainty and uncertainty. Also, see Popkewitz (1998a) as it relates to the social epistemology of educational research.
15. One way of thinking of this construction of experience is to recognize that there is always a double-sidedness to the 'I'—the historical and the biographical.

References

Alexiadou, N., Lawn, M., & Ozga, J. (2001). Educational governance and social integration/ exclusion: The cases of Scotland and England within the UK. In S. Lindblad & T. Popkewitz (Eds.), *Education governance and social integration and exclusion: Studies in the powers of reason and reasons of power (A report from the EGSIE Project)* (pp. 261–298) (Vol. Uppsala Reports on Education 39). Uppsala: Department of Education, Uppsala University.

Alonso, W., & Starr, P. (Eds.). (1987). *The politics of numbers: For the national committee for research on the 1980 census*. New York: Russell Sage Foundation.

Berger, P., Berger, B., & Kellner, H. (1974). *The homeless mind: Modernization and consciousness*. New York: Vintage.

Bledstein, B. (1976). *The culture of professionalism as the middle class and the development of higher education in America*. New York: Norton.
Bowker, G., & Star, S. L. (1999). *Sorting things out: Classification and its consequences*. Cambridge, MA: MIT Press.
Castel, R. (1991). From dangerousness to risk. In G. Burchell, C. Gordon, & P. Miller (Eds.), *The Foucault effect: Studies in governmentality* (pp. 281–298). Chicago: University of Chicago Press.
Defert, D. (1991). Popular life and insurance technology. In G. Burchell, C. Gordon, & P. Miller (Eds.), *The Foucault effect: Studies in governmentality* (pp. 211–234). Chicago: University of Chicago Press.
Dreyfus, H., & Rabinow, P. (1983). *Michel Foucault: Beyond structuralism and hermeneutics*. Chicago: University of Chicago Press.
Ewald, F. (1991). Insurance and risk. In G. Burchell, C. Gordon, & P. Miller (Eds.), *The Foucault effect: Studies in governmentality* (pp. 197–210). Chicago: University of Chicago Press.
Gould, S. (1981). *The mismeasure of man*. New York: W. W. Norton & Company.
Grek, S. (2009). Governing by numbers: The PISA 'effect' in Europe. *Journal of Education Policy, 24*(1), 23–37.
Hacking, I. (1990). *The taming of chance*. Cambridge: Cambridge University Press.
Hacking, I. (1991). How should we do the history of statistics? In G. Burchell, C. Gordon, & P. Miller (Eds.), *The Foucault effect: Studies in governmentality* (pp. 181–196). Chicago: The University of Chicago Press.
Hacking, I. (1995). The looping effects of human kinds. In D. Sperber, D. Premack, & A. J. Premack (Eds.), *Causal cognition: A multidisciplinary debate* (pp. 351–394). Oxford: Clarendon Press.
Hacking, I. (2006). *Kinds of people: Moving targets*. Paper presented at the British Academy Lecture, Paris.
Hall, G. S. (1904). *Adolescence: Its psychology and its relation to physiology, anthropology, sociology, sex, crime, religion, and education* (Vol. 1). New York: Appleton & Co.
Hanson, A. (1993). *Testing testing: Social consequences of the examined life*: Los Angeles, CA: University of California Press.
Latour, B. (1999). *Pandora's hope: Essays on the reality of science studies*. Cambridge, MA: Harvard University Press.
Lesko, N. (1995). The "leaky needs" of school-aged mothers: An examination of US programs and policies. *Curriculum Inquiry, 25*(2), 177–205.
Lesko, N. (2001). *Act your age: A cultural construction of adolescence*. New York: Routledge.
Lesko, N., & Talburt, S. (Eds.). (2011). *Youth studies: Keywords and movement*. New York: Routledge.
Lindblad, S., Pettersson, D., & Popkewitz, T. S. (2015). *International comparisons of school results: A systematic review of research on large-scale assessments in education*. Stockholm: Vetenskapsrådets rapporter.
Mauss, M. (1938/1979). *Sociology and psychology: Essays*. London: Routledge & Kegan Paul.
Meyer, J. W. (1986). Myths of socialization and of personality. In T. C. Heller, M. Sosna, & D. E. Wellbery (Ed.), *Reconstructing individualism: Autonomy, individuality, and the self in western thought* (pp. 208–221). Stanford, CA: Stanford University Press.
Morrison, T. (1992). *Playing in the dark: Whiteness and the literary imagination*. Cambridge, MA: Harvard University Press.
OECD. (2014). *Education at a glance 2014: OECD indicators*. Paris: OECD Publishing. http://dx.doi.org/10.1787/eag-2014-en

OECD. (2015). *Improving schools in Sweden* (An OECD perspective OECD Sweden report). Paris: OECD.
OECD. (2016). Improving schools in Sweden. Based on OECD. (2013c). *PISA 2012 results: Excellence through equity (Vol. II): Giving every student the chance to succeed.* Paris: PISA, OECD Publishing. http://dx.doi.org/10.1787/9789264201132-en.
Official Report from the Swedish Government. (2017). Samling för skolan. Nationell strategi för kunskap och likvärdighet SOU 2017: 35. Retrieved from www.regeringen. se/rattsdokument/statens-offentliga-utredningar/2017/04/sou-201735/.
Pocock, J. G. A. (2003). *Machiavellian moment: Florentine political thought and the Atlantic Republican tradition (with a new Afterword)*. Princeton, NJ: Princeton University Press.
Popkewitz, T. S. (1991). *A political sociology of educational reform: Power/knowledge in teaching, teacher education and research*. New York: Teachers College Press.
Popkewitz, T. S. (1998a). A changing terrain of knowledge and power: A social epistemology of educational research. *The Educational Researcher, 26*(9), 5–17.
Popkewitz, T. S. (1998b). *Struggling for the soul: The politics of schooling and the construction of the teacher.* Teachers College Press: New York.
Popkewitz, T. S. (2008). *Cosmopolitanism and the age of school reform: Science, education, and making society by making the child*. New York: Routledge.
Porter, T. (1995). *Trust in numbers: The pursuit of objectivity in science and public life*. Princeton, NJ: Princeton University Press.
Rose, N. (1999). *Powers of freedom: Reframing political thought*. Cambridge: Cambridge University Press.
Schleicher, A. (2005). *Are students ready for a technology-rich world? What PISA studies tells us.* Retrieved from www.edublogs.be/wp-content/uploads/2006/01/PISA_ICT_2.0.pdf
Shapin, S. (1994). *A social history of truth: Civility and science in seventeenth-century England*. Chicago: University of Chicago Press.
Shimakawa, K. (2002). *National abjection: The Asian American body onstage*. Durham, NC: Duke University Press.
Stigler, S. (1986). *The history of statistics: The measurement of uncertainty before 1900*. Cambridge, MA: Harvard University Press.
Varela, J. (2000). On the contributions of the genealogical method in the analysis of educational institutions. In T. Popkewitz, B. Franklin, & M. Pereyra (Eds.), *Cultural history and education: Critical studies on knowledge and schooling* (pp. 107–124). New York: Routledge.
Wagner, P. (2001). *A history and theory of the social sciences.* Thousand Oaks, CA: Sage.
Wallerstein, I. (1991). *Unthinking social science: The limits of nineteenth-century paradigms*. Cambridge: Polity Press.
Wittrock, B. (2000). Modernity: One, none, or many? European origins and modernity as a global condition. *Daedalus, 29*(1), 31–60.

14

ANTICIPATING THE FUTURE SOCIETY

The Cultural Inscription of Numbers and International Large-Scale Assessment[1]

Thomas S. Popkewitz

I begin the chapter with the emergence of the idea of society in the 18th century. Previously, 'society' was a word about collections of people in guilds and societies or associations. Its new meaning was to represent a way of thinking about the abstract relations that tie people with shared memories and social values outside the traditions of the family. Society" 'expressed an abstract set of relations about collective belonging and 'home'. This idea of society is visible in the French *philosophes* as a word to think about the changing conditions associated with the European Enlightenments. The modern idea of the citizen is perhaps the most recognizable category linked with the abstract relations embodied in the idea of society. It gave representation to the new collective relations and moral obligation that were autonomous from that of God or social positions predetermined by birth.

This general historical observation brings forth three related themes about international student assessment that structure this chapter. First, society, as is the idea of the modern nation, is not something naturally there to express human relations. The 19th century French historian Joseph Ernest Renan gave focus to the precariousness of the collective belonging as a daily plebiscite. The obligations and responsibilities of the citizen in England, Sweden and the United States, for example, are not static but continually changing. Second, this production of collective belonging is made possible through a particular kind of consciousness. This consciousness brings abstract concepts of human purpose, civic virtues, the common good and, by the late 20th century, universal human rights as principles of conduct into daily life.

Third, to bring the historical considerations into the present, there are new actors in the making of society. These actors operate in a greyzone, a shadow and social space that is barely visible yet acts in the intersection between science and nations. My focus, however, is not as much on the institutional apparatus of the international agencies performing assessments such as OCED, UNESCO and Pearson Publishing, or on the authors of the documents who pronounce the virtues of the comparative national assessments for social development. Attention is directed to the particular rules and standards that shape and fashion the 'reason' and reasonable people embodied in the assessments. The principles generated are about desired futures anticipated as the possibilities of collective belonging (society) and individuality. Numbers in the assessment are 'actors', directed to the future, that perform in making 'the daily plebiscites'. And this is my fourth point. Numbers are never merely descriptive, but rather they are cultural practices about desired futures. This is evident in the very language of improvement' in OECD[2] and the McKinsey[3] reports. The assessments are directed to how educational systems can produce the knowledge and skills necessary for students' future participation.

The first section focuses on the inscription of systems analysis in international assessments. Systems thought, it is argued, is an abstraction for ordering what is seen, thought and acted on for producing change. Models of change are not merely about the present but function to realize the desired future about an imagined society and people. Numbers are assembled in these principles of change as cultural expressions. The second section explores how the principles of systems theory order and classify populational differences. These differences embody double gestures. The magnitudes and comparisons of the assessment embody the hope of a universalized child and society that overlaps with fears of the dangers and dangerous people who threaten the future. The fourth section explores the irony of the hope of democracy and equality that instantiates the certainty of the vision in the relation of assessment research and its models of change, described as 'road maps' and 'highways' to the future and its kinds of people and society.

The analysis draws attention to a particular historical quality of the sciences of planning of Western social science from the 19th century, of which numbers have become increasingly important. The social and psychological sciences, initially called the moral sciences, were concerned with deviancy and moral disorder. The sciences were to change social conditions that also changed particular populations. Change tied the present to a desired future in Europe and North America though distinctions and division related to the 'Social Question' about the moral disorder of populations produced through urbanization and industrialization in the 19th century to the early decades of the 20th century. Today, the hopes and fears are pronounced through descriptions of globalization, national development, democracy and equality. Numbers, in this context, condense complexities of reality that interactively organize and produce that reality and its material features. Embodied in the greyzone that exists outside of the borders of nations, numbers 'act', here as technologies ordering conduct, making social spaces and envisioning future society and people and differences.

Systems as an Abstraction in Search of Data to Actualize

The common sense of research and policy are to effect strategies for planning that will bring about change. Change through science gave expression to salvation themes of modernity. The appeal of the international assessment is the promise of a democratic process. The salvation narratives create pathways that solve issues of modernization and social inequality in national contexts. Democracy is embedded in the seemingly universal and the neutral procedures and measures that chart gaps and highways produced with proper planning and coordination. The numbers of the assessments speak for themselves. Its reasoning can be applied equally for all nations and the mechanism of change is universal but tailored to each nation so all actors can follow. To follow are the standards, given as 'benchmarks' that mark the qualities and characteristics to achieve, as exemplified in the national use of teacher assessment (Mourshed, Chijioke, & Barber, 2010, p. 14). The promise is that if the knowledge learned from the assessments is applied properly, the nation, schools and economy will function at the high level of efficiency and productively necessary in achieving prosperity.

The lure of the future is so much a part of the natural quest of contemporary research that the principles that order the planning for change are not scrutinized. This anticipating the future is evident in the contemporary international assessments. The future is embodied; OECD asserts, for example, it knows the future. That future is embodied in specifying in its assessments of educational outcomes that our children will need for their economic success and well-being. The OECD asserts, for example, it measures the skills and knowledge needed for future participation. The educational management-consulting firm, McKinsey & Company, asserts, 'We provide external and independent assessments of education policy and practice, from an international perspective, to raise education outcomes'. It draws on 'OECD knowledge and data and international best practices'[4] to organize models of educational change necessary for the future perfection of modern nations.

The Lure of the Future and Systems as Its 'Actor'[5]

The lure of the future is enmeshed in particular principles that order and differentiate what is seen and acted on as change. In the international assessments, these principles relate to schools as 'systems'. Systems is a theory that underlies the ordering and classification of the assessments. The chapter will explore its distinctions and classifications to understand how the inscriptions of systems theory envision the interrelation of institutions, organizations and people. Systems analysis as a theory ordering the assessments functions at two layers. It is about processes and communication patterns of social life, while at the same time, it is about ordering the possibilities of change that anticipates what should be. The seemingly technical knowledge about people and processes as 'systems', explored in this section, are cultural inscriptions about anticipated kinds of people. Governing the present to achieve a desired future is embedded in the very idea of change. Change in the problem of reform and its research as interventions whose horizon is what society and people should be, and not merely about who they are.

Historically, the notion of social life as a system is given renewed visibility in the expansions of the post-World War II welfare states.[6] System *'thinking'* was used to manage logistics and training of US military, among others countries, during the War. It was brought into thinking about social life and change that coincided with the mobilization of the social and psychological sciences to manage the changes occurring in multiple social realms.[7] Process and method were privileged as the material objects to operate on for change. Research into the working of social systems is 'problem solving', making the social question of research as that of utility in finding the points that foster or hinder reform agendas. Borrowed from biology, social institutions are conceptualized as a *social organism*, having stages of growth and processes of development that change over time.

The idea of a system as an organism replaced earlier mechanical notions with more dynamic models of change. But the idea of machine did not disappear. Systems thought connected with cybernetics theories to relate mind and the machine, with the machine as the computer and its analogy to the mind as artificial intelligence. The school is studied as a system that has qualities of a biological organism, a metaphor to think about '*the educational needs*' in which social growth and development can be measured. The McKinsey and OECD reports embody systems thought through an experimentalist view of the individuals and society (see, e.g., Easton, 1953; Simon, 1968). The experimentalism is the collection of data and their correlations to explain results, then using the correlations to create models of changes that can anticipate better results.

The system was composed of processes and networks of communication that provided the method and strategy for change. The processes of change are given as technical and descriptive through the numbers that compare different national contexts. The system rules and standards serve as the expertise detached from people and attached to the specific elements of educational systems that have universal relevance for '*significant, sustained, and widespread student outcome gains*'. The visual culture of graphs, statistics and charts gives information as a 'communicative objectivity' (Halpern, 2014). Latour (1986) discusses how such devices as diagrams, lists, charts and graphs provide an 'optical consistency'. Techniques of measurement are to map processes as flow of information about stable objects that can move among different social spaces for administration (Halpern, 2014).[8] The visualization technologies collapse complexities into incessant calculations that seem well arranged, easily accessible and monitored to steer what is seen and acted on. Numbers are given as the transcendent ordering of what nations' need for development, growth and equity. The future appears innocuously as the 'needs' of nations.

The experimentalism seems devoid of theory, but infused with theoretical principles of systems to think about changing social conditions and people. The McKinsey report on education to employment (Moursed, Farrell, & Barton, 2013), for example, describes the system's elements as not merely a way to think about institutions or organizations. The system spoken about uses a management language but its object is people who form *the material structure that operates as to maintain the human organism*, with interdependent parts likened to a living being. People are spoken about in the image of the system; for example, making 'competent students [who] are able to participate productively in society' (OECD, 2017, p. 63) and governing conduct so families and children have 'a positive view of themselves and their future' (OECD, 2017, p. 51). McKinsey argues that the interventions are change the 'structure, resource, or process, and in terms of which *agent* the intervention is acted upon (e.g., principal, teacher, student)' (Moursed, Chijioke, & Barber, 2010, p. 14; emphasis added). 'Agent' is the people to be changed!

The Rules of Reason and Reasonableness

The epistemological ordering of systems assembles and joins five principles that connect in the international assessments: systems as an abstraction to actualize that future society and people; the abstraction embodies principles that are not empirically deduced but are a priori and *self-referential and self-authorizing* research; the categories and numerical expressions are *a fabrication* about who people are and should be; science is *problem solving* to effect that change; and reasoning is *comparative and produces differences* that compare, differentiate and divide nations and people.

(1) The school as a system is an *abstraction embodying social salvation themes*, such as those of democracy, universal progress, equality, human happiness and satisfaction. These themes are placed in the particular cultural spaces and ordered and classified by the abstraction of systems. 'What matters' is to identify, manage and maximize what people do and think to achieve efficiency of the hypothesized system. The hypothesized system links what is to what should be the characteristics of social life and kinds of people.

(2) The system principles are not empirically deduced. They are a priori, internal to the rules and standards of systems thought that form the basis of what is to be known, how it is to be known and what counts as reasonable knowledge and reasonable people. In this sense, the abstraction is *self-referential and self-authorizing*. Self-referential, in that the particular systems principles for research create boundaries about what constitutes the problem of education and the objects of schools to be distinguished and scrutinized, and what is manageable to acted on for change. The self-authorizing,

or the classification principles, act as a kind of circularity that order and classify what is possible in reflection and action. The abstraction, then, is an 'actor' to order what is known, the components, relations and effectiveness of the operation of human activities. The circularity is 'normal'. My interest is in the epistemological principles shaped through reasoning of school as a 'system'.

(3) The categories and numerical expressions are *a fabrication*. Fabrication has two qualities operating at the same time. One, it is a fiction or a symbolic way of thinking about 'the nature' of human practices, how '*things*' hold together, what matters within its boundaries and what might be possible for planning to optimize its efficiency. The fiction, however, enters into social practices and acts to produce the objects that can enable its manufacture. The categories, graphs and tables in the international assessments are inscription devices about social life and individuality that function as strategies to bring the system into being. Research codifies and standardizes its theoretical principles in order to actualize them.

(4) *Research is problem solving*. Problem solving assumes a particular strategy for understanding and planning. The problem solving is directed to securing algorithmic rules over the complexity and contingencies of life. The rules are in the measurement. Equivalences are statistically created as standards that serve as universal scales. The standards and benchmarks are invented to symbolize the imagined stages of growth and development of the organism embodied in the abstraction of the 'school system'. Problem solving is meant to standardize, codify and calculate the different qualities, characteristics and connections of the parts whose management and administration allows for growth and development. *These rules are impervious to social and cultural complexities*. Context is reimagined as the components, parts and sequences embedded in its measures.

(5) The research embodies a comparative style of reasoning about *equilibrium/disequilibrium*. The functional balance of the system is the goal. What is classified and ordered brings into being the harmony of the disparate human and organizational elements and relations for achieving maximization utility of the system. Embedded in the graphs, charts and lists are system principles and theoretical assumptions about change. They assume change as producing the optimum state of the system where its parts (processes and communication processes) can be managed to create a state of harmony and consensus. When stripped, the organizational and management language of processes and communication, the components to manage and create efficiency, are about kinds of people. The talk is about achievement and skills related to children, parents and teachers. The distinctions are social and psychological, about people: motivation, collaboration, peer and family relations, immigrants and poor populations, among others.

This is where differences and comparison are theoretically inscribed. The inherent focus of research is what disturbs and prevents the hypothesized system harmony and the utility of system performance. The two—equilibrium and disequilibrium—are mutually entwined in each other simultaneously as the same system phenomenon. That reasoning, expressed earlier and discussed ahead, creates a continuum of value in how variations produce scales of differences.

Research as a theoretical inscription in search of the future is not something of this moment and found only in the international student assessments under focus in this chapter. If examined historically, Adam Smith used the idea of 'system' as a fabrication to think about the philosophical claims about a universal (human nature) that was made into a particular abstraction (the market system). In *The Wealth of Nations* (1776), the numbers applied '*embodied [Smith's] a priori assumptions about what the market system should be*' (Poovey, 1998, p. 216, emphasis added). The empirical research would '*solve*' the problem of studying the particulars observed so as to standardize in a manner that could be projected into a resemblance of the future. Numbers appeared in Smith's political economic theory as a strategy to actualize the philosophical fictions of markets as performative standards instead of descriptions. The quantification of the effects or products of the system abstractions (labor, national prosperity, rents and profits) then became the '*social facts*' that enable comparisons of different '*systems*' (Poovey, 1998). What is important, then, is how the contemporary inscriptions of systems thought functions as a way to reason as a calculative rationality about change and the 'nature' of society, people and differences.

Benchmarks and Variations: Desired People to Be Actualized

The research to actualize the future of society has a name: 'benchmarks'. Benchmarks are indicators of organizational goals to be achieved. The benchmarks are defined through correlation whose principles are the desired interactions, communication and outcomes among the system's actors (populations that include parents, teachers, administrators, children and their social world or communities). Methods are statistical algorithms that calculate differences from the standards (benchmarks).

The benchmarks are an invented '*universal scale of calibration*' to create equivalences from, for example, several different international assessment scales of student outcomes discussed in education literature (see, e.g., Mourshed, Chijioke, & Barber, 2010, p. 7). In the Forward to OECD's most recent PISA measures of student 'well-being', it states that it is the 'world's premiere yardstick for evaluating the quality, equity and efficiency of school systems', a statement about what is desired and what is to be actualized rather than what is.

Benchmarks, as standards, are placed in scales that order elements on a continuum from '*poor/fair to good*', '*good to great*' and from '*great to excellent*'. In the report on how school systems are improving, the scale is given as a clear and linear progression that is internal to each category and then correlated across categories (Barton, Farrell, & Mourshed, 2013), such as:

Fair to good: consolidating system foundations, high quality performance data, teacher and school accountability, appropriate financing, organization structure, pedagogical models;
Good to great: teaching and school leadership as a full-fledge profession, necessary practice and career paths as in medicine and law; and
Great to excellent: more locus of improvement from center to school, peer-based learning, support of system-sponsored innovation and experimentation.

Variations are from the standardized norms to define spaces of actions. The strategy is to address deviations from the norms through mentoring arrangements, international meetings and workshops and the development of country case studies. A three-stage process is provided with scales to indicate progress (Figure 14.1).

The making of kinds of people is embodied in the self-referential/self-authorizing of the system's principles. The scales of *student performances are linked to psychological qualities of motivation and the taxonomies of skills of a kind of 'expert' or professional teacher and child* schools are to produce. The qualities of people are bounded by principles of the abstraction of the school as a system. Measures of achievement are correlated to who the teacher is, psychologies of the child and personality, school organization and norms that describe parent participation. The qualities link principles that order and classify, for example, 'peer-led creativity and innovation' and 'building technical skills of teachers and principals'—'creativity', 'innovation' and 'skills' are words that begin to form as particular kinds of people,

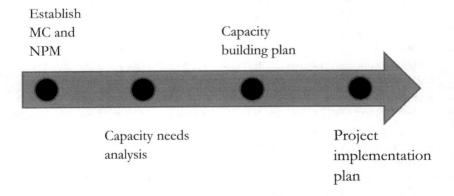

FIGURE 14.1 Stages of Participating Country Preparation

Source: (Ward & Zoido, 2015, p. 23)

their interactions and sociality. These qualities and characteristics become the normative, from which to determine what constitutes 'enjoyment of life', happiness, belonging and self-realization.

> The evidence base ... goes well beyond statistical benchmarking to examine children's 'enjoyment of life', asking 'Are students basically happy? Do they feel that they belong to a community at school? Do they enjoy supportive relations with their peers, their teachers and their parents? Is there any association between the quality of students' relationships in and outside of school and their academic performance?' Together they can attend to students' psychological and social needs and help them develop a sense of control over their future and the resilience they need to be successful in life.
> *(OECD, 2017, p. 3)*

Numbers are the inscriptions of the cultural practices that govern the classifications expressed as 'benchmarks'. The benchmarks seem as descriptions born of empirical data drawn from the present but are about people to actualize a desired future. The magnitudes of differences in the statistical correlations are placed into models of intervention that are to bring into existence kinds of people that can actualize the effectiveness of the system. The measures provide a comparative algorithm that 'tells' of a continuum of values about people and the future that enables successful school systems.

Change is using the abstract model to develop analytic devices that recognize differences. The paradox of this strategy is it normalizes differences. The logic of change embedded in the scaling creates a continuum of value. The differences are standardized, codified and ordered into hierarchies of values for comparing. The report on '*how schools are improving*' asserts that any school system can improve from any starting point. The hierarchy of values is created to differentiate nations and populations. The statistical analyses are used to '*examine why and what they have done has succeeded where so many others failed*' (see, e.g., Mourshed, Chijioke, & Barber, 2010). Scales are created to map the development and change of populations, such as to illustrate 'sustained improvers 1983–2007; promising starts, 1990–2007 (years very according to country/city); and type of system, such as nation, province, district, network, wealth, performance level, size of system (# of schools)' (Mourshed, Chijioke, & Barber, 2010, p. 14). Performance Stages are identified with sets of discrete markers about development. The scales relate to organizations that leach into the qualities and characteristics of kinds of people who 'fit' into the model of success. School districts that allow more local autonomy and looser guidelines are more successful; characteristics relate to the dispositions and sensitivities of school leaders and teachers who can 'adapt' and implement that models of change (Mourshed, Chijioke, & Barber, 2010, p. 18).

The standardizing and codifying to find equivalences, ironically, erase difference by establishing difference. The reduction of complexities to those of rational management 'systems' makes it seem that 'all' national systems can anticipate equality through the application of categories that recognize difference that inscribes difference. Differences entail comparisons through creating sets of equivalences among disparate databases.

The paradox of the international comparisons is its inscription of difference that 'makes' differences so that some can never be at the '*top*'. Different and independent assessment scales are rescaled, for example, into a single set of norms that serve as a universal of system difference (US educational spending allocates $6000 per student versus other nations) (Barber & Moursched, 2007). The spectrum makes it possible to correlate differences among factors to define system improvement that are not only about money spent or the development of mediating layers between schools and central administration. The classifications ordering the numbers of students' assessments are variations in kinds of people—successful to failing or non-performing or those who use collaborative practices.

Double Gestures: The Hope and Fears of Kinds of People

Systems thought in the international assessments is a particular style of reasoning about life and change. Research as problem solving connects with principles of equilibrium/disequilibrium in systems thought to produce particular comparative principles about people. The principles of equilibrium/disequilibrium entering into international large-scale assessments are cultural practices that have double gestures. The principle of equilibrium embodies the hope of finding universal achievement, social equality and individual "well-being".

Benchmarks provide the universals. The mode of reasoning in the benchmarks, however, entails comparative methods. This comparativeness occurs in two different ways. One is the obvious making of lists and rankings in the international assessments discussed in Chapter 3 by Hansen and Vestergaard. They argue that lists reorganize and give a visual form for reading and interpretation. They argue that the production of lists and rankings are part of the transnational struggles for truth and power. That struggle is also one of comparison as a mode of differentiating and dividing as the effects of power.

The comparison is formed through secondary statistical measures that create '*a universal calibration*' in which a spectrum of norms defines equivalencies among subsets of data (Moursched, Farrell, & Barton, 2013, p. 7). Variations established continua of values according to universal characteristics given in the abstraction of the school system. The report about how schools keep getting better, for example, discusses the need to develop a higher order statistical measure that can normalize several different international assessment scales of student outcomes (Moursched, Chijioke, & Barber, 2010). PISA-D, for example, identifies low-income and middle-income countries anticipating the future outlined as goals in The Education 2030 *Agenda for Sustainable Development* (UNESCO 2015 in Ward & Zoido, 2015).[9]

The comparison formed through the universal calibrations functions to eliminate differences then produces distinctions that divide. These divisions embody double gestures: the hope that the assessments tied to the model of change will produce more progressive societies. If I draw on the OECD and McKinsey reports, effective education travels as the gesture of hope that forecasts the good society, full employment, well-being and the progress of the nation.

These universal calibrations are not merely about 'systems'. They are about who people are and should be as well as about who does not 'fit' as part of the universal calibrations. The classifications and numbers connect to psychological categories of children's social and communicative patterns, such as family influence on children's achievement and the relation of education to employment. The indicators function to compare and develop benchmarks about kinds of people. These qualities appear to differentiate better performing and low-performing students' 'needs', such as feedback from teachers, autonomy, respect, non-disruptive behavior, parent involvement and interactions with school and other parents (OECD, 2015). Yet in these qualities are distinctions and differentiations about what is to constitute collective belonging and the kinds of people that constitute 'society'.

The social and psychological distinctions about the hopes of the future simultaneously express the gesture of fears of the dangers and dangerous populations to that future. The youth study, for example, begins with a discussion of higher education and includes all populations from universities through vocational education. But the report is not about 'all youth' and all employment! The universal category of youth is, in fact, about the poor and other populational categories related to vocational education. The delineating of stages of development are not only organizational factors but they also align with psychological qualities of youth that normalize what is functional and dysfunctional for employability, such as disengaged, disheartened, well-positioned or too poor to study (Mourshed, Farrell, & Barton, 2013, pp. 32–33).

The double gestures operate in the scaling and hierarchies to project the lower categories in the taxonomies as threatening not only to the school, but also to society. The characteristics of people who succeed and don't succeed form a continuum of value about the hope to actualize a desired future with fears of populations inscribed as dangerous to the system's harmony and consensus. Codifying and standardizing are not merely about achievement. The ranking and classification engender differences in those 'civilized' and those different in degree from that advanced stage of civilization—the school systems and nations at the top! The populations are discursively outside of the spaces of normalcy, lacking particular psychological and sociological skills for successful participation.

The dysfunctions embody a language of systems and management that reterritorialized the social and individual. The changing of people appears, for example, as the lack of coordination between educator and employer, which connect the psychological qualities of the child to the social qualities of family and community. It is the trilogy of child, family and community that order the reason of failure and change of the '*struggling youth*'. The distinctions appear, for example, as linking of organizational development stages with the psychological qualities of youth that normalize what is functional and dysfunctional for employability.

The task of research is to manage changes of the pathologies. Unless making 'sufficient investments to develop capabilities in the present, students are unlikely to enjoy well-being as adults' (OECD, 2017, p. 62). The dangers connect management qualities and characteristics, for example, poor teacher recruitment, salary and professional development, with the psychological and social qualities of youth who drop out of schools.

The double gestures embodied in the international assessment can be traced to a particular style of reasoning about representations and difference that is visible in the European enlightenments and revisioned in 19th century social science concerned with the Social Question of urban moral disorder. What is being explored here is a particular calculative rationality embodied in the numbers represented in the international assessment. Difference and the pathologies are in a social space of the greyzone that seems outside of history, nations and political theories of the good but correctable through the models of change about what the social and individuality are to become.

'Follow Me!' Knowing the Future as Taming Uncertainty

The anticipation of the future is not merely about the hope of change. The theory of systems 'acts' as both the pathways and the outcomes of what society and people will be. The future is certain, and the problem of measurement is to putting nations and people on the highways to obtain and actualize the abstraction of the school system. McKinsey uses the highway metaphor, for example, to think about the equilibrium/disequilibrium. McKinsey's language of highways, for example, posits them as the correct paths to '*scale up to delivery of sustainable skills*' (Mourshed, Farrell, & Barton, 2013). The OECD posits a similar claim about the knowable future. The OECD states, for example, that PISA measures the future participation of students in society and the skills and knowledge of science. Its more recent measures of students' well-being and their future uses the correlations of data as models of change that are to bring into being the child who can control and find satisfaction over the future:

> The challenges to students' well-being are many, and there are no simple solutions. But the findings from PISA show how teachers, schools and parents can make a real difference. Together they can attend to students' psychological and social needs and help them develop a sense of control over their future and the resilience they need to be successful in life.
> *(OECD, 2017, p. 9)*

The highways are not merely paths to the future. They embody the qualities and characteristics of the kinds of people who will inhabit that future. The highways and pathways are to 'deliver better outcomes' and are to actualize the kind of people embodied in the abstraction. Not far away from the search for harmony and consensus are fears. The McKinsey reports expresses the dangers as '*to get rid of potholes, make educators and employers part of the solution by providing "signs" and concentrate on patch of pavement ahead*' (Mourshed, Farrell, & Barton, 2013, p. 54). The making of kinds of people and differences were discussed in the previous sections. The youth unemployment report begins the discussion by referencing the category of youth, as including those who go to universities. The focus quickly shifts to the youth who are dangers to the future by not being employed. The problem to be solved is youth do not use the available information. The solution is to give youth better and more efficient information (Barton, Farrell, & Mourshed, 2013).

The systems principles inscribe what should be as what is already foretold. The universal stages, scales and inscription devices portray that the knowledge of the future at hand is needed for all nations to reach the top. The correlational statistics and its categories of relations are given as the process to arrive at the future. The pathways posit social life as a mechanism or machine whose proper alignment (equilibrium) allows it to administer system goals. The problem is how to tailor the highways individually so all can find the destination. Education-to-employment, for example, is a highway 'where three drivers—educators, employers, and young people—all want to get to the same destination' (Mourshed, Farrell, & Barton, 2012, p. 24).

While the report's language often references complexities and cultural and national differences, the principles organizing change are the destination and the right highways are known. The language about '*suggesting*' or merely reporting is accompanied with declarative statements that McKinsey has identified as '*the best practices for achieving the implementation of the management schema irrespective of the culture in which they are applied*' (see, e.g., Barber & Mourshed, 2007, n.p.). The international listing of nations functions as a GPS system for school systems so they can navigate in order to install strategies that hold the promise of coming out on top. The benchmarks of the change models establish the comparative ideals to achieve, that is, to move from academic achievement into social problems such as youth employability. Comparing is used to find '*the route by which others can get there*' (see, e.g., Barber & Mourshed, 2007, Preface, n.p.). Strategies are posited as changing existing structures, resources or processes, and also as identifying which agents the interventions are to act upon—such as the principal, teacher or student (Mourshed, Chijioke, & Barber, 2010).

The certainty of the future is embedded in the statistical methods. They are '*getting at what lies behind the numbers and are thus generating key insights* and questions, and with this report portraying the inner workings of successful pathways of reform given different beginning points*' (Fuller, Preface in Mourshad, Chijioke, & Barber, 2010, n.p.). Educational attainment, it is asserted, can be achieved within as little as 6 years (Mourshed, Chijioke, & Barber, 2010, p. 14). Innovation is applying the universal '*to navigate the challenges in their context and to use their context to their advantage*' (Mourshed, Chijioke, & Barber, 2010, p. 20). The aim of interventions are '*to gain requisite support of the various stakeholders*' for the interventions being made (Moursched, Chijioke, & Barber, 2010, p. 20).

Context, the space of actions authorized, paradoxically stabilizes the present. The analyses create superordinate algorithms that neutralize the indeterminate qualities of social life culture, politics and context (Barber & Moursched, 2007, p. 13). Social dimensions of educational systems are mapped as rationally organized and measured where humans can pursue their interests. Context is embedded in the problem solving whose solutions reduce complexity into components parts and sequences to delineate the most efficient means toward certain given goals.

Contexts are the rules of the system in which people make rational choices. It is making the right choice that prepares for entrance on the highways and helps move to high achievement (see, e.g., Moursched, Farrell, & Barton, 2013). Expressed in the McKinsey report on unemployment is that students need only to achieve the proper information in finding employment. The study of youth, employment and education deploys the language of certainty through organizing change as predefined stages that relates the school system and '*its outer environment*' (Moursched, Chijioke, & Barber, 2010). The schemas of interventions are scaled as hierarchies with precisely six interventions. Agents are described as those categories of people in the system to more efficiently implement management procedures, that is, to address those parts that are out of sync now with the optimal vision of the model.

There are no surprises except as they relate to the system coordination. The narratives and images of the OECD and McKinsey reports instantiate a practical logic that re-presents what medieval alchemists thought of as the Philosopher's Stone, the ultimate or foundation knowledge for all of humankind. The models are the elixir of change. The only issue of importance is whether school systems can actualize what is already calculated and measured. To return to the self-referential and self-authorizing qualities of its style of reason, the scaling, are continuums of development that become the boundaries within which solutions are expressed.

Making Society/Making People: The Cultural Practices of Numbers

Assessments have a materiality. *As argued in this chapter, the international assessments are 'merely' descriptive of some reality but 'act' in making or fabricating what matters; its 'nature' acts as a given to social problems and the strategies of change are to enact that 'nature'.* Statistics and numbers generate what are taken as stable scientific facts, planning and interventions. The 'facts' ordering the planning, however, are produced by 'systems' as a style of reasoning. This is said not as a constructivist argument but about how things of the world are given description and loop into the world and have material consequences. Further, numbers embody cultural theses about society and populations. They order the sciences of planning and assessments as an anticipatory reasoning about the future. The principles of systems deploy numbers as sequences and stages for nations to achieve given efficiency, perfection and equality as a seemingly mechanistic quality. The pathways and highways are spoken through numbers.

Numbers are cultural practices that are never merely about institutions and organizations. They are fabrications that embody fictions of schools as a system. The fictions, however, 'act' not only as a way of thinking and describing, but its system's categories of participation, collaboration, peer relations and motivation are about the kinds of people necessary for that governing to work. The mathematical and numerical signs in the international assessments seem transcendent, independent of social and cultural, yet they are formed as anticipatory models to actively organize and produce that reality and its material features. The systems thought acts as a style of reasoning to organize 'thought' through its a priori conditions, that is, internal rules and standards about what is to be known, how it is to be known and what counts as reasonable knowledge and reasonable people.

The numbers are not about scientific discoveries but about boundary limits of the present that simultaneously generate principles about the future and changing people to 'fit' into that future. Where previously one could argue that the counting of citizens, territories, resources and problems were acts in which the State participated, what was called political or state arithmetic, statistics—the political arithmetic of the greyzone in which OECD and McKinsey operate—embodies no visible state for governing. The governing occurs in the phenomena of counting, standardizing and codifying populations. The counting and numbers perform as expectations about universal characteristics of society and people whose composition forms a common and harmonious world. The common world becomes accessible as highways to rectify the dangers that are disruptive to the equilibrium. Context is the site where the consensus and harmony exist for maximizing school system performance. The pathologies are given as the system's context or environment.

An anticipatory future is a calculated rationality that shapes and fashions as ahistorical yet is located in a particular historical configuration that this book seeks to make visible. The international assessments are anticipatory, in the same manner as a Google, Amazon or Netflix search anticipates who you want to be. The difference with the international assessments from the web searches is that our preferences have not been registered prior to the algorithm's work on us. The preferences are prefigured in the abstraction of the school as a system. This future is embodied in the standardized knowledge of the curriculum, the kinds of people who master that knowledge and how that knowledge is to be appropriated by the child as an actor and agent in their actions to achieve a future life. The irony and paradox of the system's principles of equilibrium/disequilibrium is they morph into cultural practices of normalcy and pathology. The comparing from the universal norms and distinctions provided differences and divisions. The divisions were pathologies of populations dangerous to the system's models and highways and feared if not changed.

Notes

1. The discussion draws from Lindblad, Pettersson, and Popkewitz (2015).
2. Beatriz Pont et al. (2014)
3. The titles of these reports present the promises of comparing the performances of educational systems.
   Barber and. Mourshed (2007), Mourshed, Chijioke, and Barber (2010), Mona Mourshed, Diana Farrell, and Dominic Barton (2013).
4. On Google Scholar (March 31, 2015), the reports have a very varied impact, depending how you measure it. Measured by Google, the impact is immense—for example, 9.5 million hits on "McKinsey and School" over the world. They are non-existing on Web of Science.
   Barber and Mourshed (2007), 843 citations
   Mourshed, Chijioke, and Barber (2010), 379 citations
   Dominic Barton, Diana Farrell, and Mona Mourshed (2013), 39 citations
5. McKinsey considers itself as with a social obligation to address problems that to address global challenges of economic and human development. The societal concerns are taken as part of the larger corporate public responsibility. The non-profit McKinsey Global Institute, for example, is an economic think tank to provide management knowledge for foundations, non-profits and multilateral institutions on issues relate to disease, poverty, climate change and natural disasters. www.mckinsey.com/about_us
6. As discussed later, Adam Smith used a notion of systems to talk about the wealth of nations in the late18th century.
7. The belief in the expertise of science was captured in the thesis of '*the end of ideology*'; that is, after the defeat of the Fascism regimes, the problem was no longer ideology but finding the paths to a more progressive world society.
8. Systems theories were applied in OECD's approach to study the conditions of education in the late 1950s (see, e.g., Pettersson, 2014) and as a method for interventions in research related to, for example, the *US War on Poverty and the Great Society*, among others. The late 1960s establishment of research and development centers in the United States applied forms of systems analysis to the study of school learning, administration, classroom learning and curriculum (Popkewitz, 2011a, b).
9. http://en.unesco.org/education2030-sdg4

References

Barber, M., & Mourshed, M. (2007). *How the world's best-performing school systems come out on top*. Chicago: McKinsey & Company.

Barton, D., Farrell, D., & Mourshed, M. (2013). *Education to employment: Designing a system that works*. Retrieved from www.mckinsey.com/industries/social-sector/our-insights/education-to-employment-designing-a-system-that-works

Easton, D. (1953). *The political system: An inquiry into the state of political science*. New York: Alfred A. Knopf.

Fullan, M. (2010). Preface. In M. Mourshed, C. Chijioke, & M. Barber, *How the world's most improved school systems keep getting better* (pp. 7–8). Chicago: McKinsey & Company.

Halpern, O. (2014). *Beautiful data: A history of vision and reason since 1945.* Durham, NC: Duke University Press.

Latour, B. (1986). Visualization and cognition: Thinking with eyes and hands. *Knowledge and Society, 6,* 1–40.

Lindblad, S., Pettersson, D., & Popkewitz, T. (2015). *International comparisons of school results: A systematic review of research on large-scale assessments in education.* Retrieved from https://publikationer.vr.se/produkt/international-comparisons-of-school-results-a-systematic-review-of-research-on-large-scale-assessments-in-education/

Mourshed, M., Chijioke, C., & Barber, M. (2010). *How the world's most improved school systems keep getting better.* Chicago: McKinsey & Company.

Mourshed, M., Farrell, D., & Barton, D. (2013). *Education to employment: Designing a system that works.* Chicago: McKinsey & Company.

OECD. (2017). *PISA 2015 results (Vol. III): Students' well-being.* Paris: OECD Publishing. http://dx.doi.org/10.1787/9789264273856-en

Pettersson, D. (2014). Three narratives: National interpretations of PISA. *Knowledge Cultures, 2*(4), 172–191.

Pont, B., Donaldson, G., Elmore, R., & Kools, M. (2014). *The OECD-Sweden education policy review: Main issues and next steps.* Paris: OECD.

Poovey, M. (1998). *A history of the modern fact: Problems of knowledge in the sciences of wealth and society.* Chicago: University of Chicago Press.

Popkewitz, T. (2008). *Cosmopolitanism and the age of school reform: Science, education, and making society by making the child.* New York: Routledge.

Popkewitz, T. (2011a). PISA: Numbers, standardizing conduct, and the alchemy of school subjects. In M. A. Pereyra, H.-H. Kottoff, & R. Cowen (Eds.), *PISA under examination: Changing knowledge, changing tests, and changing schools* (pp. 31–46). Rotterdam: Sense Publishers.

Popkewitz, T. S. (2011b). *Standardizing kinds of people: The post WW II sciences and the Wisconsin Center for Research and Development for Learning and Re-education.* Paper presented at the International and National Standardization and Differentiation of Education Systems from a Historical Perspective, International Research Congress, Monte Verità, Ticino, Switzerland.

Simon, H. (1968). *The sciences of the artificial.* Cambridge, MA: MIT Press.

Smith, A. (1776/1991). *The wealth of nations.* New York: Knopf.

Ward, M., & Zoido, P. (2015). PISA for development. *ZEP—Zeitschrift für internationale Bildungsforschung und Entwicklungspädagogik, 38*(4), 21–25. Retrieved from www.waxmann.com/index.php?eID=download&id_artikel=ART10d&id_artikel=ART101865&uid=frei

INDEX

Page numbers in *italic* indicate a figure and page numbers in **bold** indicate a table on the corresponding page.

abjections 214–216
abnormality 55–57
abstraction 9, 12, 17, 39, 210–212, 233; schools as systems 226–227, 229, 231; systems as abstraction in search of data to actualize 224–231
academia: rankings and 39–41; as site of assessment and regulation by measurement 32
accountability: emerging age of 112; in public policy 39
achievement gaps 168–169, 176, 180, 207
achievement test *see* standardized achievement test
act, numbers as 2, 11
adolescence, concept of 62, 212, 213
Adolescence: Its Psychology and Its Relations to Physiology, Anthropology, Sociology, Sex, Crime, Religion, and Education (Hall) 62
agency 206–207
aggregation effect 112
Alamán, Pano 154
alchemy: analogy of 11–12; of school subjects 54
Alexander, Robin 142
American Statistical Association 141
Anderson, Charles Arnold 87
arithmetic of the state 205
artificial intelligence 225

Assessment of Higher Education Learning Outcomes 122
assessments: materiality of 235; problematics of 73; *see also specific assessments*
Astor, Ron Avi 177
audit societies 69
Australian National University 69
authors, TIMSS research and *177*, 177–178, **178**

Bachelard, Gaston 218
Barber, Michael 142–143
Barnes, Earl 60
bell curve 26
benchmarks 228–231, 234; planning development and growth to reach 80–83; *see also* indicators
Bernstein, Basil 143
best practices, PISA and 123
Beyond PISA 2015: A Longer-Term Strategy of PISA 110, 122
bias, in rankings 39
bibliometrics 69, 167, 169–175
Big Data 69–70
big data analytics 49
Biographical Sketch of an Infant (Darwin) 55
blacklisting 36–37, 41–42, 48
Bologna process 32, 186
Bottam, Norberto 94

boundary organization 197
boundary work 196
Bracey, Gerald 128
Brave New World (Huxley) 78
Brazil, PISA and 158–159
Bruner, Jerome 76
bureaucracy, lists and 36

calibration, universal scale of 228, 231–232
Canada, PISA and 158
Carnegie Endowment 95
census 28, 94, 98–99, 206
Centre for Educational Research and Innovation (CERI) 85–86, 94, 193
Chen, J.K. 178
child development 53–66, 232; abnormalities 55–57, 62; chronology 55–56; drawing 59–61, 66; linearity 56, 58–60; stages in 15, 21, 57–61, 66; statistical reasoning 58–61, 66; as way of reasoning 64–65
Child Study Movement 59
chimeras 12
Chiu, Ming 177
citizens, obligations and responsibilities of 222
CIVED 4
clinical trial, controlled 33
Cold War 75–78
Coleman report 141
collective puzzling 189–190
commerce, science and 68–69
Committee for Scientific and Technical Personnel (CSTP) 78–82; *The Need for Improved Statistics* 82; *Techniques for Forecasting Future Requirements of Scientific and Technical Personnel* conference 79
commodification 121
communicative objectivity 6
comparability, illusion of 105
comparative education, history of 3–4
comparative knowledge construction 167–169
comparative testing 187–190
comparative turn 152
comparativistic paradigm 3, 5, 6, 17
Compayré, Gabriel 55
competitive ethic 56
consequential validity 134–135
construct irrelevant variance 131–138
construct validity 134
consultants, as external irritants 70
content validity 134

contest of lists 36–37
context 111–112, 130, 235–236
control of system by means of indicators 86–89
Coombs, Philip H, 77, 81–82, 84–85
Cooperación Iberoamericana 160
Council for Big Data, Ethics, and Society 70
Council of Europe 82
countries of authors, TIMSS research and 174–175, *175*, **178**
Cox, Ian 85
Crease, Robert 68
creativity 63
credit rating 36
Crump, Thomas 68
CSTP *see* Committee for Scientific and Technical Personnel
cultural inscription of numbers 222–237
culture practice, statistics as 204–211, 216–218
curriculum models 11–12
Cussó, Roser 30
cybernetics 225

Darwin, Charles 55, 57
data behaviorism 181
datafication 49
democracy 2, 65, 152, 215, 223–224, 226
development of children *see* child development
development of international education indicators 75–89; forecasting 78–80; management 83–86; planning development and growth 80–83; development planning to reach benchmarks 80–83
digital citizenship 154
Directorate for Scientific Affairs 78, 80
Directorate General Education and Culture (DGEAC) 136, 193, 195, 197–198
dominance 40
Dominican Republic, PISA and 158
double gestures of hope and fears 231–233
drawing, children's 59–61, 66

Eagly, Alice H. 178
EBSCO Discovery 169–170
Eclipse of Reason (Horkheimer) 152
ecology of institutions 114
econometrics 190
economy: knowledge 112, 116; measures of 29–30; technological 81

Index 241

education: empirical turn in 57; as fundamental right 94; manpower planning linked to 101–102, 106; science of 55; universe of 100–101; yearbooks 96–97
Education 2030 *Agenda for Sustainable Development* 231
Educational Agenda for 2030 62
educational attainment 100, 204, **205**, 234
educational gaps 205
educationalization: of Cold War 76, 78; scientific-technological productivity 78
educational system, output of 77
Education at a Glance (OECD) 75, 87–88, 107, 120–121, 187, 203–204
education governance in Europe 185–198
Education International 122–123
education-to-employment highway 234
Eide, Kjell 80, 87
Else-Quest, Nicole M. 178
empirical turn in education 57
enjoyment of life 230
Enlightenment 9, 10, 56, 63, 207, 212, 222, 233
equilibrium/disequilibrium 227–228, 231, 233, 236
equivalences: construction/creation of 62, 65, 226–227, 231; to make comparison possible 56
Esquirol, Jean-Étienne 55
ethnicity 28
European Commission 186, 191–198
European Union 13, 30–31, 42
exit 40
experimentalism 225–226
external irritants, consultants as 70
externalization, PISA and 161

fabrications 211–213, 226–228, 236
facts 53, 56–57, 211; as external to the self 210; PISA and 160; social 9, 18, 118; TIMSS and 16, 147, 167–169, 173, 178–182; truth 94
fears 231–233
fictions, numbers as 64
Financial Action Task Force (FATF) 43
Financial Secrecy Index (FSI) 36–37, 43, 45–47, **46**
Finland, PISA and 132, **132**, 135–136, 152, 159, 161
Fitoussi, Jean-Paul 29
flatness of the world 31
Ford Foundation 77, 81, 84–85
forecasting 78–80
Forum on Harmful Tax Practices 43
Foucault, Michel 23, 24
Fourier, Joseph 26
Foville, Alfred de 28
free will, moral doctrine of 23
FSI (Financial Secrecy Index) 36–37, 43, 45–47, **46**
future: anticipating future society 222–223, 236; certainty 233–235

Galileo 25–26
Galton, Francis 26
gases 26–27
Gass, James Ronald 80–82
Gaussian normal distribution 26
GDP 29–30
Geimeinschaft 10
Germany, PISA scores in 136, **137**, 152
Gesellschaft 10
Gillispie, Charles 23
Glass, Gene 128
Global Entrepreneurship Index (GEDI) 136–138, **137**
Goethe, Johann Wolfgang von 23–24
Goldstein, Harold 79–80
Google Trends tool 155
governance: by comparison 152; by coordination 151; of European education 185–198; informational 37; by instruments 151; of international comparative testing 187–188; international large-scale assessments (ILSA) and 166; lists and 36–37; by opinion-forming 151; PISA and 151–152; statistical reasoning and 203–218; statistics as technology of governing 205–206
governing knowledge 124
Great Depression 29
Green Book 83
growth mindset 63

Hall, G. Stanley 59–60, 62, 212–213
Hans, Nicholas 97
happiness 207, 230
hashtag 154
health, application of quantitative technologies in 33
Heclo, Hugh 189
hegemony 40
Heller, Walter 81
Heyneman, Stephen 93–94

hierarchization of education 4–5
history of sciences 15, 21, 23–33
history of statistics 15, 21, 23–33
homeless mind 204, 209–211, 213
hope 231–233
Horkheimer, Max 152
Houtte, Mieke van 178
How the World's Best-Performing Education Systems Come Out on Top (McKinsey report) 142–143
Hughes, Everett 114
human capital 103, 106
human sciences 24–26, 210–211
Hume, David 9
Huxley, Aldous 78
Hyde, Janet Shibley 177

IALS (International Adult Literacy Survey) 187–188
IBE (International Bureau of Education) 96–97
ICCS 4
idiocy 55–57
Idiocy: And Its Treatment by the Physiological Method (Séguin) 57
IEA *see* International Association for the Evaluation of Educational Achievement
IIEP (International Institute for Educational Planning) 77, 82, 84, 102
IIIC (International Commission on Intellectual Cooperation) 95–96
illiteracy 97–100, 106
illustrations, cultural differences in interpretation of 130–131
ILSA *see* international large-scale assessments
indicators: control of system by means of 86–89; creating 16, 75; critical 84–85; OECD 75–89, 103, 117, 162, 190, 197
INES (International Indicators of Education Systems) 94, 103, 113
injustice 40
inscription devices, numbers as 11–12, 17
institutions, TIMSS research and 176, 176–177, **178**
instrumental reason 152
intellectual life 95
International Adult Literacy Survey (IALS) 187–188
International Association for the Evaluation of Educational Achievement (IEA) 3–4, 13, 116, 166; comparative knowledge construction 167–169; *see also* TIMSS (Trends in International Mathematics and Science Study)

International Bureau of Education (IBE) 96–97
International Commission on Intellectual Cooperation (IIIC) 95–96
international comparative assessments 187–190, 197–198
International Indicators of Education Systems (INES) 94, 103, 113
International Institute for Educational Planning (IIEP) 77, 82, 84, 102
international large-scale assessments (ILSA) 2–4; criticisms of 13; cultural inscription of numbers 222–237; governance and 166; importance in educational research 12–13; as inscription devices 17; reasoning within 13; style of reasoning 63–64; *see also* PISA (Programme for International Student Assessment); *specific assessments*
International Standard Classification of Education (ISCED) 92–95, 100–107; challenges in development, implementation and revision 103–106; classification system 101, 104–107; focus on outcomes and quality 102–103; manpower planning linked to education 101–102, 106; politics and 93; politics of nomenclature 104; story of 94–95
International Standard Classification of Occupations (ISCO) 102
International Standard Industrial Classification (ISIC) 102
International Statistic Institute 95–96
International Summit on the Teaching Profession 122–123
International Yearbook of Education 96–97
ISCED *see* International Standard Classification of Education
ISCO (International Standard Classification of Occupations) 102
ISIC (International Standard Industrial Classification) 102
Israel, PISA scores in 132, **132**, 136
item equivalence, PISA 128

Japan, PISA scores in 133, 136
journals, TIMSS research and 173–174, *174*, **178**
Jullien, Marc-Antoine 3–4

Kamens, David K. 150
Kershaw, Joseph 77, 84
Khoury-Kassabri, Mona 178
kinds of people: hope and fears of 231–233; making of 229; right 75–89

Index

kinetic gas theory 27
King, Alexander 78, 80–81
knowledge: comparative knowledge construction 167–169; expert knowledge for policy 110–125; framing of educational knowledge by TIMSS research 166–182; of future asserted by OECD 224; governing 124; for policymaking 196–197; practical 61; scholarly framing of educational knowledge 178–182; science as 24; technical 25
knowledge economy 112, 116
knowledge for policy: contextuality 121; ecologies of a project for 112–114; making and legitimizing expert 114–119; PISA (Programme for International Student Assessment) and 110–125
knowledge problematic, numbers as 2
knowledge society 116, 125

Lamarck, Jean-Baptiste 57
Lang, Fritz 78
law of falling bodies 25
League of Nations 95
learning 87
Linn, Marcia C. 177–178
lists 15, 21, 35–39, 231; alternatives to official lists 36; contested 49; Financial Secrecy Index (FSI) 43, 45–47, **46**; as non-narrative statements 38; OECD list on uncooperative tax havens 43–45, **44**; statactivism and 37, 41, 45; surveillance and 38, 47–48; *see also* rankings
literacy 94–95, 97–100, 106; competencies of 116; definition of 98–99; PISA and 116–117, 189
Liu, Xinfeng 178
Locke, John 10
loyalty 40
Luhmann, Niklas 70
Luyten, Hans 178

Madrid, PISA and 152
making differences, numbers and the paradox of planning for the future as 206–209
Malaysia, PISA and 152
Malthus, Thomas Robert 28
management: based on benchmarking 40–41; performance-based 39
management consultants 70
manpower planning 101–102, 106
Manual of Educational Statistics 101

markets, invisible hand of 10
market system 9
Marshall Plan 78
mathematics: New Mathematics 79; origins of 68–69; performance in 63–64; unreasonable effectiveness of 25; as wisdom 217
Max Planck Institute 86
Maxwell, James Clerk 26–27
McBride-Chang, Catherine 177
McKinsey report 12, 17–18
measurement 68–71; academia as site of assessment and regulation by 32; bibliometrics 69
media event, PISA as 151–155
mediatization 150, 152–153
medicine, role of numbers in 33
meta-organizations 15, 22, 69
metrification of modern world 127
Metropolis (Lang) 78
Mexico, PISA and 160
mindset, growth 63
Mohammadpour, Ebrahim 178

National Assessment of Educational Progress (NAEP) 203
National Defense Education Act 77
Netherlands, PISA and 158
New Mathematics 79
Newton, Isaac 23
No Child Left Behind 31, 215
nomenclature: in education, standardization of 96–97; politics of 104
Nova Escola Foundation 159
numbers: cultural inscription of 222–237; as educational understanding 3–11; as fictions 64; as inscription devices 11–12, 17; large-scale assessment as the production of 147; objectivity and 64–65, 124; paradox of planning for the future as making differences 206–209

objectivity 24, 30, 35, 53, 55–57, 61; numbers and 64–65, 124; objective myth of science 92–93; qualification of 112; technology based on connotations of 182
OECD (Organization for Economic Co-operation and Development) 3, 4–6, 12–13; actions against tax havens 42–47; as boundary organization 197; Centre for Educational Research and Innovation (CERI) 85–86, 94; child development 61–66; *Education at a Glance* 75, 87–88, 107, 120–121, 187,

203–204; *Education Indicators in the 1960s* 16; governance of European education, as key organization in 185–198; *Harmful Tax Competition: An Emerging Global Issue* report 43; history of 81–82; indicators 75–89, 103, 117, 162, 190, 197; International Indicators of Education Systems (INES) 94, 103, 112; international rankings and 39; knowledge of future asserted by 224; Leveraging Knowledge for Better Education Policies-GPS project 120; media strategy 153–154, 159; as meta-organization 15, 22; policymaking and 196–198; Secretariat 117; as site of coproduction 17, 185–198; status as expert organization 112; visits to website of 155, **155**; *see also* PISA (Programme for International Student Assessment)

OEEC (Organisation for European Economic Co-operation) 78–81

offshore world 42, 47

Operational Research 75–76, 85

Optiks (Newton) 23

Organisation for European Economic Co-operation (OEEC) 78–81

Organization for Economic Co-operation and Development *see* OECD

Panama Papers 36

pedagogy 55, 124

performance-based management 39

performance stages 230

performative, numbers as 1

personhood, conceptions of 58

Pestalozzi, Johann Heinrich 55

PIAAC (Programme for the International Assessment of Adult Competencies) 188, 192

Piaget, Jean 96–97

PISA (Programme for International Student Assessment) 4–5, 13, 16–18, 31, 110–125, 203; acting as factory of citizens 62; aggregation effect 112; assembling and purveying knowledge for policy 117–119; associations with other actors 119; *Beyond PISA 2015: A Longer-Term Strategy of PISA* 110, 122; broadening of PISA ecology 119–124; consensual decisions 118–119; construction of equivalences 62; construct irrelevant variance 131–138; contextualizing and framing analysis 111–112; core domains of 117; country-specific overviews 120; cross-national use 128; differentiating new subject of inquiry/policy 116–117; DIY products 121; ecologies of a knowledge for policy project 112–114; enlargement of a social-cultural matrix 121–124; European education systems and 187–189; exhorting policy emulation and policy learning 120; expert knowledge for policy 110–125; final reports 118; future of 110; goal of 61; governance and 151–152; Governing Board 114–115; indicator of success or failure of education policy 188–189; as instrument of legalization/externalization for the implementation of educational reforms 160–161; limits in providing information for policies 139–144, *140*; making and legitimizing expert knowledge for policy 114–119; multiplication of deliverables 119–120; national raw scores, scaled scores and ranks 132, **132**; as non-predictive of nation's innovativeness 138; number of students and countries part 151–152; PISA-D 63, 231; PISA for Development 122; *PISA in Focus* 120; quality of 138–41; rationalities 61–66; reliability 133, 138–139; sampling issues 133–134; sense of usefulness 111; shortcuts to knowledge 120–124; social media and 16; as social media event 149–162; as standardized achievement test 127–144; Strong Performers and Successful Reformers report 120; student performance and equity *209*; student well-being and 233; success of 112–113; TALIS and 120–123; talismatic power of scores from 127, 135; Test for Schools, PISA-based 122; trust in 112; truth telling 160, 162; Twitter and 150, 153–160, 162; validity 134–138, **137**

PISA items: context and 130; equivalence 128; illustrations and 130–131; language and 128–130; raw scores and imputed scored derived from 131–133, **132**

plane of reality 64

planning, prospective systems 84

policy: collective puzzling 189–190; evidence for 161; expert knowledge for policy 110–125; knowledge, relationship to 196–197; pedagogy for 124; PISA as indicator of success

or failure of education policy 188–189
policy mobilization 197–198
policy soup model 190
political economic theory, Smith's 228
political theory, Locke and 10
politics 27–33; lists and 36, 48–49; of nomenclature 104; of quantification 93; science and 93, 107; standardization and 92–93
Pons, Xavier 151
populational reasoning 206, 217–218
populations: autonomized management of 216; census and 28, 94, 98–99, 206; dangerous 208, 213, 237; differences 213–217, 223, 230; people classified within 209–213; statistics and 17, 26, 201, 204–206; targeting different 213
Porter, Theodore 69, 71
positivism 3–4
poverty, war on 206
poverty rates, childhood 135
power: lists and 36–37; soft 37
powers of numbers 1
practical knowledge 61
predictive validity 135–139
preparation, stages of participating country 229, *229*
problem solving 64, 210, 226–227; assessment of 53–54, 63, 129–130, 217; context embedded in 235; creativity and 63; research as 225, 227, 231; science as 226
Programme for International Assessment of Adults Competencies 122
Programme for International Student Assessment *see* PISA
Programme for the International Assessment of Adult Competencies (PIAAC) 188, 192
Progress of Literacy in Various Countries (UNESCO) 98
prospective systems planning 84
psychologies of learning 12

quantification, politics of 93
Quetelet, Adolphe 26–27
Quirantes, Arturo 160

race 28
RAND 76–77, 84–85
ranking lists 15, 21
rankings 4, 32, 36–37, 43, 48–49, 186, 231; bias in 39; in education and research 38–41, 49; Financial Secrecy Index (FSI) 43, 45–47, **46**; as performative 39–40;

PISA 64, 129, 133, 137, **137**, 150, 152, 156; ratings and rankings (R&R) 150
reasoning: comparative style about equilibrium/disequilibrium 227–228; development as way of 64–65; populational 206, 217–218; rules of reason and reasonableness 226–228; statistical reasoning and child development 58–61, 66; statistical reasoning and governing education 203–218; style in international large-scale assessments (ILSA) 63–64
reduction 25–26, 39
reflective practitioner 211
Reilly, David 178
Renan, Joseph Ernest 222
research: framing of educational knowledge by TIMSS research 166–182; as problem solving 225, 227, 231; self-referential and self-authorizing 226–227; in working of social systems 225
retweets 154
right kind of people 75–89
risk 215–216
Rockefeller Foundation 95
Rose, Nikolas 64
Roselló, Pedro 3
Rousseau, Jean-Jacques 10, 28, 55
Rueda, Mancera 154
rule by numbers 32

Sadler, Michael 143
Sahlberg, Pasi 159
Sarkozy, Nicholas 29
satisfaction 6, **7–8**, 233
Sauvageot, Claude 94, 103–106
Schleicher, Andreas 143
Schor, Paul 28
science: as basis for new technologies 23; bibliometrics 69; commerce and 68–69; fats and truths 179–182; history of 15, 21, 23–33; objective myth of 92–93; politics and 93, 107; power of statistical significance test 24; as problem solving 226; technicality and 24–25; as wisdom 217
science mapping 167
science of education 55
science/society distinction 14, 201–202
scientific-technological productivity, educationalization of 78
Scopus 169–170
secrecy justification 45–47
Séguin, Édouard 55, 57

self-authorizing 226–227, 235
self-referential 226–227, 235
Sen, Amartya 29
Shapin, Steven 68
shell company 43, 45
Shell Foundation 85
skills shortages 94
Slovenia, PISA scores in 132, **132**
slowness 55, 58, 65
Smith, Adam 9, 228
Smyth, John 93, 95–97, 99, 101, 103
social contract 10, 28
social critique 40
social dimensions of educational systems 235
social engineering 83–86
social facts 9, 18, 118
social media, PISA and 149–162
social mobilization, lists used for 37
social order, statistical model of 23
social organism 225
social physics 26–27
social question 213, 223, 233
social relations, mathematical order in 23
social science: comparativist paradigm in 3; statistics in 21, 23–33; suicide and 27
society: Adam Smith and 9–10; anticipating future 222–223; audit societies 69; discovery of 207; invention of 207; knowledge 116, 125; as living world laboratories 89; meaning of term 222; nature of 203; new actors in making of 222–223; quantification of 10; science/society distinction 14, 201–202; technological 81; urban 10
socioeconomic status and test results 208
sociology of knowledge 13–14
Soviet Union 78–79
Spain, PISA and 152
standardization 16; of measures of professional work 32; of nomenclature in education 96–97; as normative, interpretive, and performative 93, 106–108; politics and 92–93; slipperiness of standards in practice 99–100; socio-technical nature of 92
standardized achievement test: limits in providing information for policies 139–144, *140*; PISA (Programme for International Student Assessment) and 127–144; as reflective of sociological variables 139; sources of variance 139–141, *140*; talismatic power of scores from 127, 135; validity 134–138, **137**

standards 92–108; early attempts 95–96; ISCED 92–95, 100–107; UNESCO and 92, 94, 97–103
Standing Conference of European Ministers of Education 82
statactivism 33, 37, 40, 45
state: governance of education by 15; statistics as a state science 26–27, 59
statistical reasoning: child development and 58–61, 66; governing education and 203–218
statistics: abjections 214–216; as applied mathematical field 25; categories about human conditions and people 205–206; child development 58–61, 66; criticisms of 25; as culture practice 204–211, 216–218; empirical turn in education 57; fabrications 211–213; history of 15, 21, 23–33; as inscription device for governing 211; on literacy 97–100; making up people and designing futures 211–218; as moral science of the State 59; as performative 93; politics 27–33; populations and 17; in social science 21, 23–33; as technology of governing 205–206
Stigler, Stephen 27
Stiglitz, Joseph 29
student life satisfaction 6, **7–8**, 233
student performance, scales of 228–231
student well-being 5–6, 12, 228, 233
Studies of Childhood (Sully) 61
subjectivity, disqualification of 112
suicide 27
Sully, James 59–61
surveillance, lists and 38, 47–48
Sweden, OECD report on 208
Swedish Research Council 13
symbols, numbers as 1
systems: as abstraction in search of data to actualize 224–231; as actor of future 224–226; equilibrium/disequilibrium 231; as organism 225; research into working of social systems 225; schools as 224, 226–227, 229, 231; social facts that enable comparisons of different 228; social life as 225; style of reasoning 231
systems analysis 76, 84–85, 224
Systems Analysis and Education (Kershaw and McKean) 77, 84
systems theory 223–224

Takayama, Keita 178
TALIS (Teaching and Learning International Survey) 120–123, 187

taxation, lists and 36–37
tax haven 36, 38, 41–47, **44**, 47
Tax Justice Network 42, 45
teachers: affect on individual students 142; affect on standardized achievement test variance 139–143, *140*; value-added models of evaluation 141
Teaching and Learning International Survey (TALIS) 120–123, 187
Techniques for Forecasting Future Requirements of Scientific and Technical Personnel conference 79
technological economy 81
technological society 81
think tanks 70–71
TIMSS (Trends in International Mathematics and Science Study) 4, 13, 16–17, 203; comparative knowledge construction 167–169; content validity 134; framing of educational knowledge by TIMSS research 166–182; overview of data and analysis *172*
TIMSS corpus 170–178; analyzing research 170, 172–173; authors *177*, 177–178, **178**; characteristics of 173–178; countries of authors 174–175, *175*, **178**; institutions *176*, 176–177, **178**; journals 173–174, *174*, **178**; most cited articles **171–172**
Tönnies, Ferdinand 10
transparency, in public policy 39
Trends in International Mathematics and Science Study *see* TIMSS
trust: in PISA 112; in science 24; in teachers and researchers 39
Trust in Numbers (Porter) 30
truth 210; facts 94; lists and 36–37; TIMSS and truths 167–169, 173, 178–182
truth speech 63
Twitter and PISA 150, 153–160, 162; excellence and equity or how 'truth is said' about society and schooling 159–160; as instrument of legalization/externalization for the implementation of educational reforms 160–161; number of tweets per day *156*; number of tweets per location **156**; reception of PISA on Twitter 155–162, *156*, **156**; voice of winners and losers on Twitter 156–159

uncertainty, taming 233–235
unemployment, youth 234
UNESCO 4, 82; Education for All initiative 103; Institute of Statistics 105–106; International Institute for Educational Planning (IIEP) 77, 82, 84, 102; *Progress of Literacy in Various Countries* 98; standards and 92, 94, 97–103; Sustainable Development Goals 107; Universal Declaration of Human Rights 99; *World Handbook of Educational Organization and Statistics* 98
United Nations Population Commission 98
United States, PISA scores in 132, **132**, 134–139, **137**
United States' National Assessment of Educational Progress (US NAEP) 203
Universal Declaration of Human Rights, UNESCO 99
universe of education 100–101
US NAEP (United States' National Assessment of Educational Progress) 203

validity: consequential 134–135; construct 134; content 134; PISA (Programme for International Student Assessment) 134–138, **137**; predictive 135–139
value-added models of teacher evaluation 141
variations, from standardized norms 229
voice 40
VOSviewer 170, 172–173

Ward, F. Champion 87
War on Poverty 206
wealth, Smith's science of 9–10
Wealth of Nations, The (Smith) 9, 228
Web of Science 169–170
well-being, student 5–6, 12, 228, 233
Werfhorst, Herman G. van de 178
Wigner, Eugene 25–26
wisdom, science and mathematics as 217
Woods Hole Conference 76–77
Woolf, Leonard 68
World Bank 4, 13, 94, 196
World Education Survey 99
World Handbook of Educational Organization and Statistics (UNESCO) 98
World Illiteracy at Mid-Century (report) 100
World in the Balance: The Historic Quest for an Absolute System of Measurement (Crease) 68
world of tomorrow 79, 86, 116
World War II 75–76, 112
Wossman, Ludger 178

youth unemployment 234

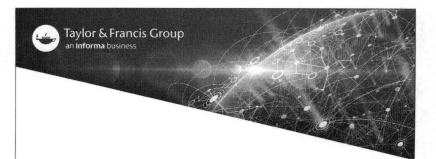

Taylor & Francis eBooks

www.taylorfrancis.com

A single destination for eBooks from Taylor & Francis with increased functionality and an improved user experience to meet the needs of our customers.

90,000+ eBooks of award-winning academic content in Humanities, Social Science, Science, Technology, Engineering, and Medical written by a global network of editors and authors.

TAYLOR & FRANCIS EBOOKS OFFERS:

- A streamlined experience for our library customers
- A single point of discovery for all of our eBook content
- Improved search and discovery of content at both book and chapter level

REQUEST A FREE TRIAL
support@taylorfrancis.com